BEYOND MEDIA:
NEW APPROACHES TO
MASS COMMUNICATION

BEYOND MEDIA: NEW APPROACHES TO MASS COMMUNICATION

RICHARD W. BUDD, Ph.D.

Chairman, Department of Human Communication
Rutgers University
New Jersey

BRENT D. RUBEN, Ph.D.

Director, Institute of Communication Studies
Rutgers University
New Jersey

HAYDEN BOOK COMPANY, INC.
Rochelle Park, New Jersey

In memory of
Robert J. Kibler
colleague, friend, and
conscience to our field

Library of Congress Cataloging in Publication Data

Main entry under title:

Beyond media.

   Includes bibliographical references and index.
   1. Mass media.   I. Budd, Richard W.   II. Ruben,
Brent D.
P90.B487   301.16′1   78-12432
ISBN   0-8104-5644-5

1 2 3 4 5 6 7 8 9 PRINTING

79 80 81 82 83 84 85 86 87 YEAR

PREFACE

It is abundantly clear that communication is the fundamental process of human existence as we know it. It is equally clear that the ways in which we understand this basic process will dictate the extent and direction of any possible influence we as human beings have on our future. No small part of that future course will be determined by the functions performed by our institutions of mass communication and, of greater import, the manner in which we respond to those performances.

While the mass communication function has existed for as long as human beings have lived together in organized communities, it has only recently become a subject of study for scholars and an object of concern for practitioners. Unfortunately for both, it was primarily the invention of radio, followed shortly thereafter by television, that gave impetus to the study of mass communication. Therefore, it was not totally without reason that the preoccupation with these two quite powerful and novel media led most scholars and practitioners to the current state of confusion between the *process* of mass communication and mass media *technologies*. Today, the terms mass media and mass communication are used interchangeably, and, most frequently, both are used to refer primarily to television, radio, newspapers, magazines, and, occasionally, film. Even those scholars who have sought to point out the difference between mass communication and mass media (the technologies of mass communication) invariably fall back on one or more of the four or five popular media as the focal point for their studies. To be sure, the products of these basic media often serve the functions of mass communication, but it is our contention that they represent only a small segment of legitimate mass communication institutions operating within our society, a fact that seems to have eluded most students of mass communication.

Traditional thinking, we believe, has severely restricted the understanding of the mass communication phenomenon, and to a large extent prevented many other legitimate mass communication enterprises from the benefits of such study and research. What we are dealing with here and throughout this volume is more than a problem of semantics, but rather a fundamental conceptual issue. In response to the limited and often constraining classic view of mass communication, our book offers a dramatically unique look at contemporary society and its key decision-makers. This volume contains a variety of new and quite different perspectives of mass production and mass consumption seldom before thought of as mass communication. Our own view of mass communication, presented in Chapter VI, flows from a basic systemic conceptualization of the process of human communication. Mass communication is presented here not as an awkward appendage to the study of communication, as has all too frequently been the case, but as a fundamental and endemic function of the more basic process.

Simply stated, our work represents a fresh attempt to substantially broaden and redefine the concept of mass communication and, concomitantly, of mass communication institutions. Our basic concept is one in which the one-to-many model that distinguishes mass communication can be applied to a variety of public enterprises in which communication with mass audiences is not only an organization's prime function, but its means of survival. This extended view includes such activities as architecture, religion, popular art, museums, libraries, legitimate theater, restaurants, and political image-making, to mention only the few presented in Part Two of this volume.

The message units and the delivery systems employed by each of these enterprises differ markedly perhaps, but the generic processes of decision-making ("message" design and "audience" analysis) involved in each are virtually identical. We believe that offering this enlarged view of mass communication will provide a basis for much needed interaction among institutions which, by virtue of their existence, depend on the mass communication function for their effectiveness.

It is not our intent to minimize recognition of what we traditionally think of as the mass media—radio, television, newspapers, magazines, and film. Rather, we are attempting to provide a framework to place these more commonly studied media in a broader context of mass communication and mass communication institutions. Our hope is that the comparisons and contrasts might generate new ways of looking at some current problems experienced by each, and suggest new avenues of study and research toward the solution of those problems.

This book, then, seeks to explicate the generic process of mass communication on two levels. On the most general level, we are attempting to establish the notion that mass communication is a broad phenomenon which is communicationally indigenous to all social organizations, and that the number of institutions serving that function in our society is far greater than heretofore recognized. On another level, we support this notion by including eight presentations by active professionals who by virtue of their positions are, on a day-to-day basis, involved in decision-making vis-a-vis a mass audience, and are, in every sense of the concept, presiding over the operations of a mass communication institution.

RICHARD W. BUDD
BRENT D. RUBEN

CONTRIBUTORS

Dr. Victor J. Danilov is Director of the Chicago Museum of Science and Industry and a frequent contributor to museum journals and the American Association of Museums.

Dr. David Davidson is Professor of Communication at Rutgers University. He holds his Ph.D. degree in information science and also teaches graduate courses at the Rutgers University Graduate School of Library Science.

Dr. James Hitchcock is Professor of History at St. Louis University, specializing in the Reformation. He is author of *The Decline and Fall of Radical Catholicism* and a number of scholarly journal articles.

Leslie G. Moeller is John F. Murray Professor and long-time Director of the University of Iowa School of Journalism. He has taught and written extensively about mass communication for more than thirty years.

Robert Mueller is both a scientist and artist and contributes significantly to both fields. He is author of *Eyes in Space, Inventors Notebook, The Science of Art,* and *Mind Over Media.*

Richard Redman is head of Redman Resources, a political consulting and research firm headquartered in Des Moines. He has been highly active in the Republican party on both state and national levels since 1960. He has lectured widely on his special area of expertise, political financing.

Vincent Sardi is owner and director of the internationally famous Sardi's restaurant, located in the heart of New York City's theater district. More than an entrepreneur, Vincent Sardi has been and continues to be an active spokesman in a number of New York City citizens' groups.

Paolo Soleri is a universally renowned architect. He is vitally concerned with what he calls "arcology," the union of architecture and ecology. His best known treatise on the subject is his book, *Arcology: The City in the Image of Man.* Soleri heads the Cosanti Foundation in Arizona, where much of his time is devoted to the construction of Arcosanti, his city of the future.

Dr. Lee Thayer is Professor of Communication at the University of Houston. He has authored and edited numerous books and scholarly articles, including the influential *Communication and Communication Systems.* He is the founder and editor of the journal *Communication,* and was organizer and moderator of both the First and Second International Symposia on Communication.

Ken Waissman and Maxine Fox are the producers of Broadway's longest running hit musical, *Grease*. When *Grease* opened in early 1972, this now husband and wife team were the youngest of Broadway's successful producers. Aside from *Grease,* Waissman and Fox produced the Broadway musical *Over Here,* which featured two of the three Andrews Sisters.

CONTENTS

PART ONE

DIALOGUE

CHAPTER I

Mass Communication: Media, Messages, and Myth

It is said that one of the giants of the communication field used to open his graduate seminar in mass communication, each semester, by describing the phenomenon thusly: "It builds our buildings, it makes our morals . . . it colors our sky." These are perhaps among the more modest claims concerning the influence of mass communication and the impact of the mass media in our society. Depending upon what you read and to whom you listen, the mass media also cause violence, elect senators, destroy presidents, breed intolerance, subvert children, sell toothpaste and Cadillacs, ignite riots, end wars, teach medicine, administer justice, and on ad infinitum.

During the past 40 years, and particularly during the past 25 years—primarily since and because of the advent of television—great powers have been attributed to mass communicators for effecting both good and evil in our society, while alternately sharing the blame and the credit for our social failures and successes. In spite of the outcomes, the mass communicators continue to be held in public awe as master arbitors of our social behavior. Walter Cronkite is perceived as a more credible source of information than the President of the United States.

The Genesis of Concern

As a natural consequence of all this, two distinct but related areas of interest to us have developed around the media. First, an immense and extensive multi-million dollar research effort focusing upon mass media and mass media effects, and secondly, burgeoning programs, departments, and colleges of mass communication at secondary and higher educational institutions. The two are frequently related because much, if not the overwhelming majority of research is being

3

conducted by academicians. This research, which spans the last 40 to 45 years, ranges from laboratory experiments to field studies observing a range of so-called media-related behaviors, including the use of opinion studies, viewership/readership patterns, content analysis, audience analysis, message design, studies in persuasion, credibility, diffusion networks, (not to mention the complicated and often confusing labyrinth of research on media effects concerning violence), election outcomes, preventive health, to name only a few from an inexhaustible list.

In colleges and universities, as well as in an increasing number of high schools and junior colleges, course work in mass communication and mass media has grown both in number of offerings and in student enrollment. The increased popularity of the subject matter has, of course, spawned an enormous number of textbooks, some of which include the following: *The Mass Media;*[1] *Media;*[2] *Mass Media;*[3] *The Mass Media and Modern Science;*[4] *Using the Mass Media;*[5] *Mass Media and Communication;*[6] *Mass Communication;*[7] *Theories of Mass Communication;*[8] *Mass Media and Mass Communication in Society;*[9] *Introduction to Mass Communication;*[10] *The Process and Effects of Mass Communication;*[11] *Mass Media in America;*[12] *Media, Messages and Men;*[13] and *Men, Messages and Media.*[14]

In the main, most of these books typically cover the same general territory. They characterize mass communication as the human interface with the media and as primarily a stimulus-response, cause-effect interaction; discuss the transfer of information through a linear source-message-channel-receiver-effects paradigm; enumerate the major source/channels as television, newspapers, radio, and magazines (sometimes books and records, but as Moeller will point out, only marginally); focus upon the functions which, by various names, include information, entertainment, cultural transmission/socialization, and prescription/influence/persuasion; outline traditional problem areas including control, ethics, responsibility, legal ramifications, and in many instances enumerate and describe mass media technologies and demographics. Nearly every one of the books (of which the ones enumerated are simply instances) carries a perfunctory chapter or section on communication/communication theory elaborating upon the process—what it is and how it works.

The mystery lurking in the midst of all this activity is that despite the accruance of some four decades of research and writing, we appear to know little more about the process and effects of mass communication than we did when Harold Lasswell prescribed the basic source-message-channel-receiver model. In fact, more than 55 years ago Walter Lippmann's *Public Opinion*[15] (as yet reasonably unexploited as a source of researchable hypotheses) presented what perhaps remains the most comprehensive and integrated understanding of mass communication to date. The past history of study and research in mass communication is virtually isomorphic with the field's present state (the notable exception, perhaps, is the increased sophistication and complexity of its research tools).

There are, of course, a plethora of researchers and academicians who take great exception to such an assessment, pointing to an increasing body of research and theory under the subject heading of mass communication. But such criticism misses the point, because the assessment is not made to belittle or point up the futility of that research; the doing of that research has, in fact, made such an assessment possible. What must be acknowledged, however, is that the bulk of research findings and writings about mass communication and/or mass media has neither brought us closer to an integrated, comprehensive understanding of what the subject area consists of, nor has it appeared to have any significant effect upon either the operations of the mass media or the nature of consumption of mass media fare by their audiences. Considerable evidence of both the weakness and confusion in our current understanding of mass communication stands as perhaps one of the major infra-findings manifested in the few major compendia[16] synthesizing nearly 50 years of mass communication theory and research.

Part of the reason is that mass communication/mass media research has never been very well orchestrated. Students of the field have been swamped by a profusion of findings from a variety of disconnected, or at best loosely connected, sources. Too often, research questions have been determined more by who was paying the bill than by more generic research questions growing from prior cumulative research. We are not questioning the legitimacy of such research. We do question whether mass communication research can focus on primary issues of concern to the majority if it limits itself to concentrating on more specific questions of particular interest to a relatively few.

A compounding factor has been our compulsion to rush to "scientific" explanations of the ubiquitous nature of mass communication which has frequently stampeded scholars to an uncritical acceptance of often simplistic and unsupportable findings of "media effects." The consequences of this condition are two fold. First, the illusion of having discovered "root causes" or "underlying processes" often serves to delimit or obviate the apparent need for further research regarding the conditions under study. In addition, and perhaps of greater significance, adoption of a set of seemingly logical and highly explicative findings leaves unresolved the important questions of prior assumptions, research design and appropriateness of methodology undergirding the research findings. Second, wide-scale adoption of explanations of "how mass communication works" become integrated and embedded in subsequent mass communication theory and literature as "fact" rather than as "suggestive." Perhaps one of the most obvious examples of this process is the so-called "two-step flow of communication." The concept emerged as a subsidiary finding of a 1940 voting study by Lazarsfeld, Berelson and Gaudet,[17] and was later embellished by Lazarsfeld, Katz, Trodahl and others.[18] The theory holds, essentially, that mass media messages pass from the media to "opinion leaders" to followers (less active, low-users of the media). And while subsequent studies have all but annihilated the concept, still today, more than three decades later, the "fact" of the process lives on in much of the literature of the field, albeit frequently now disguised as a "multi-step flow."

Yet another contributor to what seems, at best, an uneven research effort overly concerned with isolating mass media effects can be found in the history of the field's development. In large part, the origins and heritage of research on mass communication are rooted in (certainly legitimized by) popular and governmental hysteria and misconception about what it is media can do to people. By way of background, the popularity of ferreting out effects of mass communicated messages followed closely on the heels of the development of radio broadcasting. The search was given added flavor and legitimization as a result of the public panic and subsequent concern triggered by the NBC Mercury Theater's presentation of H. G. Wells' "War of the Worlds" in 1938.[19] Study of mass communication was further intensified as a result of the U.S. Government's continuing study of enemy propaganda during World War II, and further spiced by what appeared to be an astoundingly successful media-inspired response to a marathon radio War Bond drive, featuring Kate Smith.[20] Within a relatively short time, television emerged as a new medium generally available to the public, and both rekindled and magnified the concern for media effects. Its two major foci were the effects of political reporting and the notion that crime and violence portrayed on television caused crime and violence among viewers. The controversial

nature of the issues raised by these concerns has generated considerable funding from interested parties involved in these debates, besides providing an expansive and lucrative playground for mass communication scholars. The expenditure of such a disproportionate amount of the field's research talent and energies on such popularly created issues has yet to be proved worth the investment.

The Substance of the Response

Perhaps we are, after all, too ambitious and too impatient. The research findings of mass communication effects has not been without consequence. It has resulted in an increased ability to describe, at least in part, some evolving conventions of the audience-media interface, and an emergent language for talking about those conventions.

We know, with respect to the popular media, much more than we did about:

Who watches/listens/reads.
How much they watch/listen/read.
What they watch/listen/read.

Additionally, we have been able to find out where and when they watch/listen/read, and with whom. What is more, from all these data, we have been able to construct a number of theories about why they watch/listen/read and design our research to tell us what that means in terms of social and individual behavior.

Some of the more accepted findings regarding the audience-media interface are:

- People watch/listen/read what they most like, and will attend most to the medium that does the best job of presenting it.
- With respect to television, viewing is likely more appealing to persons lacking broader interpersonal links, less than average education, and fewer options for occupying leisure time (although more recently television was also found to be equally appealing to those with higher than average income/education and more than normal options for filling free time).
- Regarding the mass media audience, important information is diffused more rapidly amongst the population than unimportant information, but "importantness" is a dependent rather than an independent variable. At the same time, the more important the information being disseminated, the less important the media as an initial source for that information, and the more important interpersonal channels become.
- The flow of media-disseminated information is not simply explained as a direct-line transmission from media to individual (the so called "bullet" or "hypodermic needle" theory of mass communication), but is mediated, either by being passed through another party (or parties), or received by an individual whose understandings are colored by a network of "primary" and "secondary" group memberships.
- An important influence of the media is their apparent "agenda-setting" function—i.e., what the media choose to focus upon is likely to determine what society at large will consider important and current.

Regarding whether media messages can also tell us *how to think*—i.e., their power to influence and persuade:

- Those who believe the media can influence and persuade, at least commercially, spend in excess of $10 billion for advertising in newspapers and magazines and on radio and television each year.
- If an individual is predisposed toward some action, television information may well be effective in motivating action in the predisposed direction.
- Further, people deal with persuasive messages in a similar manner: they tend to evade messages not in accordance with their beliefs (or find ways to understand such messages as supportive of their beliefs). Moreover, if people trust and believe the

source of a message, they are more likely to accept what he/she says. At the same time, attitudes of family and friends have much to do with the individual's acceptance or rejection of information.

- Media-originated messages become more influential when transmitted through "opinion leaders" than through direct attendance to the media source—although the concept of opinion leadership is, at best, somewhat confused.
- Mass media are believed to be most effective in creating opinions on topics where no opinion (or little information) was previously held by an individual; the media are relatively ineffective in changing opinion.
- In a related fashion, under highly ambiguous circumstances, people are more likely to utilize pertinent information provided by the media than under normal conditions.
- The mass media—neither through advertising nor through the reporting of election returns—appear to have little effect upon how people vote.
- There is no evidence that portrayals of violence in the media either cause viewers/listeners/readers to engage in violent social acts or provide a cathardic outlet for potentially violent behavior.

Among more general findings of mass media research:

- The mass media confer status (both to media personalities and to those who become mass media subject matter), enforce social norms, and sometimes "narcotize" (knowing about a situation becomes a substitute for doing something about it) audience members.
- The mass media are a major component of leisure time use and a significant organizer of individual living patterns.
- The mass media serve as the chief source (as well as selector) of public knowledge.
- While long-term effects of the media are difficult (if not impossible) to isolate from related causes of behavior, two generalizations seem tenable:
    (a) mass communication builds upon existing attitudes
    (b) an ongoing effect of mass communication is the systematic, albeit slow, structuring and coloring of the individual's view of the world, providing a backdrop against which one views and validates his/her place in that world.

The Persistence of Unrest

The above narrative makes no pretext of being either meticulously exhaustive or painstakingly detailed. Not only was that not its purpose, but there exist already a number of encyclopedic recitations of communication research findings. By contrast, we sought to skim only the mainstream of mass communication research, admittedly excluding the many tributaries of exploration that have branched from these more central findings, and to set out in fairly bold relief what it is we claim to know about mass communication.

From that context, two things about the field become inescapably apparent and speak quite clearly to our earlier supposition. If anything, perhaps we have been too patient and too uncritical of our research efforts in mass communication. Our foregoing summary of findings, while perhaps revealing some rather elegant and laborious descriptions of media/audience conventions, reinforces the criticism that our research has contributed little to legitimate theory-building at a level that is likely to fuel any significant breakthroughs in our understanding of the phenomenon. And most of those tributaries left out of our summary seem pointed even less so in that direction. In short, mass media research is and has been in a rut, and a theory of mass communication non-existent.

Secondly, as a consequence, our failure to establish any sort of comprehensive theoretical framework for mass communication has had serious implications for the field of study in general, for the stability of the many burgeoning programs in mass communication, and for the growing body of literature which purports to serve both. The patchwork nature of research in the field has left open the question of how those pieces fit together, or whether they fit together at all. As a result, the substantive content of the field of study is frequently reduced to a set of loosely strung platitudes, aphorisms, and proclamations which seem to gain credence and acceptability more through age and repetition than through empirical substantiation. What is more, they have served as a launching pad from which often untenable generalizations are derived and insolvable debates mounted: Is television viewing debasing our culture? Do magazines cause social frustration and class warfare by presenting the "unobtainable ideal" to their readers? Are the mass media performing a homogenizing function leading us closer to the "society of sheep" concept? Do violent acts portrayed in the media incite members of society to commit actual acts of violence? And when one of these proclamations catches the public fancy, the cycle is completed, and we have yet another area to research.

It has been the deep and persistent concern for the rather disparate and amorphous state of knowledge of mass communication that ultimately led to the development of this book. What we present herein most decidedly will not offer *the* solution to some of our main concerns, but a blend of concepts, notions and criticisms that will perhaps offer some new perspectives and suggest some alternative ways of addressing anew some of the explanations we seem for so long to have taken for granted.

Perhaps no small part of the problem (at least a place to begin) is the fact that almost nowhere in the writings about the field is a clear distinction made or maintained between the terms *mass communication* and *mass media.* They are used interchangably. In our view, the problem is greater than a semantic one and the consequences have been more than trivial. For one thing, as will be obvious in reading the Moeller chapter which comes next, the formulation has been extended thus: mass communication = mass media = the "big four" (where: the big four = radio, television, newspapers, and magazines). The consequence of this is that work in mass communication theory and research has been constrained through preoccupation with the channel as the entry point into the system. The constraint has been, in the main, that the objects of study in mass communication have in turn been limited to the big four, and to the contents and the audiences of the big four. On top of that, a great deal of energy and debate have gone into developing criteria—mostly arbitrary—for defining what constitutes a legitimate member of the big four. Some of those "rules" include:

1. the requirement that a mechanical or electronic device be interposed in the system to carry the message
2. that there be a regularity in the availability of the media products
3. that the media experience be public, rapid and transient
4. that the audience be large, heterogeneous, and anonymous. The list goes on, extended and subscripted to cover special cases and accommodate new technologies.

In our view, this unfortunate confusion has had a much more significant impact on our field than we might imagine. It has conceptually blocked potentially productive expansion of the definition of mass communication to include numerous other one-to-many communication situations. In doing so, we have denied ourselves the opportunity to develop alternative explanations of the phenomenon. At the least, we have blinded ourselves to a variety of one-to-many communication formats that would allow us to focus upon dimensions of the process that are not always prevalent or obvious among the big four. Indeed, it is that very set of circumstances this volume addresses head-on.

To be sure, many of the content areas covered in Part Two of this book have been considered elsewhere, under the heading of "mass culture," a term that has long intrigued us. McQuail says mass culture has two main features:[21] First, it enjoys wide popularity and an appeal predominantly to the working classes; secondly, it involves mass production for dissemination on a mass market, and is therefore standardized, and involves mass behavior in use. Like most global phenomenological definitions, this one is not without its problems. At the same time, it's possibly the best that could be done with a concept as ambiguous as mass culture. But perhaps of more interest is the fact that the definition, with equal facility, can account for hula hoops, pop art posters, Walter Cronkite, *The New York Times,* or Crest toothpaste (either the product or the advertisements for it). Of what value, then, is the concept of mass culture? In our view, the attractiveness of the concept to media scholars stems from the inability of the traditional model of mass communication to accommodate such events. It will be our contention that mass communication is a far broader concept than currently defined, that such a conceptualization grows quite naturally from a less esoteric understanding of communication in general, and that an expanded view could open more productive areas of exploration to researchers, ultimately leading to a more comprehensive and pragmatic theory of mass communication.

But, we are getting ahead of ourselves. A number of issues introduced in this chapter are discussed at greater length in the next two chapters, and from two quite different perspectives. We invited Leslie G. Moeller, an influential media scholar, and Lee Thayer, a contemporary and often outspoken communication theorist, to set out their views on mass communication. By virtue of their differing opinions on the issues and problems involved in the field of study, the next two chapters form a natural continuum of dialogue against which a number of alternative approaches to mass communication can be weighed. Following their respective presentations, Moeller and Thayer get the opportunity to write commentaries about each other's position, thus helping to highlight the differences between the two. Finally, before we close out Part One of the volume, we will stimulate further discussion by including some of the major issues raised in the work of other writers in mass communication.

Notes and References

1. Wm. L. Rivers, (New York: Harper and Row, 2d. ed., 1975).
2. P. Sandman, D. Rubin and D. Sachsman, (Englewood Cliffs: Prentice-Hall, 2d. ed., 1976).
3. R. Glessing and Wm. White (Chicago: Science Research Associates, 1973), or R. Hiebert, D. Ungurait and T. Bohn, (New York: David McKay, 1974).
4. Wm. Rivers, T. Peterson and J. Jensen, (San Francisco: Rinehart Press, 2d. ed., 1971).
5. S. Chaffee and M. Petrick, (New York: McGraw-Hill, 1975).
6. C. Steinberg, ed., (New York: Hastings House, 2d. ed., 1972).
7. C. R. Wright, (New York: Random House, 1959).
8. M. DeFleur, (New York: David McKay, 2d. ed., 1970).
9. F. Whitney, (Dubuque, Iowa: W. C. Brown, 1975).
10. E. Emery, P. H. Ault, and W. Agee, (New York: Dodd, Mead, 1970).
11. W. Schramm and D. Roberts, eds., (Urbana: University of Illinois Press, rev. ed., 1971).
12. D. R. Pember, (Chicago: Science Research Associates, 1974).
13. J. C. Merrill and R. L. Lowenstein, (New York: David McKay, 1971).
14. W. Schramm, (New York: Harper and Row, 1973).
15. (New York: Macmillan Company, 1922).

16. I. DeSola Pool, F. Frey, W. Schramm, N. Maccoby, and E. Parker, eds., *Handbook of Communication,* (Chicago: Rand McNally Co., 1973); G. Lindsey and E. Aronson, eds., *The Handbook of Social Psychology,* 2d. ed., Vol. V (Reading, Mass: Addison-Wesley, 1969); B. Berelson and G. Steiner, *Human Behavior: An Inventory of Scientific Findings* (New York: Harcourt, Brace and World, 1964).

17. P. J. Lazarsfeld, B. Berelson and H. Gaudet, *The People's Choice* (New York: Harper and Row, 1944).

18. E. Katz and P. Lazarsfeld, *Personal Influence* (New York: Free Press, 1964); H. Menzel and E. Katz, "Social Relations and Innovation in the Medical Profession: The Epidemiology of a New Drug," *Public Opinion Quarterly,* 19:337–352 (1955); E. Katz, "The Two-Step Flow of Communication: An Up-to-Date Report on An Hypothesis," *Public Opinion Quarterly,* 21:61–78 (1957); V. C. Trohldahl, "A Field Test of a Modified 'Two-Step Flow of Communication' Model," *Public Opinion Quarterly,* 30:609–623 (1966).

19. See in particular H. Cantril, *The Invasion From Mars* (Princeton: Princeton University Press, 1940).

20. See in particular R. K. Merton, *Mass Persuasion* (New York: Harper and Row, 1946).

21. D. McQuail, *Towards a Sociology of Mass Communication* (London: Collier-Macmillan, 1969).

CHAPTER II

The Big Four Mass Media:

Actualities

and Expectations

Leslie G. Moeller

The Nature of Mass Communication: The Communicator, the Audience, the Experience

The major media of mass communications saturate most of the modern industrial world; and they wield some or much or an excessive amount of power, depending on the point of view of the observer. They are discussed, fought over, praised and cursed, and almost no one disregards them.

In discussing this servant-or-master, tyrant-or-sponge entity, it seems important to consider meanings for the term *mass communications,* the functions which the media are expected to perform, the context in which the media operate, the nature of media performance and the effects of the media, and, finally, trends and possibilities.

The term mass communications most commonly refers to communication through a medium to an audience, usually relatively large, and ordinarily on a continuing basis.

But there are a welter of definitions and of points of view, and considerable differences of opinion about such various factors in the process[1] as these three major elements: First, the nature of the medium and of the mass communicator, secondly, the nature of the audience, and thirdly, the nature of the communication experience.

The Medium

The medium itself, a mechanical device which "mediates" between source or communicator and audience, whether the medium be a printing press or a transmitter or a projector, is an indispensable but not solely sufficient element. Technology is essential (Innis declares that the prevailing technology of communication is central to all other technology[2]), and it made mass communications possible, but it is of itself not enough: One communicator with a microphone and transmitter reaching an audience of one does not constitute mass communications.

For me, it is important that the medium be "continuing," that it operate regularly and consistently, producing an expectable product which can be relied upon rather well (whether hourly or daily or weekly or monthly) as to time of production. In this sense, newspaper, magazine, radio and television (including cable) for me constitute "The Big Four," and this discussion is essentially confined to them; the film industry is nearby, the book industry is on the edge, and other elements are still farther toward the fringe.

The presence of "a medium," the mediating element which is "between" the source and the audience, means almost always that fewer senses come into play than with interpersonal or even small-group communication; in mass communications usually the senses involved are sight and sound, although in printed matter the tactile quality is rather nominally present. At the same time, it is possible to think of the medium as being an enlargement of, or an intensifying of, or an attachment to, the human sensory system.[3]

After the message is prepared, dissemination of the product should be rapid, a condition met readily by newspapers, radio, and television, and met relatively well by magazines, but much less readily by film and books. Dissemination should be "public," in the sense that, while there is a monetary cost for access (although the cost is usually relatively small as compared to annual personal income), this payment is the only requirement for access, as distinguished from a closed access in which selected or other restricted membership is a requirement.[4]

It is obvious that mass communication is highly organized communication, almost always through an organization. Production and the product are then influenced by all the factors which influence an organization of size and complexity.

One of these factors is that the total cost of setting-up and of operation are usually relatively high, which reduces the ease of entry into the field and the diversity of content which is available to the society, with some reduction also of individual access to expression. At the same time, production in quantity usually sharply reduces unit cost to the citizen.

The mass media are often spoken of as agencies of social control, but it is important to realize that they are almost always effective indirectly, through transmission of material from others, rather than themselves being self-deciding effecters of change. The media do transmit much material of value to the status quo, the establishment, whether it be business or government, but the end results may not be quite as intended. Consider the war in Vietnam. Both the administration and, to judge by voting records, the Congress, were long in favor of that enterprise, and the media transmitted much of their material, but even so there developed, on the basis of other content, intense feeling against

the war. Further, most media for the past quarter century have probably been strongly in favor of improved treatment for Blacks, but actual progress, though real, has been uneven and relatively slow. Perhaps the term "social affairs impact" is more precise than the term "social control."

The mass medium is almost always a part of the marketing process (exceptions, of course, are public television, some publications, most films, nearly all books) in the sense that the medium carries paid messages designed to sell merchandise or services or to present ideas which have commercial overtones. Some observers insist that the mass media are primarily marketing devices, that they are tailored intensively to provide the best possible settings for increasing the selling effectiveness of advertising, and that other content factors are primarily adjuncts to the merchandising process.[5]

One overtone of this point of view, held also by other observers who do not see marketing as the central thrust of the mass medium, is the feeling that many or most media are driven constantly toward seeking and holding a relatively high proportion of within-range pertinent audience. ABC network president James Duffy spoke of an ever-sharpening three-network competition for national audiences when he was trying to persuade ABC affiliates to carry as many ABC shows as possible (when an affiliate refuses to carry a network show, there is no audience for that show in that area and network revenues are cut; losing 1 percent of national audience for an hour of evening prime time may cut income $150,000).[6]

This drive for audience then tends to push a medium toward a "mass common denominator" approach to the selection of content. For example, in a television news show, it is important that practically every item have some appeal to most of the audience; low-appeal items run the risk of tune-out, which reduces the audience for all succeeding items.

Still another view, relatively more applicable to print, finds the media seeking high intensity pull from each of a variety of types of content, diverse in nature, and each appealing strongly to an audience segment, even though appeal to other elements in the audience may be very low. Haskins, writing of the use of this approach in magazines, speaks of how maximum audience reach may be attained with a minimum of items.[7]

The fact that the mass medium is usually large brings specialization of labor, so that most workers are involved in only one small part of the process and few, if any, carry the whole process through from beginning to end.[8] The worker then usually has only a small share in the final product, at the same time that he is removed from any major direct contact with and personal responsibility to most of the audience. This is the case even though the specialist dealing with content is often a very major gatekeeper, at times for audiences of millions, making decisions on inclusion or exclusion of material and on degree of emphasis given to content. At the same time this professional or semi-professional is subject to policies set by management, often determined unilaterally, and/or to the content decisions made by superiors. Currently this situation is resulting in relatively more discussion on how much voice the direct-contact news worker should have in management and in implementation of policy.[9]

The Audience

As for the nature of the audience, it is, first of all, thought of usually as very large. Cutting points on relative size are cloudy and/or arbitrary. One rule of thumb is that the size is such that the communicator cannot interact face to face with each individual in the audience; this guideline is not very meaningful, since audiences are usually measured in tens or hundreds of thousands, or in millions, rather than in dozens or hundreds. A related factor on audience is anonymity, in that the individual in the audience, considered in the generic sense, is

not known to the communicator (although the communicator may know some few persons in the audience).

The relationship is also such that the audience does not usually show much disposition toward direct feedback (so common and even essential in interpersonal communication) to the communication medium or to the communicator. If more than one-fifth of 1 percent of a station's listeners comment in a day, that's unusual. At the same time, there is indirect feedback, often without detailed knowledge by the medium, such as turning to another channel or stopping the paper.

Another characteristic of the "ideal" audience for mass communications is that it is essentially heterogeneous. It is made up of a wide variety of persons so far as age, sex, education, occupation, economic class, and geographical location are concerned. (We do tend to accept some limitation by geographic area; a station or a newspaper covering 100 or even 50 square miles is still thought of as a mass medium.)

A problem does arise in the middle-ground area of audiences of specialized interest, whether they be teenagers or hardware dealers or supermarket operators; such an audience is certainly not heterogeneous in the broadest sense, but it can be considered a mass communications audience within that specialized interest area, and in such enterprises most of the other circumstances of mass communications operations are found.

Since audiences are thought of as not known to the communicator, and for other reasons, there has been some tendency to see audience members as isolated, in a sense atomized, members of the society, but this is clearly not the case. Audience members do not usually attend to mass media as atomized persons; they almost always attend with a consciousness of their membership in groups, and indeed often attend consciously to mass communications content for the purpose of later re-consumption of the material with other members of their own groups.

The Experience

As for the nature of the mass communication experience, the fact that it is "public" is of much importance. In a sense, the message is addressed "to whom it may concern," and is open to public examination and inspection.

The message is usually distributed rapidly, and this rapidity is a factor in another characteristic, the relatively transient nature of the product. A broadcast disappears at once unless recorded, and the low usefulness of yesterday's newspaper is traditional.

In contrast to interpersonal communication, where feedback is constant and almost immediate, feedback in mass communications is almost always low, and usually involves only a small and perhaps rather constant part of the audience; that is, the reactor is more likely to produce added feedback response, while the non-reactor will probably continue in that no-response pattern. It is true also that feedback is in part minimized by adherence to a pattern of content recognized by management as almost unchangeable, such as always running a certain amount of sports news about recognized topics, and always running certain comics. Deviation does produce feedback: e.g., a TV listener calling in about substitution of Henry Kissinger on an international crisis for a morning soap opera: "If I knew this trash was going to be on, I would have done my shopping."

Almost always, a part or much of content has entertainment value, and some definers of mass communication hold this to be an essential. An important overtone is that often information content is dramatized or livened up so that an entertainment factor is introduced, as part of an effort to make the news more widely appealing.

Most of the content, in addition, is not directly experienced; it is unusual when a government committee hearing is covered live and in full; almost always the product is excerpted and is processed by a communicator who then becomes a crucial gatekeeper.

Mass communications content also tends to saturate the audience. There are thousands of stimuli available, many of them offered almost continuously through the day, and the citizen is almost constantly faced with the need to select, to make innumerable choices.

Major Functions of the Mass Media

Like all institutions, the mass media exist because they fill a need or needs felt by the society and by individuals. As Katz declares, ". . . media-related needs are not, by and large, generated by the media."[10]

Obviously many of the needs could be filled otherwise, such as through the private employment of information gatherers (as medieval bankers did on many occasions), or by family and by associates, but the increased efficiency and lowered per-unit cost of the mass media have been the major determining factors in building the media.

Surveillance–Information–News

In any discussion of the needs which are filled, and of the functions which are important, it is usually assumed that the primary function, from the standpoint of the welfare of both the society and the individual, is to fill the need for information. Even though a substantial portion of the audience seems to place low value on at least certain phases of information, nearly everyone has a need, often urgent, for at least some types of information. Modern industrial societies live on information; they live well, and survive, only if their citizens are well enough informed. Lippmann declared that it is the function of communications in society "to make a picture of reality on which men can act."[11] (Swanson, commenting on the New England Newspaper Survey, said, "If there is one common lesson in newspapering available from the survey, it appears to be a command to print all the information possible. . . .")[12]

In essence this means knowing what's happening; a common term, first used by Lasswell, is "surveillance of the environment," which involves seeking out and then transmitting information about the society and all other relevant elements.[13] Most of this is "news," a term which includes some advertising and a part of the product of public relations.

There are at least three major phases, not totally demarcated, in the surveillance-news-information package:

1. The "instrumental" news, of direct help in the day's operations, including working news of the immediate community (when taxes are due, when the zoning board will meet, retail ads, classified advertising, TV and radio timetables, and so on).
2. Material for the continuing updating of the citizen on major developments, changes, and needs in the society.
3. Warnings about imminent threats and dangers, such as major changes in weather, or transportation; sudden major changes in government policy, or threatening social developments (escaped criminals, harassment of children, hijackings, kidnappings), or warnings about the economy (the *Wall Street Journal* reports that commercial paper may be becoming more risky[14]).

Certain sub-phases of the surveillance-news function deserve mention:

(a) Personal esteem can be built through the prestige which comes from knowing the news; in interpersonal relationships, there is a social gain from being first with the news.

(b) An individual needs a social base for personal interchange: what will my friends be talking about? What parts of this conversation will be based upon mass media content which it is highly desirable to know about?

(c) For some individuals, there is a gain also from merely having a feeling of knowledge, of knowing the score, of satisfying curiosity, as distinguished from any actual usefulness which this knowledge might have.

(d) Being the subject of media coverage (to some extent, even negatively) confers status, builds prestige.

The surveillance-information-news function also has dysfunctional facets. Some news from outside may be seen as a potential threat to the social structure: actions of other nations which are potentially harmful; impacts on one's currency of the actions of other nations; interruptions to the flow of oil. Uninterpreted or misinterpreted warnings may cause panic; the classic case is the invasion-from-Mars broadcast. There are comparable impacts on the individual, in the form of heightening anxieties; some years ago "atom bomb nerves" was a not unusual personal problem. An important overtone here is the tendency of some citizens to blame the media, rather than the news, for the nature of the accurate bad news which these citizens do not want to face.

Still another impact can be that of privatization, when the individual, overloaded or even overwhelmed by the flow of information, turns aside from the flood of public life, and retreats to private life, where he has more control. A less extreme reaction of this type is found when the citizen becomes apathetic, a condition originally referred to by Lazarsfeld and Merton as "narcotic dysfunction"; the situation of simply knowing the news may provide an adequate (the term false is perhaps extreme) sense of mastery, so that the citizen takes little or no further action in public affairs.[15]

Correlation–Interpretation

This function has traditionally been referred to as "correlation," a term first used by Lasswell. Commonly this function is seen as calling for the interpretation of information; seen positively, the purpose is to improve the quality of usefulness of the information for the citizen; seen negatively, the purpose is to prevent some of the undesirable consequences of communication, including over-stimulation and over-mobilization, in the case of news which might first be seen as threatening. Interpretive writing is a major manifestation of the effort to fulfill this function.

Correlation is also at times seen as "prescription," in which the medium tells the citizen what to think, and what line of action to choose. Usually this advice appears in editorials; less frequently it's found hidden in the news text itself. The Bethlehem (Pa.) *Globe-Times* in a front-page editorial endorsed a slate of 11 candidates for election to a government study commission. While the local Democratic party endorsed an entirely separate slate of candidates, from a field of 32, all eleven supported by the newspaper were chosen.[16]

Entertainment

The function of entertainment is distinguished from information; this distinction should not be seen too sharply, since the line between the two often blurs, and much information has entertainment value and much entertainment does also inform or otherwise contribute to the value system of the individual.

Entertainment fills time, often enlarges the citizen and is even more important because it provides releases from modern mankind's tension, stress, present and future shock, and other real or imagined difficulties.

Is entertainment important? The U.S. Senate, referred to as the single most important legislative body in the world, took time to decide whether major professional sports should be blacked out on local television in cases of a sellout.[17] Basketball star Bill Walton received over $2 million for a five-year contract.[18] Rodney Allen Rippy, then age 5, made six hamburger commercials and his sponsor's sales went up more than $140 million in one year; his face was better known to the public than the Vice President's.[19] Associated Press Managing Editors surveyed members for reader reaction to cuts in newspaper content because of the newsprint shortage: there was little reader complaint. "Those who did gripe said they missed the comics most of all."[20]

Entertainment is a major factor in the ludenic, or play, theory of mass communication advanced by Stephenson, which holds that the individual plays with the products of the mass media in much the same way a child plays with toys, or "plays house." Though often "attended to with seriousness," notes Stephenson, "it is not really important" since it falls outside an individual's "world of duty and responsibility."[21] Such communication pleasure does, however, contribute to both individual and cultural development.

Socialization

This function is seen as assisting in the process of socialization. In this context, the media tell the citizen about the expected common elements of the society: this is the way we do things. Media workers may not often think consciously of the fact that they fulfill this function, but that non-awareness does not reduce the impact of the process, and may, in fact, enhance it.

This socialization process then helps to unify the society by providing at least some common base of norms, of values, of collective experience, and at the same time it helps the individual to know the current common base; the citizen may not choose to match up with the common base, but that variation is then a more knowing one.

Marketing

The next function is that of marketing, in the sense that the mass media are currently an irreplaceable element in the marketing process. We are a market society and the maintenance of a smoothly operating market system is important to all of us (as witness the fast-spreading problems raised by even minor dislocations in the long-range trucking industry during the oil shortage crisis).

As a result, the media carry advertising which influences consumers and which to a considerable extent also informs them. The news sections of many of the media also carry product information which, while it is useful to the citizen, is also of great service to the maker of the product.

It is important to note again that some observers feel that the mass media exist primarily to deliver an audience for commercial messages, so that other aspects of media operation are secondary and viewed by operators as really important only to the extent that they contribute to the effectiveness of delivery of the advertising content.

Initiating Social Change

Another function is leadership in social change, although some observers think the media should be relatively passive in this role and feel that the media should be essentially transmitters of socially relevant information, without a leading role in initiating or in attempting to direct social change.

Carrying out this function calls for the media to carry on a continuing survey of the needs of society, and to transmit an accurate and complete picture promptly to the community. Further, the media should encourage the process of formal social planning.

The media should go beyond the earlier function of listing current agenda, and should provide an "ought to do" agenda for the soci-

ety. In this sense the media are an early warning system for the society, a conscience urging attention now to problems which promise to be major.

It may be that the media may also be under the obligation to work directly and specifically, over and beyond content in the medium itself, for the adoption of important social changes considered to be of crucial import. The point can be made that almost no major element in society is working thus on behalf of individual social changes. Because of their information-gathering experience and capabilities, the media are well placed to take on this responsibility. At the same time, the point can be raised that such a step puts too much power into the hands of the media, and that this power should be diffused.

A subphase of the leadership-in-social-change function is the developing and the recognizing of new leaders for the society. The media expose potential leaders to the public and so help them face public testing grounds. The media for centuries have appraised potential leaders and given them more or less exposure; it seems reasonably clear that a formless and nonorganized but perhaps self-reinforcing aggregation of journalists based in Washington has a major voice in determining what persons are seen seriously as candidates for the presidency.

The media also serve as a communication belt between actual and potential leaders on current developments and on points of view; this function is especially important in such large and complicated enterprises as the federal entity in Washington. And lower level functionaries have been known to leak news to the mass media in order to reach superiors who previously hadn't listened.

Creating Social Style

This function is important in setting a style for society, of providing an example of the approach to public affairs, literature, culture, and the life-style in general. My own feeling is that the mass media, among other factors, need to work for an operating attitude of civility, not only in their own conduct but in the conduct of public affairs. By civility I here mean something more than the mechanisms of courtesy; I am referring to an effort to carry on discussion, and public activities, generally in a rational rather than in an emotional manner, and to stress a concern for human dignity and for the treatment of persons as human beings rather than as mechanisms or stimulus-response entities.

Watchdogging

Perhaps subsumed under news-surveillance, but deserving special mention, is the function of watchdogging the society, of constantly being on the lookout for malfunctions of importance which should be brought to the attention of the society. Such examples as Watergate and My Lai are obvious.

Education

Another function, somewhat related to socialization, is that of continuing the educational process in organized fashion. Programs over educational and commercial television, and to a lesser extent over radio, are examples. Mass media play an important part in the new Open University in Great Britain. Newspapers also are being brought into continuing education activities.

Related Functions

There are other functions as well. Research by Katz in Israel found citizens listing as a function of the media the capability of building a greater faith in the nation and in the quality of its operations.[22] The media safeguard civil liberties; often it appears they are by far the most consistent and the most vigorous of the fighters. In a much more mundane area, but one important to many citizens, the media provide a routine or a ritual for the day ("this is something I do every morning after breakfast"). Two other related functions, also important, are the structuring of time (people don't know what else to do, so they attend to the mass media), and the introduction of variety or novelty (the media bring something different; they provide a break). The media provide a great part, perhaps the major part, of the base for the historical record of the society; they are almost unavoidably the starting point for much of that record.

Different media, of course, have always had different capabilities for performing these various functions. Supporters of newspapers will perhaps wish to stress Katz (". . . the centrality of the newspaper for knowledge and integration in the socio-political arena cannot be overstated"),[23] while supporters of other media will in turn have their favorite encomiums.

Factors Influencing Media Performance

How well are the mass media performing? What are the factors which influence their performance?

This task of appraisal is very difficult. There are objective data on some phases of media performance, such as quantity (and perhaps direction) of material on given topics, but most of the conclusions are subjective, which is not to say that they are without value.

In such an appraisal, it is important to know the social, business, political, and economic context in which the mass media operate.

Here these context elements will be treated as (a) those mostly internal—the nature of the medium and of the mass communications system, including economic factors, advertising, and mass media personnel; and (b) those factors which are essentially external—the nature of society and of audiences; government, pressure groups, advertisers, news sources, public relations, appraisers, financially related factors, suppliers, and schools of journalism.

Internal Factors: The Nature of the System

The mass media system itself tends to set certain boundaries on performance, not rigid, but usually bendable only with some specific effort. The system is business-oriented, in great part, because this is a market society.

The mass media exemplify most of the attributes of the business system, including the tendency toward concentration of ownership. The percentage of daily newspapers owned by groups rises steadily, and so does percentage of total circulation controlled by groups. Conglomerates are picking up communications units. Large communications units are tending to diversify, which protects against disruptions, such as strikes, but does centralize control. (The Department of Justice does show increasing interest in breaking up cross-media concentrations in a given city.) Big units tend to have much or major influence; Hayden has written of the need to break the influence of *The New York Times* and *The Washington Post* on other dailies.[24] Epstein has declared that *The New York Times* is the every-morning starting point for planning the major TV network evening newscasts.[25]

Stability The media system is complex, and usually requires the processing of a large body of content rapidly, and within a rather short period of time. The system must perform day after day in expectable fashion: the news broadcast is expected at the appointed hour, the newspaper should arrive by 5:15 p.m., Magazine *M* should reach us about the 20th of each month.

There has been some departure recently from the standard approaches to news processing: a few large papers have set up continuing task forces charged with following an issue without daily deadline pressure. Wire services are changing their approach, over time, as well (witness the decision of the Associated Press, a few years ago, to give more attention to younger readers), but the changes will come rather slowly. Individual wire service members and clients exert little impact on content and meantime are faced with using wire services material as it comes into their offices.

Media Influence on Events To what extent do media determine what "happened" in the public area through choosing "events" and shaping them? Molotch and Lester declare that "news assemblers" are very influential, so that news can often be looked upon as a "constructed reality" which is "assembled in the context of what has gone before and anticipated in the future."[26] Segal asserts internal struggles between newspaper "desks" for "our share" of space produce a not always logical division of emphasis on content.[27]

A change in the daily newspaper field is an increased concern with accuracy, and a greater willingness, at least on some major publications, to print corrections (often prominently). Tied with this change is the move toward a greater number (even though not large) of ombudsmen or public editors, usually on larger newspapers, who respond to complaints and may also take a lead in explaining operations to the public.[28]

There is media concern also over treatment of news of minorities, an extremely complex field to appraise. A study of Fedler indicates that in Minneapolis minorities generally received more news treatment than matched units from majorities. What is more, minorities were not totally happy with the nature of coverage, which often dealt with demonstrations.[29]

Increasing concern by the media for the audience, a topic to be discussed later under concern for outside elements, was apparent. The American Newspaper Publishers Association (ANPA) Foundation commissioned a number of important studies in this area.[30] A few individual newspapers began their own studies of the audience, one of the most sophisticated by Philip Meyer for the *Detroit Free Press*.[31]

Ethics, Personnel, and Profits Newspaper association executives agreed that credibility of newspapers is "the issue of the hour,"[32] and ethical performance is a genuine concern for the industry. Harold Taylor, the board chairman of ANPA, in his 1974 chairman's address, stressed the need for continuing concern with credibility, accountability, accuracy, integrity, and fair play.[33]

Seen by some observers as an attempt to overcome ethical and other weaknesses in the conventional establishment media, the so-called alternative press—small and often politically-motivated papers—seems to have lost much of its appeal over the past few years (perhaps in part because of the winding-down and end of the Vietnam war), and to have lost much of its impact.[34]

The competence and attitudes of personnel are obviously key factors in the operation of a medium, and a worry today is whether the quality is being maintained. Indications are that quality is being maintained, although at least one major factor in employee attitude does seem to be changing: there is more push from lower-echelon staff for greater participation in determination of policy matters. Tied with this development is the question of attitude of workday staff toward management; there seems to be more of an adversary relationship than in the past. At the Liebling Counter-Convention (an annual meeting of working reporters held in response to, and at the same time as, annual management-owner meetings), a paid attendance of 1,850 lower echelon news people recently set a record for a journalism convention in the United States.[35]

Perhaps as a result, many media do appear to be more concerned with internal communication and more steps are being made toward employee participation in decisions concerning ethical matters. There continues to be, however, strong opposition on part of management to formalize such a right in labor contracts.

It is probably true that the nature of staffs, especially on newspapers, is changing. Peter Clark, publisher of the *Detroit News,* has stated that working news people are nowadays more upper-middle class; not long ago they were from lower economic levels. This upward change, he says, has resulted in a loss of feeling for the situation faced by most of the daily newspaper audience, the majority of which is from a lower socio-economic status.[36]

Relatively more of today's staff writers believe that the writer should have the right to present his own version of events in his or her story; that is, to be an advocate. An example is found in an *Editor and Publisher* headline: "Our reporter finds session at Liebling C-C a real bore."[37] Serious problems arise in instances where the advocacy of the reporter is not made headline-clear, yet is subtley expressed throughout the report. In some media, more notably certain types of magazines (*New York* is an excellent example), there is increasing use of the "new journalism," involving both great depth of field work and the effort to select and vitalize impact phrases, which seem to the reporter to present the essence of the story as he feels it—and the word *feel* is important.

As for supply of personnel, the media are in a much better position, generally, than several years ago; journalism schools, an increasingly important source of supply, have boosted enrollment sharply (as much as 150 percent), and most media have many applications for openings.

The major mass media generally show more concern for adopting modern, highly sophisticated management methods, which increase efficiency and provide more flexibility in facing fast-moving challenges to profitability. Some observers see this change as tending to mechanize internal relationships which they feel should be on a very human basis.

New technologies, especially those involving print media composition and printing (lasers may be the next phase), are pushing in rapidly. Their increasing adoption, with new stresses for most employees (even though perhaps short-term) and certain high threats for production personnel, are temporarily disrupting factors which usually have an end result of improved cost-effectiveness and the possibility of either better service or cost reduction, or both, for the consumer.

Increased concern with costs and other economic factors has been a major interest for most media, even though many have been very profitable. For many magazines, increased postage costs are crucial; they were a factor in the death of *Life*. For newspapers, newsprint price increases have substantial impact, especially on the bigger dailies with large circulation and generally large daily issues. Print media are sensitive about circulation price increases, since price increases cut circulation, and for many publications this reduces advertising volume and income.

All of these factors have a special impact for media which have (recently this has been mostly newspaper groups) "gone public," that is, made some or much of their stock available for general public ownership. When stock is owned publicly, security analysts take more interest. They ask questions, beginning with "What's your profit picture going to be next quarter (year)?" Unrelenting pressure from analysts and investors produces a steady everyday squeeze on management to produce better bottom-line results.

Each day dozens of decisions are, even though not openly, viewed in the light of effect on profits. Here's how management consultant James B. Kobak phrases one of the possible reasons for merging or selling magazines: "The requirement of the professional manager in publicly held companies to continuously increase the earnings (possibly to the detriment of the longer range future of the company, in some cases)."[38] (An ironic twist is that many social critics, who deplored closely held ownerships as not susceptible to the public, will now find that when such ownerships go public the "public will" focuses strongly on the making of more money so that the price of the stock will go up.)

External Factors: Social, Political, Economic

Of the factors outside the media which influence media performance, the general attitudes of the society rank high in importance.

In a society which is highly pluralized, power is then rather widely divided, but there is also the possibility that relatively small elements may thwart public concerns (example: gun control). It is important also that so many elements in society now recognize the powers of the media and are prepared to "use" the media for their purposes (example: Wounded Knee).

At the same time, society does not have clearly in mind a policy toward or about the mass media, a situation which may well be preferable to a clearly known but undesirable policy. The range of attitudes toward the media is wide. It is probable that a substantial majority of the public would approve a compulsory "right of reply" law—on the surface such a law seems very "right." In the absence of any considerable evidence of social damage, large numbers of citizens are willing to limit access of all persons to certain types of content called pornographic or obscene.

Public opinion polls show consistently disturbing tendencies toward a willingness by many to limit freedom of speech and of the press (although, in a crunch, such as Watergate, the public backs the media). Nor have attitudes improved greatly. The Tennessee legislature passed (Senate 28 to 1, House 54 to 15) a law which requires that any biology text used in the public schools must state that evolution is a theory, and not a scientific fact, and that such a text, if it considers this topic, must, in the same section, give "commensurate attention to" other theories, including the Genesis account.[39]

Media Audience As for the audience of the mass media: the increase in education level has been pronounced recently, but the knowledge level may not have changed greatly. A rather well grounded rule of thumb holds that in public opinion surveying on a major current public issue about 25 percent of adults will be rather well informed, 50 percent will recognize the issue but not know much about it, and 25 percent will not have heard of it. As for topics read about in daily papers, an ANPA survey found those top topics, and percentages of readership, for men: accidents, disasters, 37 percent; U.S. government, Vietnam, armaments, 36 percent; taxes, 34 percent; crime, 33 percent; letters, 31 percent; for women: accidents, 41 percent; letters, 38 percent; advice columns, 38 percent; obituaries, 37 percent; general non-local human interest, 35 percent.[40]

The amount of time devoted to the media continues to be large, and for most persons time devoted to media ranks close behind time for work and for sleep. An A. C. Nielsen Television Index report indicates non-white total-household usage averaging 56 hours 2 minutes per week, and white usage 48 hours 45 minutes, in mid-winter. However, the amount of non-adult viewing has been declining since 1967.[41]

Surveys indicate most citizens say they are willing to pay more for media, but whether this works out in practice is uncertain. After circulation price increases, daily newspapers lose circulation for a time, then regain most of the loss rather slowly. But U.S. daily newspaper circulation in general, while rising, has been falling on a per-household basis.

In considering the impacts of higher print-media rates, and of the coming of cable television (with a cost usually of at least $60 per year) and of pay television, it is interesting to note that a superbly detailed study by McCombs indicates that the percentage of gross national product spent for mass media has held rather constant at 4.1 to 4.2 percent for most of a 20-year period. Apparently as new media have come in, funding has come from previous expenditures for other media.[42]

Feedback from the audience continues in the main to be indirect and nominal. On most media there is no "facilitating entry": how does the audience member know whom to reach or how to make the approach to this possibly distant, probably faceless organization, where he probably knows no one and into whose building he may never have gone? Recently several major daily newspapers, with increasing concern for accountability, have set up ombudsmen or public editors to receive audience response, and have vigorously publicized routes of approach to make contact easy. Broadcast outlets have consumer advertising and some newspapers are running "how we do it" self-explanation and self-criticism columns.[43]

The impact of the audience on the media is inescapable and substantial. Without an adequate audience, the modern commercial medium is lost. So the medium does respond to the audience, and media management and staff attend intensively to their concern for audience. For TV networks and stations especially, audience is a life-or-death matter, and advertising agencies are intensely concerned too (a minute on "All in the Family" now sells for about $120,000), as witness this *Broadcasting* magazine headline at the time of the crucial fall line-up announcements: "Agencies lay heavy odds on CBS's fall line-up, but see tight race for second place/Madison Avenue media types predict this season's winner will lengthen lead over other two networks when new shows premiere, but nevertheless they agree all three will sell out."[44]

But a major point must be made with some force: in the main, the audience seems at least to accept, and perhaps to like, most of what modern commercial mass media provide. Berelson's comment of 1959 is still sound: "It is a fact that people generally like what they get in the mass media."[45] Audiences show this by the manner and extent to which they attend to the mass media, and the manner in which they respond to advertising (especially local retail and classified).

Media and Government The relationship between media and government has been generally symbiotic—each needed the other (the media needed audience-arousing content, and the government needed dissemination of certain desired messages), and over the years there was an uneasy cooperation which worked to the advantage of both; it produced a great flow of information on public affairs, probably the best in the world.

Most governments, like nearly all news sources, manipulated the news after a fashion, within ground rules that were rather well recognized between the press and government, with the understanding that the manipulation would not go too far. Occasionally there were sad exceptions—Eisenhower and U-2, Kennedy and the Bay of Pigs—but usually the "rules" were observed.

But recently problems have developed, as this relationship seems to have changed subtly. Government manipulation of news has been more extensive through controlling release times and quantities released, through withholding information, through releasing diversionary information, through occasional deception,[46] and, at the federal level, through extensive use of classification. There have been attempts to harass the press, for example, through investigations and through use of the subpoena; there have been efforts, as through speeches by Agnew and statements by Nixon, to either intimidate the media or to reduce faith in it; Nixon, displeased by Watergate news efforts of the *Washington Post,* declared [it's] "going to have damnable, damnable problems" in its efforts to get *Post* television station licenses renewed.[47]

At the same time the media have become more active, perhaps more belligerent, in pushing for news, and in demanding access: passage of the various open records/open meetings laws in many states, and the federal Freedom of Information Act are examples. Publication of the Pentagon Papers and the airing of "The Selling of the Pentagon" were examples of more pronounced probing into "how things are in government."

Government forces of various kinds have increasingly challenged the contention of journalists that they must be able to keep sources confidential, in the interest of maintaining the fullest possible flow of information. News workers have gone to jail, some for indefinite periods, under contempt-of-court citations for refusal to give information. These government challenges have caused much recent interest in "shield" legislation which would permit news workers to refuse to divulge sources and would also protect against efforts to obtain notes and notebooks, unused stories, and processed but unused news film (outtakes). Such laws exist in many states.

Pressure from Groups and Advertisers Pressure groups, a not too satisfactory term for the cluster of pressure related to news content, want media to include adequate material about their interests. Such groups have always existed; now they include a wide range of interests, and especially minorities of many kinds. Such ethnic groups as Blacks, and more recently Chicanos and American Indians, come readily to mind; the largest minority, women, has recently been much more ac-

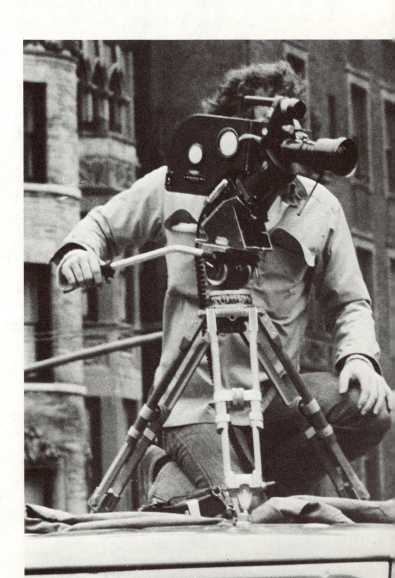

tive; consumerism is an increasingly vocal force (a monthly magazine, *Media and Consumer,* is now devoted to news about consumerism and how media treat it), and there are special interest groups of many kinds, many pushing for their own interests, such as business and professional associations, and others such as the League of Women Voters and Common Cause working for what they consider the general welfare.

Essentially these groups push for two things: news or advertising setting forth their points of view (many also desire a reduction in opposing material, but it's much more difficult to work for this), and the right attitude in editorial and other opinion content.

Increasingly, some of the groups attempt to manipulate to make more certain that they get attention for their points of view. They use the "pseudo-event," so aptly christened by Boorstin[48]—the announcement luncheon, the often not so meaningful press conference, the ribbon cutting, the acronymic group as a front for expressing views, and the physically "visible" event, such as a demonstration (often aimed at attracting television), or confrontation (often announced in advance to secure more media attention).

In the process, these groups use the media as subtly as possible, but on occasion very openly. Many observers feel that the Wounded Knee manifestation was planned essentially to manipulate the media into providing continued coverage which on a words-only basis might have gone nowhere, especially since the story would have died quickly.

The impact of the advertiser on the mass media system is essentially indirect rather than direct, although there are exceptions.

Media management is conscious always that if the end product is not seen by enough advertisers as at least adequate in terms of audience-impact desirability, that the medium will lose advertising, and if enough is lost the problems intensify, especially since a follow-the-gang-and-let's-get-out downward spiral often develops.

In most newsrooms there is subtle awareness of advertiser concern about the nature of news content, although there is also an increasing tendency toward presentation of public welfare news which at least some advertisers might dislike (for example, media investigations of bacterial count in supermarket hamburger).

Pressures from Sources of News Without adequate news sources, the modern mass news medium is dead; the quantity and quality of source material provided are crucial to the medium and the journalist. (Hersh got his My Lai story on a volunteered tip from a friendly source inside the Pentagon.) If sources are generally unwilling and reluctant, the ease of acquiring news is reduced, and cost factors can go up sharply and at the same time service to the audience may be reduced.

If a source shifts from open-contact to the use of news releases, whether oral or written, the nature of media control over output changes, perhaps a great deal; costs for the medium may go down because of the ease of using material, but may go up because of the greater difficulty and complexity of followups which try to go behind the news-release screen.

If previously open sources begin, even on a casual basis, to give better news material to a medium which is relatively more favorable, complications arise. *The Washington Post* almost certainly did not enjoy the exclusive interview former President Nixon gave *The Washington Star*. If a reporter becomes too palsy-walsy with a news source, the ease of flow may increase, but the quality of the product may be lower.

Another source of news that exerts pressure on the media, although usually more subtle, is public relations workers who create pseudo-events, then submit material which is well prepared, suited to the needs of the medium, and blessed with sufficient news value to warrant distribution. Ralbovsky was amazed at the number of press releases he was given to handle on *The New York Times* sports desk.[49]

Often skilled public relations workers can have a considerable impact on the flow of the news: Twohey and Rosapepe declare that superb public relations work, much of it through the Air Transport Association with an annual budget of $6 million, has been responsible for increased air fares at a time when service quality was declining.[50]

Media Appraisal The number of agencies or individuals formally appraising the media has been increasing, and they exert an increasing influence, even though most media managements are inclined not to admit this.

New journals of appraisal, headed by *Columbia Journalism Review* and *MORE*, are the major element. There are also broadcast critiques; schools of journalism provide some analysis;[51] individuals speak and write about the media; scholars write about their own analyses, usually in scholarly journals, and news councils or press councils consider current developments. Foundations (most often, Markle and Twentieth Century) enter the picture through grants for appraisal by others.

Usually the product will consider specifically mass medium or media treatment of a given event, or the trend of performance by the mass media in a specific area. A more recent development is a statewide survey, such as the Massachusetts Newspaper Survey, or the regional study, the New England Daily Newspaper Survey, in which 13 observers studied copies of dailies, conducted interviews on site, and wrote appraising essays which were presented along with much information from individual managements.[52]

Accuracy in Media, a private organization seen by many as having rather conservative sponsorship, follows up on specific instances of maltreatment or of inaccuracy, and Freedom House carries on a continuing study of press performance.

The National News Council, set up through efforts of the Twentieth Century Foundation, is getting under way with formal appraisal of the worthiness of complaints against performance of nationally distributed media or wire services.

Media Financing Financing from outside the enterprise itself has become relatively more important for most media in recent years, which tends to produce steady pressures for increases in dollar volume and in profit levels, especially on media in which ownership is open to the public. Public stock offerings have increased by chains of newspapers, anxious for expansion funds; *Broadcasting* magazine in each issue now carries a two-page table of current financial information, including current price-earnings ratios and price changes during the week, on more than 120 firms in or adjacent to the broadcasting field; *Editor & Publisher* in each issue lists prices on twenty or more newspaper-related stocks and devotes a page or more to financial news of newspaper stocks.

Now that more newspaper stocks are publicly held, security analysts are showing more interest in them. Fifty attended a seminar held by a security firm specializing in newspaper stocks, where executives of major enterprises told of plans ("we are tailoring our newspaper magazine for specific groups of readers") and answered questions about problems, often those affecting profitability.[53]

The influence of suppliers is crucial for most media. A worldwide shortage of paper, apparently to continue for some time, is hitting magazines and newspapers.[54] The Decatur (Ill.) dailies dropped all advertising for several weeks when projections showed anticipated newsprint to be inadequate; hundreds of dailies have cut the size of their issues. Newsprint supplies for the mid 1970s are seen as barely adequate; mill stoppages, strikes, railroad delays, or natural disasters which result in even two percent loss in expected production would cause shortages for some newspapers. Magazines are having similar problems.

In the same way all media are influenced by the capability level, innovativeness, anticipativeness, and reliability of all suppliers, whether broadcast package producers, the postal service, wire services, equipment producers and maintainers, or energy producers.

Schools of journalism exert a long-range influence on the media through a subtle and unintended screening mechanism. As media move gradually toward a preference for journalism graduates, in part because they are easier to break in, and as the cost of attending college continues to increase sharply, graduates available for new hirings increasingly come from the middle and upper-economic levels.[55] The consequences of this situation for the relationship between the media and their audiences was discussed earlier.

Educators are welcomed at media association conventions. There are educator-media joint committees of various kinds. And educators carry on more and more appraisal of the media, mostly in their own scholarly journals (the *Columbia Journalism Review* and a few others are major exceptions). But educator impact on media performance can best be described as nominal at top management levels and slightly greater at other levels.

Assessing Mass Media Performance

In considering the performance of the mass media, it may be helpful to talk of the quality of the fulfillment of the various functions described earlier, and some of the so-called "general" effects of the mass media. In discussing fulfillment of functions, it is useful to have in mind the five "ideal demands" made upon the media by the Commission on Freedom of the Press, the so-called Hutchins Commission, still very pertinent, even though phrased more than 30 years ago:

1. A truthful, comprehensive, and intelligent account of the day's events in a context which gives them meaning
2. A forum for the exchange of comment and criticism
3. The projection of a representative picture of the constituent groups in the society
4. The presentation and clarification of the goals and values of the society
5. Full access to the day's intelligence.[56]

In appraising performance, there are certain questions: Performance on behalf of whom? Who is the audience? Since the audience is large and wide-ranging, not homogeneous, there are very different answers for different parts of the audience. My estimates here are concerned with the citizen who is slightly above the middle on a scale of concern about major issues in public affairs, and, to a lesser extent, with the elite. I focus on this group because they are most likely to have the greatest political impact. In appraising, I rely on my own impressions and observations, on the impressions of other scholars, critics, and practitioners, who have shown an informed interest, and upon results of research. Usually my comparisons on changes relate to differences since, roughly, the late 1950s.

Fulfilling the Functions

Surveillance-information Facing up to the major social function of the media, information flow, I am astounded anew at the colossal task, at the vastness and complexities of the "informations" which the media are to transmit, in the words of the Hutchins Commission, in "a truthful, comprehensive, and intelligent account of the day's events in a context which gives them meaning." Appraisal is difficult, and my effort here is only to give general impressions, without detailed analysis of each of the media, with their differing built-in capabilities, not to mention lock-ins on audience expectations.

Accurate and Truthful Nearly all the time the accuracy level on factual content in most of the mass media is high, or very high. There seems to be very little lying or deceit by reporters or the media (although they may transmit the lies and deceit of others, a circumstance which is itself a form of "truth," and thus accurate). There are exceptions: Richard H. Stewart, a journalist who served on Senator Muskie's presidential campaign staff, detailed threats, pressure, distortions, other malfeasances by news people.[57]

And almost certainly some segments of the establishment, especially business, sometimes consciously, often unconsciously, get favored treatment in quite a few media. At the same time, more and more staffers are resisting this approach.

The picture of media quality grows more murky when "supporting" data and "background" are considered. These help provide the "truth" which the Hutchins Commission saw as going well beyond the bareness of accuracy about facts (which might mean one man's accuracy is another man's distortion).

There are many opportunities for bias and deceit, especially in the exercise of advocacy and first-person journalism. The Commission sought a clear differentiation of fact and of opinion.[58] This boundary has tended to become cloudier and the distinction is less clear than it was fifteen years ago, a change which is a net loss for both the public and the media.

There is evidence of increasing manipulation of the news by many sources, especially those in government. For example, NASA on several occasions denied reporters needed access to news, delayed information, and suppressed information (medical condition of astronauts, the Apollo fire story).[59]

An important factor is a greater willingness on the part of media to make corrections openly, clearly and quickly, so that there is some chance of the correction catching up with the error it is meant to rectify. The fact that this has not been generally true has been one of the more serious problems of mass communication. Once an error gets into the system, it is very hard to get it out or even to get it altered.

Comprehensiveness Comprehensive coverage of any given current major story is well handled by most major media. At times, the problem may even be overkill, or supersaturation, in a follow-the-leader wolf-pack pattern, which means the media have fewer resources and less time-space to devote to other news events occurring at the same time.

As for the "total picture," the media do less well. Most have a greater concern for speculations about the future consequences of current events than was the case fifteen years ago. Again, such activities deprive the media of valuable time-space for establishing current contexts. The situation is compounded by the current philosophy that the media need to present differentness, crisis, and urgency in order to seem worthwhile to their audiences. On balance, preoccupation with seeking out such events may have a considerably distorting effect upon comprehensiveness in a more global sense. In general, the print media are able to do a considerably better job than the broadcasting media in providing the larger picture, simply because the latter are so often locked into the "here and now" treatment of events except when it's possible to break time loose for a major documentary. Almost by definition, the major broadcast documentary rarely comes about until a problem becomes relatively immediate and rather clearly visible. In spite of what might seem to be an apparent contradiction, there is a considerable difference between isolated speculation regarding future consequences of a single event and a careful exploration of the relationship among events that have been given appropriate backgrounding and context.

Attention must also be paid to the paradoxes of comprehensive coverage of important local news. The paradoxes include comments that the media are: first, too local, at the expense of other important news; secondly, not local enough, or thirdly, local in the wrong way (not attending to the deeper long-range problems). Solid generalizations are not possible, but an ANPA research study in 1971 covering dailies with 5 percent or more circulation in 200 geographic areas representative of the 48 contiguous states showed that state and local news make up about 13 percent of news items 5½ inches or longer, compared to 10 percent international and 6.5 percent national. Sports occupied 14 percent of total news space.[60]

Intelligent and Meaningful As for the requirements that the presentation be "intelligent," the capabilities of reporters and desk workers are generally higher than they were fifteen years ago (although Kristol feels they are not high enough[61]), and quality of content is higher. Because education levels of the audience are up and their demands on the media are greater, the effectiveness of media performance is also improved. The media are in general doing better on "context that gives meaning," at a time when such an assignment becomes increasingly difficult as the complexity of the news increases from almost every field of human endeavor.

Often the information content and the depth of treatment of news are above the general level of either the concern or the capability of much of the audience; in the print media, where this is more often true, it is the hope that this factor will not drive away non-involved audiences and, instead, other elements of content in the medium will serve to hold such readers.

The whole matter of quality of surveillance-information is touched by several traumas. Do the media in general have an overall world view of happenings, or do they too often present insights essentially from the point of view of the United States? Other traumas include the almost constant demands for conciseness and brevity; the urge for "newness," pushing reporters at times to emphasize less important content, or distortion in order to get a new angle for the next broadcast or edition. The urge to be entertaining, to give the audience the illusion that they can easily understand complex problems and that becoming informed should not appear to have elements of work, is also a twisting factor.

Correlation–Interpretation Satisfying the call for correlation, interpretation, and prescription means torrents of material for the citizen. As a forum for the exchange of comment and criticism, the print media do quite well. Electronic media are improving, but are bounded by time limitations and remain overly subject to the demands of audience. Performance is considerably better than ten or fifteen years ago; most major points of view get a certain amount of exposure, especially in print media, and there is an opportunity for public criticism of those views. How to spell out "all the important viewpoints and interests in the society" (the Hutchins Commission goal) remains a very difficult question, but allowing rebuttals to controversial shows, (as CBS did in its *Guns of August* program) or allowing reporters to discuss a major political speech, show movement in the right direction.

As for presenting a projection of a representative picture of the constituent groups in the society, it is true that many stereotypes still persist on the news. Slurs on Blacks are reduced, however, and research studies generally show that exposure for most minorities has increased; the treatment of news about women has generally improved. The entertainment side of television, in particular, has made significant efforts with shows centering on and reflecting minority view points. There are more explanatory articles about the problems of occupational groups (the consistent work of *The Wall Street Journal* has been especially helpful and interesting).

The presentation and clarification of the goals and values of the society is a major assignment, even though the Hutchins Commission disposed of this Requirement No. 4 in some 150 words. The Commission saw a great responsibility for the media, "perhaps the most powerful educational instrument there is," in the goals-values area, but offered no advice on how to determine the current day-to-day goals and value of the society—the "actuals," as distinguished from the ideals, the "ought-to-be's."

Today the media aid increasingly by presenting continuing frank discussion which is in line with the Commission's belief "in realistic reporting of the events and forces that militate against the attainment of social goals as well as those which work for them."[62] Moynihan declares the media have gone too far with negative news, in part because so many reporters now come from universities associated with the "adversary position" (its better to criticize than to approve),[63] and many other observers hold much the same view. (In fact, because Senator Proxmire of Wisconsin became much concerned with the "pervasive feeling of public cynicism about the nation and the federal government," he gave a series of public speeches on "What's Right with America."[64])

Change, Entertainment and Life-Style The function of providing leadership for social change draws much media attention, primarily through the providing of information on major topics of concern, but also increasingly through providing an "ought to" agenda directed toward the needs of the future. Cohen declares the press may not be successful much of the time in telling people what to think, "but it is stunningly successful in telling its readers what to think *about*."[65]

As for the function of entertainment, many media long thought of as primarily informational appear to be giving more attention to making more of their content entertaining. There has been a strong push toward making television news more entertaining and "easier to take." (This move has also been strongly resisted, even though the entertainment approach has often netted notable gains in audience.)

In aiding in the setting of a national life-style and in the process of socialization, it seems to me that the mass media are reasonably positive, but a very different view comes from Joseph Epstein, who declares America is a "nation under psychological assault," with the chief assaulter being the media, which "require trouble" and "thrive on scandal and aggravation." He adds, "In America the media's influence is particularly strong, and significant to the tone of the nation's public life beyond reckoning."[66]

Effects of Mass Media

In considering effects of the media, a prime conclusion is that of uncertainty; it is rather easy, if time-taking, to produce data on media content, but it is much more difficult to establish that there has been a distinctive influence which comes solely from the media.[67] The listing provided is, then, considerably subjective; it is also so condensed that it is in no sense all-inclusive.

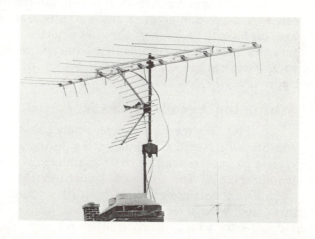

Knowledge Level, Especially of Public Affairs

This level of knowledge is almost certainly improved, but since such factors as awareness, cognition, and comprehension are intertwined, along with selective exposure and selective perception, it is difficult to appraise how much improved. Appearance of material in the mass media, of course, does not guarantee attention, or even awareness, as is apparent from the readership study cited earlier, and from much experience of public opinion pollsters. The great intangible is the "will of the citizen" to know or not know. A major question, whether an individual does or does not tend to avoid material not consonant with present beliefs, is still unresolved.

The Production of "Reality"

Beyond the sphere of local primary contacts of the citizen, the mass media provide most of the "reality" for the perceived world. Roberts writes that ". . . the way a child defines and approaches his world is to a large extent a function of the information communicated to that child,"[68] and the media certainly contribute a great deal to that input. If the citizen gives as much attention as he gave five or ten years ago, his picture of "reality" should be better, because of increased accuracy and interpretive competence from the media. With added attention to a wider variety of media, the quality of the reality is even more improved.

Setting the Agenda for Society

Here the media are increasingly effective. A study by McCombs and Shaw of North Carolina voters during an election campaign indicated that "voters tend to share the media's *composite* definition of what is important."[69] The comment quoted earlier from Kahn is also pertinent. The media are effective both in determining what's talked about now, and what's seen as urgent for future consideration. Although media performance quality is lower on future agenda, the media are an increasingly better early warning system, and the citizen who uses an adequately wide range of mass media can get a quite good picture of nearly all upcoming major social problems.

Impact on Values, Attitudes, Life-Style and Taste

Most of the effects here are seen as reinforcement of existing factors, and Weiss declares that evidence suggests "that people do not ordinarily use the media to seek out new experiences. . . ."[70]

The media effect values and life-style through reporting the attitudes, behavior and values of others. But the media alone have no substantial influence of their own; they have impact through a nexus of many forces, many of them outside the media. Economist Tilford Gains declares consumer reaction against the midi-dress, pushed by *Women's Wear Daily,* was the crucial turning point in consumer attitudes and began a questioning of the "match-the-Joneses" mentality.[71]

Effect on Behavior

John Robinson of the University of Michigan Institute for Social Research, after studying campaign results and daily newspaper presidential candidate endorsements over twenty years, asserts that endorsements have substantial positive impact, adding that "The political stand of the country's newspapers may be among the most underestimated forces in campaign politics."[72] In 1972, independent voters reading newspapers which endorsed Nixon were twice as likely to cast their ballots for him as for McGovern.

There is little evidence that exposure to violence in the media has produced catharsis, and there is an increasing feeling that under some circumstances for some persons there may be greater tendencies toward aggressive behavior, especially through cumulative exposure to media.

Consumer response to advertising continues high, and, within limits, media have high impact on the buying patterns of many sections of the public.

Other Effects

Do the media build empathy? There does seem to be a desire to get the "inside story" of how other persons feel and react, and soap operas, perhaps for this reason, hold large audiences. But whether effective concern is increased by such viewing is very much in question. As for mass culture, the culture that isn't disseminated isn't mass, so what the media choose to distribute tends to determine much public taste. Whether the media create new trends is in doubt; essentially they often appear to ride trends which are developing. In the field of social change, they do increasingly well in distributing anticipatory material, but there is no hard evidence as yet that they have succeeded in reducing levels of shock due to change. The media also increasingly take leadership in attempting to direct and control change and so, at least, expose more new ideas to the public. Without question, for most citizens, the media do absorb large proportions of time, obviously at the expense of other activities.

Prescriptions for the Future of the Mass Media

In this situation, what of the future? What ought to be done?

Here are a few possible lines of action in the public interest, and comments on the directions and possibilities of change (obviously many other items could be included, but these seem among the most important):

1. It seems important to develop and to maintain measuring sticks, a series of "media indicators," comparable to social indicators, which can provide a picture of at least some phases of media activity: What are the proportions of local, regional, state, national, and international news? Are there changes in the level of time-space devoted to

violence, crime, the future, and so on? What portion is devoted to "early warnings"?

2. All individual mass media should be encouraged to develop internal committees on "planning for our future," charged with examining the needs of the society for future mass media performance, assessing the demands which these needs place upon the medium, and considering possible alternative plans of action for meeting these needs. Such a committee should have a membership widely drawn from within the enterprise, and should be advisory to management. At the same time, management should be bound to act upon a minimum number of their suggestions.

3. In much the same way, each field within the mass medium should set up a "Committee on the Future" concerned with considering major problems of the society, current and anticipated, and developing a list of problems and a statement of urgencies and priorities. This committee would then go on to consider what action the field should take with regard to news and other coverage of each of these problems, and what other steps might well be taken. Such a committee again should be widely based, with at least some rotation of junior staff members.

4. Society and the mass media, separately, and perhaps jointly, should be reconsidering the concept of Freedom of the Press. Specifically, what kind of a free press does the society now desire, and, especially, what can be done about the major areas of concern in the relationships of the mass media and government? Two important asides: the mass media should not be penalized, or even criticized, for soundly bringing forth important news not pleasant to major elements in the society, and the mass media should be constantly careful not to overreach the now rather wide ranging areas of media freedom, such as a considerable and generous freedom from legal action for libel.

5. Currently, major problems exist on media access to sources of news which the media at least consider important for the public welfare. In great part these sources are within units of government, very often of the federal government. Compulsory disclosure through the Freedom of Information Act has been of help. But there remain such problems as overclassification of documents, and a very different concern in the form of widely distributed and increasing pressures on news persons to disclose details of confidential relationships with news sources, which somehow are in litigation (and also details of material gathered but never disseminated). The Supreme Court has made clear, in an unhappy boundary-setting decision on the Pentagon Papers, that under some circumstances prior restraint on dissemination is permissible, and increasingly, lower courts are attempting to apply such restraint. Society, the media, and many other elements have a concern in developing proper, and balanced, public policy in this area.

6. What is the attitude of each individual medium toward the society as a whole and the nature of the news about the society? Is there an adequate balance in the medium's picture of the developments in the

society? Does the medium have in mind clearly enough what the attitude is, and what the possible impacts may be? It is probable that many media managements need to think through these matters. The media should be critics of the society, and even super-watchdogs, but need also to be able to recognize and adequately present the major satisfactory developments as well. Of concern here is the tendency of many media to develop and encourage a pattern of conflict in the news, and to present portions of the news in a crisis context which may not be real. The media need to worry too about the perils of over-demanding 20-20-hindsight second-guessing; as Reeves phrases it: "We, the press, have become a little terrifying in our search for perfection or imperfection; I'm glad I never covered Abraham Lincoln."[73]

7. The work of the mass media should be continuously appraised, preferably in a formally organized manner, by a variety of appraisers. Studies such as the annual Alfred I. duPont–Columbia University surveys of broadcast journalism, and the New England Daily Newspaper Survey are highly desirable, both from the standpoint of the public and of the media. Such studies offer possibilities for much more rational appraisal of the work of the media. There is also urgent need for another type of appraisal, that is now being initiated nationwide by the National News Council, dealing with individual instances of media's so-called dys-performance, and at the statewide level by the Minnesota Press Council. Such bodies, especially those with non-media majorities, can speak also on behalf of the media and the public interest more effectively than the media themselves, and so can serve the society well.

8. Both the society and the media must face up to the increasing, and at times not necessarily logical, demands for access by the public to the media. The sound philosophical basis for this demand is the social desirability of exposing to the society all important points of view on public affairs. Numerous factors—defining "important," considering feasibilities, assessing social losses through compelled access—must be faced, since this problem will not go away. Although media generally do much for minority views, greater and very open initiative by media to seek out and offer forums would seem highly desirable, not only from the standpoint of society and from the self-interest of the media.

9. Both mass media and their audiences need to pay more attention to each other, in very specific fashion. Most media do not know their audiences as well as they should. In turn, the audience does not know nearly as much about the media as it should, and easily might. Most media should give more explanation to the public of media methods and procedures, "how we did it and why we did it the way we did it." (Ombudsmen and public editors should be much more numerous.) Usually the media will find a high degree of public interest and concern, at the same time that there is an atmosphere of considerable distrust. The public should not only know more and understand more, but should cooperate more with the media, and should offer support

more openly. Much more research about the mass media is needed. (A not small sidelight: Sooner or later the public, and government, will develop even greater concern over increased concentration of media ownership.)

10. The further growth of the professional spirit, with an attendant concern for ethical conduct, should be a major development of the media. Relationships with news sources of certain types, the worries of "freebies," carelessness, overstepping the bounds of reasonably good taste, and breaches of major tenets of codes of ethics are not common, but are apparent enough to cause concern which must be activated. Professional associations, trade associations, schools of journalism, management, and the public should all be concerned and can be helpful.

11. Until we have such considerable changes in the society that they amount to a revolution, changes in the mass media must fit into the market system at least moderately well. The changes must be salable to the various publics involved, whether citizens, news sources, government, advertisers or whatever. In general, we'll get from the mass media what the mass audience is willing to accept, or, perhaps, tolerate (most of the time, we get more and higher quality performance from most mass media than *most* of the audience is really concerned about). If the audience is to pay, the product must be seen as worthwhile.

12. Most of the changes in the mass media will be slow, and most of them will not be extreme. This will be true in part because of management caution, as well as the unaggressiveness and non-initiative of staffs, but also because the audience doesn't seem to be in the market for substantial change. Although some of the public is unhappy, most citizens find most of the media quite workable as they are. Even though levels of approval seem to be low, there are no great public outbursts for specific changes in the media.

13. The full impact on the media of new technologies is not clear. It probably will be slow in coming and turn out to be less than revolutionary. Laser composition methods may still further cut print-media production costs and allow easier entry for new magazines and newspapers, but advertisers will still be pushing for fewer large-circulation entities. Satellite transmission will cut broadcasting costs but will not necessarily or automatically change audience attention patterns, which are the major determinants of broadcasting content unless there is substantial non-commercial subsidy. Cable television will make gains but almost certainly will not be the wide ranging super-medium its strongest advocates foresee; start-up costs are high in major urban areas, which will slow expansion. The so-called local channels on cable television thus far have usually pulled rather small audiences; they will be costly to administer, program, and operate; they will not be the great and almost universal panaceas some supporters see them to be.

Since the media are an integral part of society, we are all the losers if they die, or suffer any reversals.

So there must be a heightened public concern over the mass media, and a greater public willingness to do much for and with the media. Beyond this is the need for greater public appreciation for the rights of free expression, and the knowledge that restrictions on freedom of the press tend also to bring restrictions on freedoms of the individual.

In turn, in this time when the mass media seem under greater attack than for many decades past, the media and all journalists must make many changes, and make them briskly.

With application, and a bit of luck, we can all increase our chances for survival.

Notes and References

1. Helpful discussions of definitions of and the nature of mass communications will be found in John C. Merrill and Ralph L. Lowenstein, *Media, Messages, and Men: New Perspectives in Communication* (New York: David McKay, 1971); Charles Wright, *Mass Communication* (New York: Random House, 1959); Wilbur Schramm and Donald F. Roberts, *The Process and Effects of Mass Communication* (Urbana: University of Illinois Press, 1971); J. Edward Gerald, *The Social Responsibility of the Press* (Minneapolis: University of Minnesota Press, 1963); Alex S. Edelstein, *Perspectives in Mass Communication* (Copenhagen: Einar Harcks Forlag, 1966); Bernard Berelson and Gary A. Steiner, *Human Behavior* (New York: Harcourt, Brace & World, 1964); Ithiel de Sola Pool and Wilbur Schramm, *Handbook of Communication* (Chicago: Rand McNally, 1973).
2. Harold A. Innis, *The Bias of Communication* (Toronto: University of Toronto Press, 1964), passim.
3. A helpful summary of the often confusing and much challenged Marshall McLuhan doctrines, including the sensory system concept, is found in William Rivers, Theodore Peterson, Jay E. Jensen, *The Mass Media and Modern Society* (San Francisco: Rinehart Press, 1971), pp. 30–31.
4. "Full access to the day's intelligence," presumably referring to cost as well as physical availability, is the fifth of five ideal "requirements" upon the mass media set out by the so-called Hutchins Commission, the Commission on Freedom of the Press. See *A Free and Responsible Press* (Chicago: University of Chicago Press, 1947), p. 28.
5. Rivers, Peterson, and Jensen declare that "the primary fact about the mass media in the United States" is that "they are oriented to marketing." *Op. cit.,* p. 33.
6. Michael J. Connor, "Network Tug-of-War With Stations Decides What You See on TV," *Wall Street Journal,* June 3, 1974, p. 1.
7. Jack C. Haskins, "The Editorial Mix: One Solution to a Magazine Editor's Dilemma,"*Journalism Quarterly,* 42:4, 557–62 (Autumn 1965).
8. Gerald, *ibid.,* pp. 54–57.

9. Carla Marie Rupp, "Some news stars don't show for Liebling III convention," *Editor & Publisher,* 107:20 (May 18, 1974), p. 42.

10. Elihu Katz, Michael Gurevitch, and Hadassah Haas, "On the Use of the Mass Media for Important Things," *American Sociological Review,* 38:180 (April 1973).

11. Quoted by Douglass Cater, "A Communications Revolution," *Wall Street Journal,* Aug. 6, 1973.

12. "The Black Book: A Region's Press," *Seminar,* No. 32, June 1974, p. 3.

13. "The structure and function of communications," in *The Communication of Ideas,* Lyman Bryson, ed. (New York: Harper, 1946).

14. Edward P. Foldessy, "Money-Market Critics Say Commercial Paper Less than Risk-Free," 54:150, May 16, 1974, p. 1.

15. "Mass Communication, Popular Taste and Organized Social Action," in Bryson, *op. cit.*

16. "Paper's choices sweep election in Bethlehem, Pa." *Editor & Publisher,* 107:22 (June 1, 1974), p. 24.

17. *Newsweek,* Sept. 17, 1973, pp. 79–80.

18. "Walton Signs Portland Contract," Associated Press story in *The Daily Iowan,* Iowa City, May 3, 1974, p. 10.

19. "Burger Kid," *Newsweek,* April 1, 1974, p. 70.

20. "Newsprint, news and ads," *Changing Times,* March 1974, p. 29.

21. William Stephenson, *The Play Theory of Mass Communication* (Chicago: University of Chicago Press, 1967).

22. *Op. cit.,* pp. 164–81.

23. *Op. cit.,* p. 180.

24. Martin S. Hayden, "Let's edit our own newspapers," *Seminar,* June 1973, pp. 4–8.

25. Edward Jay Epstein, *News from Nowhere* (New York: Random House, 1973).

26. Harvey Molotch and Marilyn Lester, "News as Purposive Behavior: On the Strategic Use of Routine Events, Accidents, and Scandals," *American Sociological Review,* 39:101–112 (Feb. 1974).

27. Leon V. Segal, *Reporters and Officials: The Organization and Politics of Newsmaking* (Boston: D. C. Heath, 1974).

28. Keith P. Sanders, *"What Are Daily Newspapers Doing to be Responsive to Readers' Criticisms?"* (ANPA News Research Bulletin, No. 9, Nov. 30, 1973.)

29. Fred Fedler, "The Media and Minority Groups: a Study of Adequacy of Access," *Journalism Quarterly,* 50:109–17 (Spring 1973).

30. Sanders, *op. cit.;* see also ANPA News Research Bulletin No. 5, 1973, *News and Editorial Content and Readership of the Daily Newspaper,* as well as No. 1, 1974, Edelstein, *Media Credibility,* and No. 3, 1974, McCombs, Mullins, and Weaver, *Why People Subscribe and Cancel.*

31. Philip Meyer, "Elitism and Newspaper Believability," *Journalism Quarterly,* 50:2, 31–36 (Spring 1973).

32. Robert U. Brown, "Over-riding Problem," *Editor & Publisher,* 107:20 (May 18, 1974), p. 52.

33. Philly Murtha, "More compassionate reporting urged by ANPA chairman Taylor," *Editor & Publisher,* 107:18 (April 27, 1974), pp. 9, 15.

34. See also Daniel Ben-Horin, "Quo vadis the alternative press," *Bulletin of American Society of Newspaper Editors,* May/June 1973, pp. 10–12.

35. For added detail on this convention, which probably had more top-ranking speakers than any journalism convention held previously in the United States, see Carla Marie Rupp, *Editor & Publisher,* loc. cit., and *MORE,* May, 1974.

36. Peter B. Clark, "Journalists' ideals and readers' doubts," *Bulletin of the American Society of Newspaper Editors,* No. 568 (April 1973), pp. 1, 6–8.

37. Jane Levere, *Editor & Publisher,* 107:20 (May 18, 1974), p. 11.

38. James B. Kobak, "How much is your magazine worth:II," *Folio: The Magazine for Magazine Management,* 2:9 (Nov./Dec. 1973), p. 52.

39. "Evolution: Tennessee Picks a New Fight with Darwin," *Science,* No. 4113, p. 696 (Nov. 16, 1973).

40. *"News and Editorial Content and Readership of the Daily Newspaper,"* (ANPA News Research Bulletin No. 5, April 26, 1973).

41. *Nielsen Newscast,* No. 1, 1974, p. 5.

42. Maxwell E. McCombs, *Mass Media in the Marketplace* (Journalism Monographs, Association for Education in Journalism, No. 24, Aug. 1972).

43. Phyllis Murtha, "Shop talk type columns keep readers informed," *Editor & Publisher,* 107:16 (April 20, 1974), pp. 46, 52, 56.

44. Broadcasting, May 27, 1974, pp. 18, 19, See also pp. 20 and 21 for detailed "oddsmaker" predictions.

45. Norman Jacobs, ed., *Culture for the Millions?* (Princeton: D. Van Nostrand, 1961), p. 166.

46. David Wise, *The Politics of Lying: Government Deception* (New York: Random House, 1973).

47. "Watergate tape points to White House complicity in challenges to Post-Newsweek," *Broadcasting,* May 20, 1974, p. 25.

48. Daniel J. Boorstin, *The Image* (New York: Atheneum, 1962), pp. 9–12.

49. Martin Ralbovsky, "Flacks and Hacks on the 'Times' Sports Page," *New York,* Aug. 6, 1973, pp. 26–30.

50. John Twohey and James Rosapepe, "Public Relations, Coast-to-Coast: The Airlines Take Us for a Ride," *The Nation,* Jan. 29, 1973, pp. 142–4.

51. For a detailed survey, see: Herbert Strentz, Kenneth Starck, David L. Anderson, and Loren Ghiglione, *The Critical Factor: Criticism of the News Media in Journalism Education,* (Journalism Monographs, Association for Education in Journalism, No. 32, February 1974).

52. Nieman Reports, 27:4, (Winter 1973); pp. 3–11; Seminar, No. 32, (June 1974), pp. 3–8; Loren Ghiglione, ed., *Evaluating the Press: The New England Daily Newspaper Survey* (Southbridge, Mass.: 1974).

53. Earl Wilkin, "Lee Newspapers plan to target supplements to specific readers," *Editor & Publisher,* April 20, 1974.

54. See Grace Magney, "The Paper Crunch," *Quill,* 62:4 (April 1974), pp. 20–24.

55. A variety of information and interesting comment on the nature, place, and impact of journalism education is found in *Proceedings: Education for Newspaper Journalists in the Seventies and Beyond* (Washington: ANPA Foundation, 1974).

56. Commission on Freedom of the Press, *op. cit.,* pp. 20–29.

57. Richard H. Stewart, "When a journalist becomes a flack," *The Bulletin of the American Society of Newspaper Editors,* No. 70:1 (July/Aug. 1973), pp. 8, 9.

58. A reader of the Kansas City (Mo.) Times filed a complaint with the National News Council that a syndicated article by Anthony Lewis was not clearly labeled as an opinion piece (*Editor & Publisher,* March 30, 1974, p. 80). The Council decided the complaint was unjustified but several members described the confusion created when opinion and news articles are not clearly differentiated.

59. Chris Ortloff, "Man in Space: A Media Odyssey," *Michigan Journalist,* 47:3 (Jan. 1974), pp. 2–3.

60. ANPA News Research Bulletin No. 5, *op. cit.*

61. A view which holds that the capabilities of many reporters are not great enough is expressed by Irving Kristol, in George F. Wills, ed., *Press, Politics, and Popular Government* (Washington: American Enterprise Institute for Public Policy Research, 1972), who says that journalists so often emphasize procedural matters and conflicts in government because they do not possess the capabilities for the much needed analysis of the events themselves.

62. Commission on Freedom of the Press, *op. cit.,* p. 27.

63. *Aspen Notebook on Government and the Media* (New York: Praeger, 1973), p. 22.

64. *Des Moines* (Ia.) *Sunday Register,* Section A, May 5, 1974, pp. 1, 6.

65. Bernard C. Cohen, *The Press and Foreign Policy* (Princeton: Princeton University Press, 1963), p. 13.

66. Joseph Epstein, "American Chronicle: Anyone for Paranoia?" *Encounter,* 42:5 (May 1974), p. 31.

67. Walter Weiss, "Effects of the Mass Media of Communication," in *The Handbook of Social Psychology,* second edition, Gardner Lindzey and Elliott Aronson, eds. (Reading, Mass: Addison-Wesley, 1969), pp. 38–195, is probably the best available summation on effects, and contains an extensive bibliography. See also Joseph Klapper, *The Effects of Mass Communication* (New York: Free Press, 1960), and Schramm and Roberts, *Process and Effect of Mass Communication, op. cit.*

68. "Communication and Children, a Developmental Approach," in Ithiel deSola Pool and Wilbur Schramm, ed., *Handbook of Communication,* p. 177.

69. Maxwell E. McCombs and Donald L. Shaw, "The Agenda-Setting Function of Mass Media," *Public Opinion Quarterly,* 36:176–87 (Summer 1972).

70. Weiss, *op. cit.*, p. 110.
71. "Midi-dress Revolt Era," *Des Moines Register,* May 17, 1974.
72. "Newspapers Play Important Role in Recent Elections: Help Nixon in '68 and '72," *Institute for Social Research* (University of Michigan) *Newsletter,* Winter 1974, p. 3.
73. Richard Reeves, "Is Jerry Ford Big Enough?" *New York,* 7:18 (May 6, 1974), p. 52.

CHAPTER III

On the Mass Media and Mass Communication: Notes Toward a Theory

Lee Thayer

We do not have a theory of mass communication. What we do have is a rapidly-increasing pool of assumptions, conjectures, rationalizations, hypotheses, after-the-fact explanations, and beliefs. What is often masqueraded as theory in all that is being written and said about mass communication is not theory at all; it is folklore and myth.

Nor do we have a theory of advertising or public relations or propaganda or persuasion. We tell a good story about these matters. But the illusion that we are talking theory comes mainly from wishful thinking and the mania to be "scientific" (*viz.,* "respectable").

We not only do not have a theory; what we do have is sterile. The dominant myths and the persistent folklore are not only largely without theoretical substance; they are wholly unlikely to generate any such substance.

Let us set aside for the moment the questions of whether there could be, or should be, such a theory. And these are large questions, indeed. It will be enough here to realize that if we *want* to have a theory of mass communication, we are not going to get to it by travelling the path we are on, and then to suggest the basis for an alternative path.

The Seductiveness of the Cause → Effect Orientation

Kuhn[1] has argued that there are dominant "paradigms" in science at any point in time; that these paradigms encourage certain kinds of explanations of facts and discourage others; and that real progress in scientific understanding comes not from the weight of facts as such, but from the displacement of one dominant paradigm by another. This may or may not be the case. It is still hotly debated. But it is useful for looking at the present predicament in the study of mass communication.

Those who gave the study of mass communication its initial impetus in the U.S. were apparently convinced of the "scientific" validity of the cause → effect approach.[2] Not only was this paradigm deeply imbedded in our general cultural outlook on the world, but was (mistakenly) assumed by most social and behavioral "scientists" of that day to be the guiding paradigm of the physical sciences, to whom they looked for model and legitimacy. The assumption was wrong on two counts: physicists had never been constrained by so simplistic and naive a version of the cause → effect paradigm as that imported by psychologists of the 20s and 30s; and, even in the less constraining form held by physicists of that earlier day, the cause → effect paradigm was giving way rapidly to a much different kind of basic orientation.

But the myth that the reductionist, cause → effect approach is the only true way to do "scientific" research and build "scientific theories" has persisted in the social and behavioral sciences up to the present day. That it has persisted in spite of the fundamental changes that have occurred in the physical sciences attests to its seductiveness as just that—a myth. In the physical sciences, it had the status of an hypothesis. Its status in the social and behavioral sciences has been, for the most part, that of an ideology. Look at most of the current "research" journals, or "research"-based textbooks or reviews; what cannot be studied by cause → effect methods is, by default, considered largely irrelevant.

So it was consonant with the intellectual climate of the day in the social and behavioral sciences that the study of mass communication emerged firmly anchored to a cause → effect orientation. The dominant paradigm from the field's inception, the Lasswellian formula, "Who . . . Says What . . . In Which Channel . . . To Whom . . . *With What Effect?* has frequently been elaborated upon; it has even been stood on its head. But it has never been much displaced from its dominant position.

The Present Situation

DeFleur has concluded, on the basis of his study of contemporary "theories" of mass communication:

> The all-consuming question that has dominated research and the development of contemporary theory in the study of the mass media can be summed up in simple terms—namely, "what has been their effect?"[3]

He goes on to point out that there has been "progressive change" in our thinking over the years about the impact of the media on the "mass":

This change has for the most part been a continuous and cumulative discovery of important intervening processes between media and mass, that is between the stimulus and the response sides of the S-R equation.[4]

But what has persisted is the S-R equation itself. It would seem that the more we place that equation in jeopardy by the facts, the more faith we have in it. Some do seem at times frustrated by sheer inability to fit the facts to the model. But, according to the bogus "science" we presume to, it is as if we need only to persist and refine our tools, and we will eventually be able to fit all the facts to the unaltered "theory." But never the other way around! In this we are indeed "true believers."

Nor are we, in this, alone. Faith in a cause → effect orientation is basic to Western, and particularly, perhaps, to American, culture.[5] This faith has led us, in most domains of our lives, to reify the means of power and control, and to thing-ify or objectify people—that is, to view the *means* of doing something as the cause or "independent variable"; the *ends,* human or social or otherwise, are assumed to be given in whatever "effects" will or do accrue from those "causes," and these are viewed as merely "dependent variables." The Shannon and Weaver "model," which has been and continues to be unjustifiably influential in both communication and mass communication studies, is not a model of human communication, but a control model. In a control model, the "message" or the "information" sent is presumed to "cause" the appropriate response or reaction; otherwise, there is presumed to be some "malfunction." We have deluded ourselves into believing that human communication works in this way; that messages have an objective "content" or "meaning"; and that certain "messages" will have (or "should" have) certain "effects" on certain people under certain conditions. This belief enables us to predict almost nothing of human behavior that we couldn't predict quite as well by our unaided common sense. It may put us at a disadvantage even when trying to explain what happened after-the-fact. But we cling to it.

Consider the review of the "Effects of the Mass Media of Communication" in the second edition of *The Handbook of Social Psychology*.[6] The author of this review labels as "pallid and useless" the conclusion of one set of studies that "some movies have some effects considered to be adverse on some viewers." When one knows there are going to be measurable effects from measurable causes, then any research which doesn't support that faith is obviously just "useless." The multi-million-dollar Surgeon General's report on the effects of television violence offers the same conclusion: that certain types of violence on television may have certain kinds of adverse effects on certain kinds of youngsters who are already predisposed. . . . Undoubtedly more "pallid and useless" findings. The author of the *Handbook* review does mention the study conducted in Cincinnati, in which a well-planned and supported multi-media campaign had apparently no effect at all on public awareness of the U.N.[7] But this rates very little of his attention or interest; two pages later he reverts to the faith: ". . . the media through their effects on awareness tend to confer. . . ." The ten million dollars spent on the recent presidential campaigns in the U.S. seemed to have had little effect on the outcome; Hershey has had the lion's share of the chocolate market for many years without benefit (until quite recently) of media exposure; eight out of ten new products are never successful, seemingly regardless of promotion strategy or investment. What kind of a "theory" is one which cannot be disproved?

Popper has suggested that science progresses mainly through the falsification of hypotheses and theories.[8] It is relatively easy to find confirmation for almost any reasonable hypothesis; and that confirmation is therefore not proof. One can "test" a theory substantially only by attempting to disprove it. What distinguishes an article of faith from a theory is the immunity which the former has from refutation.

The dominant conceptual framework, the dominant paradigm guiding research and "theory" in mass communication for the past several years, has not been a theoretical statement; it has been an ideological commitment. Perhaps for this reason, its defects have not often been openly scrutinized.

Some Defects in the Dominant Conceptual Framework

To focus only on the dominant conceptual framework guiding mass communication research and theorizing should not suggest that it is the only approach that has been or is being used. Nor should it suggest that others have not recognized the limitations and sterility of that dominant conceptual framework. McQuail has reviewed some of the alternative formulations that have been inspired at least in part by a disappointment in the dominant paradigm (in addition to offering one of his own),[9] as has DeFleur.[10] Other alternative formulations are to be found in Innis,[11] Mendelsohn,[12] Katz,[13] Stephenson,[14] Brouwer,[15] Lippmann,[16] and McLuhan.[17] And even those who have espoused the dominant paradigm most strongly have sometimes spoken to its weaknesses or to alternative formulations.[18]

Nonetheless, the bulk of the study of mass communication is heavily infused with the "effects"-of-the-media-on-people orientation; and the sheer inertia of so pervasive an orientation is likely to spell the future of the field for many years to come.

Its pervasiveness notwithstanding, that orientation is flawed. In spite of the readiness by which it is taken for granted, it has logical as well as theoretical defects. Four of those can be specified here:

1. In the extensive review of the "Effects of the Mass Media of Communication" referred to above, Weiss concludes that the primary methodological criterion for research on the "effects" of the mass media is "replicability." Even without bringing such a criterion into question on the basis of its faulty interpretation of how the physical sciences operate, this is quite a prognosis: If there are "effects," it would be impossible to replicate them on the same people, for "effects" by defini-

tion would be tantamount to changes in the people involved. Nor could replication in a different setting with different people constitute a valid test, for the statistical assumption in such sampling would have to be that of an infinite number of homogeneous classes, a condition which obtains nowhere in human societies. So if the primary methodological criterion is that of replicability, there is an immense logical and self-defeating defect in the dominant cause → effect orientation to mass communication research and theory.

2. For the unwary, there is more than a little deception in the terms themselves. "Mass" is likely to imply something that may not exist; one may be led to do research on a "mass" because the terms of the enterprise require that he do so. Then there is "communication." For many, in both mass communication and communication studies, the casual use of the term "communication" implies that something already has been, or inevitably will be, "communicated."[19] There is something compelling about this way of using the word "communication." It permits the user to ignore everything but the "message," the medium employed, and the "effects." He needn't be troubled by the fact that the "message" the reader or listener "gets" is not *in* the medium *or* in what is presented, but is *in* the receiver. Then there is the word "media." To say that the "media" *as such* have social effects makes about as much sense as to say that automobiles or brains or paintings *as such* have social effects. No human tool or artifact has any social effects except those produced by the uses to which they are put by people. In a McLuhanesque sense, the ways in which people traditionally or conventionally use their tools and other artifacts may have some influence on the evolution of the species; but such influence would hardly be detectable by the methods and the time frames used by our usual research on these matters. If people began to use the millions of transistor radios now in existence as weapons to be thrown at one another, what would we want to say about the "social effects" of that medium? The way people come to *use* a medium is not *just* another "intervening variable" between the "stimulus" and the "response." It is the underlying dynamic. The attempt to elaborate the S-R model into even some minor relevance to human behavior has been as sterile in the study of human communication and mass communication as it has been in psychology.

3. Limiting the concept of media to the more recent popular media of newspapers, magazines, radio, television, and film is not only extremely arbitrary; it is theoretically unfortunate. Its arbitrariness likely contributes to assumptions such as Weiss' that concern with media effects on moral, sexual, and social behavior began with the introduction of movies and television! Such arbitrary classifications blind one to the history and evolution of communication media in human societies. There have been instances in human history when speaking to a crowd was considered to be so potentially evil that only sanctified persons were permitted to do so. Even more important, however, is the theoretical disadvantage such as arbitrary classification

imposes. There are phenomena that look very much like "mass communication" in some animal and insect societies. Doesn't the dancing bee bring "the news"? When he spreads his glorious tail feathers as an invitation to any willing peafowl, isn't the peacock "advertising"? If we would but loosen our anthropomorphic and ahistorical and mystical posture vis-à-vis popular media like television, we could see that the media are little more than the means or techniques or technologies for storing, transporting, or displaying "messages" (i.e., appropriately codified data). In what sense are greeting cards not mass media? In what sense are fairs and shows and expositions and galleries and museums and libraries not mass media? The most popular entertainment medium in the U.S. today is not television, but music; the record industry is larger than the television industry.[20] In what sense, then, are phonograph records not a mass medium? It will be appropriate to extend this list below when considering other "Definitions." The point to be made here is simply that we discount the major historical and social foundations of any theory of mass communication when we limit the concept of the "media" to the press, movies, television, and radio. If we want a relevant theory of mass communication, it will have to be based on the ways in which people of all cultures and times have used all of the media for human and social purposes. To base a theory on relatively *ad hoc* analyses of an arbitrary few of those media is simply to limit its relevance.

4. Finally, any attempt to construct a theory of "mass" communication which does not accommodate the conditions of human *communication* is empirically indefensible. In this regard, those who purport to study and theorize about communication have strayed as far afield as those who purport to study and theorize about "mass" communication. The dominant model of communication assumed in both fields is—shorn of its various filigree—this one: $A \rightarrow B = X$. This is a formula which says that there is a source (A) which transmits a message $(\rightarrow)$ to a person or group (B), with (X) effect. For all of the scientistic appeal and for all of the widespread acceptance of this model, this is just not the way human communication works. Those who subscribe to one or another of the variants of this model seem, sooner or later, to indulge in a shorthand way of talking: they may say, as Weiss does, that the media transmit "information" or "influence." There is little empirical justification for talking about communication in this way. No person can "transmit" meaning or significance or information, and certainly not influence, via any medium. There is no medium, including the human ear or human speech, which is capable of transmitting or receiving anything but codified data. If such codified data is to have any meaning or significance, if it is to be "informative" in any way, that meaning or significance or informative import will have to be attributed to it by *some* receiver; and that receiver, given his peculiar intellectual and culturally-derived competencies for doing so,[21] must be the *de facto* creator of whatever meaning, significance, or informativeness a message has for him. One's cognizance of a message directed to him *may be*

a necessary condition of his response (or nonresponse), but the *sufficient* condition is always and invariably a product of that receiver. In addition, the conditions of human communication are by nature systemic. For example, there are those who purport to study the "credibility" of certain speakers. But by what logical or theoretical or even commonsensical rationale can the "credibility" of a speaker be assessed independently of the "credulity" of his audience?[22] Empirically, no human utterance taken out of its human context has any meaning except that assigned to it by some observer for *his* purposes in talking to someone else. We can talk to each other at great length about the "meaning" of a statement such as "I love you." But the meaning it has in any given circumstance exists only *in* the people directly involved. When we abstract components of a communication system (speaker, message, medium, receiver, etc.) out of the social system in which communication occurs, we mutilate them for the purposes of talking in some *other* social system. All human communication is systemic in nature, and no theory or model of the process which does not accommodate this empirical fact has claim to validity.

There are other defects in the dominant conceptual framework which guide research and theorizing in the field of mass communication. But these four should suffice to show that we do not have a theory, and that what we do have is destined to be sterile. In his recent book, *Human Understanding,* Stephen Toulmin writes:

> The true measure of the insight which any serious theory provides lies, above all, in the richness and variety of the novel questions it forces on our attention, and in its power to reveal significant connections between elements, or fields of inquiry, that had previously appeared entirely independent. This means not just the power of the theory to generate additional questions for investigation, but also its capacity to discredit questions left over from earlier accounts and to replace them by other, more operative questions.[23]

What, then, are the possibilities for a more productive and heuristic alternative?

Some Preliminary Definitions

Definitions do not make a theory, of course. But some preliminary redefinitions of terms consistent with the preceding analysis may help to set the stage for an alternative conceptual framework.

Media

By the term *media,* we should be referring to *all* of the means—all of the devices, technologies, etc.—utilized for acquiring, storing, transporting, or displaying "messages" (i.e., codified data). The human ear is thus a medium, as are human languages.[24] The microscope and the telescope are media. A piece of parchment, like the wall of an inhabited cave, when used to inscribed "messages," is also a medium. Most of the popular media are compounded: radio requires not only the devices which broadcast and which receive codified signals, but the natural "medium" of "air waves." Historically, the most ubiquitous and significant of all of the media have been people themselves: people may be utilized, or utilize themselves, as a *means* of storing, transporting, acquiring, or displaying "messages" presumed to have some potential relevance or meaningfulness for others.

There are many ways of categorizing media. Some we take ourselves to (e.g., museums and churches); others are more portable (e.g., radio, photographs). Some can be privately utilized (e.g., books); others are necessarily more public (e.g., circuses[25]). Some are simple (e.g., the human ear, the newspaper); others are compound (e.g., roads and highways, which are used to transport people, who store and transmit "messages," and television, which displays people talking to each other by telephone). But the essential point is that the media include *all* means of acquiring, storing, transporting, or displaying "messages."

Communication Messages and Mass Communication Messages

A communication message is one which is addressed to a specific person or to specific persons who are functionally related to the source in some way. A communication message always involves a personal reciprocal relationship. A mass communication message is of the sort: to whom it may concern; the addressees are essentially anonymous; and a mass communication message neither implies nor requires a personal relationship, even though the conventional uses to which people put the media or media fare over time establishes a reciprocal relationship, a special form of "institutionalization" which will be discussed below. A piece of mail addressed to John Jones by a friend or a legitimate creditor is a communication message. A piece of mail in his mail box addressed to "Occupant" or to "John Jones" from someone unknown and unrelated is a mass communication message. By its nature, a television network cannot transport communication messages; it can transport only mass communication messages. The telephone and telegraph systems, like the postal system, can transport either kind of message. The ultimate distinction between the two is this: a communication message involves two or more people reciprocally, and in terms of their relationship; a mass communication message is of the sort: to whom it may concern; it is impersonal in the sense that either or both the source and the consumer are anonymous.

A weakness of existing formulations is the typical assumption that non-mediated (e.g., "face-to-face") communication is always personal, while mediated communication is generally impersonal. A letter or telephone call between friends is certainly mediated; but it can be extremely personal. On the other hand, the ritual pleasantries we exchange at cocktail parties, although "face-to-face," are typically impersonal, such "messages" as "The weather has certainly been unusual," or "Hello, how are you?" can be addressed to anyone who cares to listen; they are therefore essentially impersonal, in the manner of "to whom it may concern."

Communication Media and Mass Communication Media

Whether a given medium is a communication medium or a mass communication medium therefore depends entirely upon how it is used. By their nature, some are more "usable" one way than the other. For example, the print and electronic media may lend themselves more to the transport and display of mass communication messages. While the major use of the telephone is for the transport of communication messages, it can be used the other way too. Film may be used to transport a movie to be viewed by millions; or it can be used to capture a special moment having special meaning for only one or two people— as when an absent lover sends a picture of himself. Memos between two principals of the "Watergate affair" may have been a communication medium prior to the investigation; but, if read by others, they become a mass communication medium.

So the distinction between the two is neither a dichotomous nor a mutually exclusive one. Entertainment media typically become more specialized over time by the uses to which their audiences put them. Specialized media having specifiable audiences are somewhere in the middle of the continuum from the exclusively personal to the indiscriminately impersonal.

Any means of storing or transporting or displaying what people say is a communication medium. The distinction is not in the technologies used, but in the uses to which they are put. Using two-way television for personal conversations in lieu of using the telephone doesn't alter the devices used; it merely alters their use.

Communication Networks and Mass Communication Networks

A much more important distinction, theoretically, is that between a communication network and a mass communication network. A communication network emerges from people talking to each other about matters that make a difference to them. It connects or links people functionally "in series." A mass communication network is superimposed or overlaid on existing communication networks (*viz.,* social structure) to the extent made possible by the available technology. It networks or connects people nonfunctionally "in parallel." *What is* and *what matters*—indeed, all human reality, all human values—are products of communication networks. There is more to be aware of in our physical and social environments than we could possibly be aware of; there is more to be known than we can possibly know. One function of a communication network is to sort out what we need to be aware of from what we don't, and what we need to know from what we don't. The mass media and their fare are ultimately no more than a part of our social environment. What aspects of that fare we need to be aware of depends generally upon who we talk to; what we need to know of what is provided by a mass communication network depends generally upon the communication networks to which we belong. In a free society, the relationship between people and the mass communication media is the same as that between people and their communication media— adaptive, emergent, and evolving. Therefore, the more subcultures (communication networks) there are in a given society, and the more heterogeneous they are, the more "selectivity" there is or the more specialized the mass communication media become. The demise of *Life* was but one of a long list of examples in recent U.S. history of what happens when a "something-for-everyone" medium fails to adapt to changing social conditions. Would the disciples of the cause → effect approach want to argue in this case that the "effect" of *Life* was to kill its audience?

Mediators

A mediator is someone who, intentionally or not, mediates for others some world, some domain of existence, some knowledge, etc., which is presently or permanently inaccessible to those others. Parents are, of necessity, mediators of the adult world for their children. Teachers are, by choice, mediators of knowledge and value for their pupils; priests are the mediators of other worlds for their parishioners, as movie and television and stage stars are for their followers, as sports or music celebrities are for their publics, as reporters and broadcasters are for their audiences, and as scientists are for laymen.

The nature of the relationship between a mediator and his constituency is such that what he says or how he acts about those inaccessible worlds he is mediating cannot be directly verified by those who, by necessity or by choice, comprise that constituency. Whether what we take to be public beliefs about "the Establishment" or about "Hollywood" are well-grounded or not cannot be decided by direct inspection. They can be validated only in communication with other persons, and these are typically other members of the same constituency. Whether a given public's image of the President is truly "accurate" cannot in fact be determined; it is acceptable as "true" to me or to you to the extent that its relevance to others confirms that image. "Is it true? Is it true that President Kennedy was shot?" was the question that was asked of millions by millions. There were, of course, the radio and television and newspaper "reports." But did the event in fact occur? And, if so, what does it *mean?* When we cannot see for ourselves, and often even when we can, we can determine the truth and the relevance and the *human* meaning of something or some event only by talking to each other. What the child's mother or teacher tells him about sex may be interesting; but is it *true?* For this, most children must turn to their peers.

Mediators may create, in what they say or what they do, some possibilities. But the social significance and the social reality—whether of Vietnam or Santa Claus—has to be created by those for whom given social realities have reliable social utility. Thus the distinction between "reality" and myth is a blurred one. The beliefs and opinions of various publics about Vietnam, like the beliefs and opinions of various publics about the sex lives of movie stars, emerge not directly out of what our mediators of those worlds say and do, but out of the ways in which we talk to other people about those worlds. The assumption made— whether by reporters or researchers or parents or preachers—that what we say as mediators of an inaccessible world determines the image that people will have of it, or the opinions they will develop about it, is a grossly naive one. The opinions and images that various publics hold of mediated worlds are products not of what mediators say, but of the ways in which their constituents come to talk about what those mediators say.

It will occasionally be useful to distinguish two kinds of mediators. There are *instrumental* mediators—those who perform their function more or less anonymously. There are also *consummatory* mediators—those who mediate other worlds for us by embodying those other worlds. The local weather forecaster reports the weather news; Jane Fonda *is* news. An instrumental mediator is one *through* whom we are enabled to see or vicariously experience other worlds which are at least at that moment inaccessible to us. A consummatory mediator is one *in* whom we see and vicariously experience those other worlds. The consummatory mediator is a celebrity; the instrumental mediator is a functionary. The two are not mutually exclusive; many mediators, for example parents, function as a little of both. But, in the extreme, the distinction is useful. For example, the industries which arise around the revelation of the lives of celebrities may be eco-

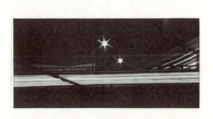

nomically far more important than what the celebrity actually does. For example, the President of the United States has a fixed salary. But the time and money invested in reporting on and reading and hearing and talking about the President undoubtedly runs to many times what the President makes.

Consummatory mediators are *institutionalized*—taken together with their constituencies and the beliefs and images that their constituencies have of them, the whole is as much a social institution as any other. Bob Hope is an American institution; can you imagine how difficult it would be for most people to take him seriously at the opening of his regular "specials"? Or how difficult it would be for us to accept Doris Day as a serious character actress? Or to accept the Pope as a practical joker? Or one's own parents as being lascivious?

The Basic Dynamic

The basic dynamic in the phenomena of mass communication, the pivotal mechanism out of which all else evolves, is not the technology, awesome as that has become. Nor is it the "message," or the implicit culture imparted in the "content" of the media. Nor is it the "effects" which the media are purported to have. The basic mechanism inheres in the *social and personal uses* to which people put the media and their fare.[26] It is this basic dynamic which any relevant theory of mass communication will have to be based upon.

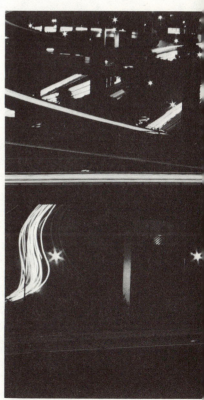

The historically and theoretically significant phenomenon, and the measurable and explicable one, is not that of the "effects" of the media on people, but that of the effects *on* the media of the *uses* to which people put the media and their fare.[27] Books, as such, have had no measurable effect upon people, for example; but the uses to which books have been put by people have altered the structure of that industry over the years, and have had identifiable social and human consequences. So it has been with radio, and with movies and museums and the greeting card and recording industries. The change and evolution of mass communication systems in the context of particular societies, and the change and evolution of particular human societies networked by certain kinds of mass communication systems having certain kinds of characteristics: these are matters of central theoretical importance. And they can be validly approached only from this point of departure: that the basic dynamic is the uses to which people put the media and their fare. All the rest is incidental to this.

The producers and distributors of mass communication messages can and do use the media for the transportation and display of those messages. But in the same way that "I love you" has no relevance for the people involved apart from the way they use it, no mass communication message has relevance apart from the ways in which it is taken into account by people. And our ways of taking mass communication messages into account hinge generally upon the personal and social uses to which they can be put.

Uses of the Mass Media and Their Fare

The uses to which people put the mass media and their fare, in approximately descending order of importance or magnitude, are these:

1. The primary use to which people put the media and their fare is that of providing something to talk about in ritual, non-vital encounters with other people. The more complex and the more mobile a society, the more frequent are such encounters, and hence the more functional the media and their fare. Bertrand de Jouvenel wrote:

> The more society is mixed, the more a man needs to know what to expect of the unlike-seeming stranger. He needs security for and against the behavior of another.[28]

Using media fare as something to talk about provides just this kind of security. People who live in relatively non-complex, non-mobile societies have little occasion to use the media and their fare in this way, except perhaps for the purpose of talking to an occasional tourist or anthropologist from this culture! Thus having a radio or a television has a quite different meaning for such people than it does for us. A businessman drawn into a casual conversation with a tourist in a Hong Kong bar will need to know the current ball standings, the current "front page news," the names of the characters in the currently "in" TV programs (e.g., Archie Bunker), or something of that sort which would serve as a basis for the conversation. Wherever you go today, whether to your own village or shopping center, or to any of the world's cities, it will be possible to talk with almost anyone about current news events or media celebrities, in the same way that we use talk about the weather to ease through such ritual encounters. And the fact that people can talk to each other without threat using media fare as a basis has some very real consequences for what media producers can and cannot do, as we shall see below. So this primary use that people make of media fare—that it gives them something to talk about—is not trivial; it is, in fact, of major theoretical import.

2. The second use to which people put the mass media and their fare, in order of importance or magnitude, is as the central component of personal identity or reality *rituals*. There are two aspects of this use that deserve attention. First, more than is often recognized, the routinization of our lives around certain regular, predictable happenings on a day-to-day basis is crucial to the maintenance of a sense of personal identity. The marking of time by certain rituals is common to people in every culture. Those who have the media available for such rituals can use them in this way: I know it's Saturday (or whenever) because "All in the Family" is on tonight. "You know I don't like to talk in the morning until after I've had a chance to look at the paper." There is "travelling music" and special traffic news during commuters' hours, silence in church, the indestructibility of Little Orphan Annie, the unchanging pulchritude of Daisy Mae, and the "profundity" of Peanuts. There is the "six o'clock news" which reliably comes on at six o'clock and structures that end of the day. There is knowing what to expect in the latest issue of your favorite magazine, with only the details to be filled in. And there is listening to (but not hearing) the "top forty" pop records over and over again for several days in a row. And so on. We need to know that we're in a structured and predictable world, and that the world is as we remembered or expected. The media and their fare can go far toward providing such props for our personal identity rituals.

There is another aspect to the ritual uses of the media and their fare. To the extent that we have our sense of being "in" the world through being like "others" and doing as "others" do, we will feel constrained to attend to the media and their fare according to our beliefs about how "others" are attending to the media and their fare. To the extent that we believe "everyone else" takes a daily newspaper, and to the extent that being like "everyone else" is vital to our own sense of being "in" the world, we will go through the ritual of "taking" a daily newspaper. If large numbers of people believed that "everyone else" attended a museum once a week, more people than now do so would go through the ritual of attending a museum. Suffering the nth repetition of a "top ten" tune being played that day, young people are no longer hearing it; they are performing a ritual—one which keeps each one tacitly in touch with all the "others."

Thus there comes to be a structuring of the media and their fare more or less consistent with the structure of the lives of those who use them in similar ritualistic ways. We speak of "curling up" with a good book. And most people comprehend the image of watching the late night television shows over one's bare feet. There are sermons on Sunday, but rarely any lectures. People go to see movies that other people are going to see, with likely little or no thought as to real personal preferences. Expressions like "Would you believe?" become public rituals.

In a complex society, these rituals are more and more frequently identification rituals for those who belong to the same "epistemic communities" or the same "interest groups" or the same "communication networks." But there are still some which are more national in scope. What adults in the U.S. do not feel a stirring of emotion when witnessing a colorful street parade? In 1973, what American could afford not to know *something* about the Watergate "scandal," even though he may have had no vital interest in it one way or the other?

All such rituals in which we engage the media and their fare provide us a sense of reality, and of being "in" the world with others, which is the only way we *can* be "in" the world. What is real to people, and what is indispensable to their sense of being "in" the world is of fundamental theoretical importance. The fact that what is real to people and what is indispensable to their sense of being "in" the world more and more involves ritual uses of the media and their fare makes it no less important.

3. The third use to which people put the media and their fare is the *mythical.* There are three levels at which this use of the media and their fare can be observed.

First, because no "recipes" for living are given in man's genes—as they are totally or largely given for all of the other creatures of the earth—these "recipes" have to be created and perpetuated in some way. No one of us can for long go without a feeling that our way of living is reasonable, just, proper, and "right." Whether in matters of morality, esthetic sensitivity, value, ideology, or of just everyday comportment, we need to be able to find in our social and/or physical surrounds some regular confirmation for our own "recipes" for living. All cultural and subcultural "recipes" for living are like myths: they are created and sustained by tacit covenant[29] and behavior. They are not absolute. Nor is there any ultimate test of their "rightness" beyond self-affirmation. To the extent that such cultural or subcultural "recipes" for living are functional and operative, they must be pervasive in that culture or subculture. Those "recipes," or aspects of them, must pervade what the members of that culture or subculture do and do not do, the manner in which they do and do not behave, the way they invent and deploy their artifacts and technologies, the stories they tell and the generic beliefs they hold, and so on. Thus, to the extent there are operative cultural "recipes" for living, they will be, covertly or overtly, intentionally or inadvertently, built into the fare of the mass media.[30] And we will sense them there; we will find there confirmation of the "recipes" for living by which we are guided, and we will find there alternative recipes for living, some of which may be feasible, as well as others we can only fantasize about. We may be surprised to learn that the Russian people are not that much different from us. But most of us can only fantasize about the "recipes" by which native islanders of the South Seas or the "beautiful people" of the "jet set" live.

Second, there are many aspects of our human existences which can be explained *only* by metaphor or myth. Humans are by nature the only creatures on earth who must explain the inexplicable. How are we to explain just what we are, where we came from, where we are going? How are we to comprehend death? Or life? Or love? These are questions whose ultimate and absolute answers must seemingly be always just out of reach. What we don't or can't know, we make up; myths undergird the existences or people of every culture.[31] Watts defined myth as follows: "Myth is to be defined as a complex of stories—some no doubt fact, and some fantasy—which, for various reasons, human beings regard as demonstrations of the inner meaning of the universe and of human life."[32] Again, to the extent these myths are cultural, they will necessarily be pervasive, and largely covert or tacit. Those who create and produce the fare of the mass media will not be able to avoid imbuing what they do with cultural myth. And those who consume the media and their fare will not be able to avoid finding in that fare some confirmation—or disconfirmation—of the "recipes" upon which their ways of seeing and knowing and being are based.

Third, neither of these mythical uses of the mass media and their fare is limited to "content." To the contrary, it seems altogether likely that the "deeper" and hence the more influential myths are sensed not in the "content" of the myriad of "messages" and "stories" to which the average person in the U.S. subjects himself every day, but in their individual structure and their aggregate patterning.[33] For example, it has been suggested that advertising (always good news) represents heaven, juxtaposed with "the news" (almost always bad news) which represents hell. The "story" which embodies the cultural myth of the western hero is not to be found so much in the plot or even in the theme, but in the structure of the action. And there is presently some research into the structure of the total pattern of television programming as being the mythically important aspect of television.[34] Whatever the outcome of these more contemporary approaches to the study of myth, it is clear that the most fundamental cultural myths are codified in the *patterns* of the things we say and do, and that being socialized into one culture rather than another means that we are empowered to "read" the patterns of our own culture and thus nurture those guiding and orienting myths within ourselves. To the extent that these patterns or "structures" get codified in the media or their fare, people will be able to "read" them there, and to use them for the purposes to which all cultural myths are put.

4. People use the fare of the mass media also for the purpose of providing varied experiences. In their book, *The Functions of Varied Experience,* Fiske and Maddi conclude that there are three broad positive functions of variation in experience: (a) it contributes to the normal development and to the normal functioning of organisms; (b) it is sought out for its own sake; and (c) it is one factor contributing to the affective state of human beings.[35] Some of this seeking out or "tuning in" may derive from pure curiosity—from a sheer curiosity to know what's "there" or what's "going on." Such curiosity may or may not be socially-inspired, may or may not be expected to produce socially-useful experiences or knowledge. But, just as the laboratory rat which explores a maze out of curiosity, then learns how to "run it" in order to reach food at the other end, the varied experience that one has in exploring the fare of the mass media out of curiosity becomes a part of that person and therefore has potential utility for personal ritual or as social currency.

Perhaps the major impetus behind this particular use of the fare of the mass media, however, is that of *compensation.* Although we all work out individual patterns, our psychological and social equilibrium depends upon compensating for too much, *or too little,* uncertainty, chance, risk, variety, etc.[36] There are many activities which we can turn to for such compensation: drinking, wilderness vacations, hobbies, eating, travelling, etc. To achieve that pattern of stimulation which, intuitively at least, seems "right" to us individually, we turn to what is available. The more available the fare of the mass media, the more possibilities there are for more people to use the media and their fare to compensate for too much, or too little, uncertainty, chance, riskiness, variety, etc., in the balance of their lives. This use of the media and their fare is related to people's individual life patterns, and not to any particular set of demographic factors, such as age or income level. A highly paid executive might be as bored with his everyday life as a housewife might be with hers. Yet their compensatory uses of media fare, or of any other compensatory activities, are not a function of "boredom" as such, but of the total life patterns of the two particular individuals. The fact that it is presumed to be "manly" in the U.S. to be interested in certain sports should not, therefore, be viewed as "mass" compensation or as a sufficient explanation of why more men than women watch professional football on television; different viewers may be putting this "same" fare to different uses. Or, to take another, perhaps too obvious example, the subscribers and readers of *Playboy* magazine do not constitute a homogeneous audience, except perhaps in a very naive microeconomic sense. Different subscribers and readers put *Playboy* to different uses. Some may use it as a status prop; others for purpose of phantasy; still others as a basis for confirming "nonconventional" values; and so on. It makes considerable theoretical difference whether we differentiate audiences by use rather than, for example, age or geographic location or social position, as is customarily done.

All audiences and all consumer aggregates of media fare are thus self-selecting. If a medium or one of its products were to be said to have an "effect" on people, it would have to have that "effect" on a *random* sampling of people. If the "effect" is discernible only in the case of a self-selected audience or consumer aggregates, the direction of the "effect" is the other way around. It is the *uses* to which people put the media and their fare that differentiates audiences and consumer aggregates, not demographic "variables" and not the "content" of that fare or the static "personality characteristics" of the people involved.

5. People make other uses of the media and their fare, certainly. A television set may be used as a status symbol; a head-set radio to isolate oneself from the rest of the world aurally; a library as a place to sleep or meet; a particular stereo amplifier or a trip to a particular art gallery for prestige; a highway as a challenge; a book to press leaves or a newspaper to wrap garbage; a particular magazine dropped on a suburban coffee table for snob appeal; a greeting card to hide indifference or inarticulateness; and so on and on. The "hardware" can be put to many diverse uses, in the same way that the "software" can be put to many diverse uses by people in the context of their personal and social existences.

People do use the media as a source of information for purchases they are going to make, have just made, or might make. There is the housewife whose primary use of the newspaper is that of clipping supermarket or other sale ads. There is the fellow who carefully reads advertisements for a certain Chevrolet automobile or a certain tour because he has just bought one. And there are those who use certain media as a source of information about next fall's or next spring's fashions—whether in clothing, party-giving, travel, reading, or office decor.

People use the media as a source of information about work- or hobby- or leisure-time-related interests. There is the executive who scans particular newspapers for news and ideas pertinent to his company. There are those who have a low attention threshold for ideas about golfing or woodworking or skydiving or mink-breeding or baby-raising or car repair, whatever the medium. And there are those who gain access to diffused subcultures like recreational vehicle owners by paying attention to media fare on that subject.

Some people may use media fare for educational purposes. This is not related to enterprises like "educational television," which serves mainly the purposes of those who make their living in it, or in related industries (e.g., "educational technology," which is a euphemism for all kinds of products and services that are sold primarily to schools and to "educators" and not to students). Rather, this refers to the *systematic* use of the media as a means of carrying out one's own educational plans and goals. Someone who could not afford books, for example, might set out to become an Elizabethan scholar by using the public libraries. Or, one might invest his time in media fare on the basis of his intent to become an expert on public affairs. It has been said that only about

15 percent of the people in the U.S. *can* learn from books. Whether it is the same 15 percent who *could* learn from television or from museums, or some other 15 percent of the people, remains to be determined. In any case, this use of the media is relatively minor.

And people do, of course, sometimes use media fare for purposes of pure entertainment. But in the overall view, this is also a relatively minor use of media fare, contrary to much popular belief. For a media experience to be used as sheer entertainment, it would have to remain personal. The experience would have to be the end in itself. When one talks to others about media fare, he is using it not only as "entertainment," but for social purposes or ends as well; and the latter may be the more important. We may "enjoy" a movie; but most people sooner or later talk to others about the movie's relevance, its "truth," its artistry, its "meaning," or its quality relative to other movies made by the same director or producer. Americans give considerable lip service to the value of communication "work" over communication "play."[37] Regardless, almost, of how we may individually use television fare, we find it easy to agree that there should be "better" television programs. When you ask people how "good" television is in their part of the country or their part of the world, they will most likely describe to you the public affairs programs, the documentaries, the different ethnic programs, and the like. But if you ask them what they in fact "watch," you hear a different description. Given the alternative, a majority of Britons seem to prefer cops-and-robbers shows to ballet, domestic comedy to news analysis. Even so, there is no basis for assuming that "Gunsmoke" is entertainment and that a documentary is not. People can use either one in many ways. And it is these uses which define mass communication systems, mass communication audiences, and future alternatives, not arbitrary form or "content" classifications.

The several uses of the media and their fare described here do not exhaust the possibilities, of course. Nor are such uses mutually exclusive. One may put media fare to several uses simultaneously. And consumer uses of media fare are not always obvious or specific. We may not even be aware of the uses to which we put the media and their fare. And certainly the importance of one use relative to another may change over time. Nevertheless, for all such reservations and qualifications, the key to any empirically-sound theories or generalizations about mass communication lies not in the "effects" which the media have on people, but in the uses to which people put the media and media fare.

Institutionalization of Media and Media Fare

The uses to which people put the media and media fare have consequences for the future possibilities of those media and their fare. This is a condition of social life; it is a condition of social order. From a casual friendship to the largest, most complex human society, there must be order, structure. And this order or structure comes from the reliable expectations people have about how other people are going to behave. It comes from being able to depend upon what one expects, whether of other people, of oneself, or of things. Out of necessity for their own continuity, people base their lives on the dependability of their conceptions of the world. How we conceive of tables and cabbages may be as important socially as how we conceive of ideas and kings. The only difference is that, as far as we know, it doesn't make any difference to the table how we conceive of it. But it does make a difference to other people how we conceive of them. If other people don't behave according to our expectations, we have no way of relating to them. And this is as true for every other person as it is for us.

For example, someone in a community who has come to be known as the "town gossip" over a period of time will be expected by people who "know" this to continue providing "the gossip." If for some reason the "gossip's" resources dry up, or if he or she wishes to change from that expected role in the community, it will be at the considerable peril of losing the security of a known role and a reliable set of expectations; and this would threaten the psychological continuity of those people who had these expectations as much as it would the psychological continuity of the one "known" as the "gossip." Our expectations of others over time serve to *institutionalize* our relationships with them. It happens with husbands and wives. They come to expect certain behaviors of one another, and these expectations function as real constraints on the other. Husbands and wives *institutionalize* their relationships with each other. Or, consider the case of Joe Namath: it is conceivable that he could revert to a withdrawing, family-man type of role if he wanted to; but who could accept that image immediately beyond those who didn't already "know" who he is? We who "know" him have *institutionalized* him. We get impatient quickly with an automobile we have come to expect to start easily; we have more patience with one which we are less familiar with, in the same way that we have less patience with the unexpected behavior of others we "know" well than we would have with the unexpected behavior of strangers. We want the world to fit our expectations of it, and most of us are ready most of the time to exert whatever influence we can to *make* the world fit our expectations of it, for good or ill, right or wrong.

It is so for all humans in all human societies, and it is so in our relationships with the media and their fare. The crux of the matter is this: The conventional uses to which the media and media fare are put by people *over time* constitute an *institutionalization* of those media and of that fare. That is, when the uses to which people put particular media and particular fare become an integral part of their everyday lives, or an integral part of the basis on which people relate to each other over time, then those media and that fare have become institutionalized. When we can take our expectations for granted, we are relying upon a social institution. Joe Namath is a social institution, in much the same way that "the news" is a social institution; what we get is what we expect, and what we expect is what we get.

Consider ball game scores or stock market reports. If it becomes conventional for people to use this information as a basis for starting or sustaining a conversation (in a bar, a subway or train, or barber shop, etc.), then such "knowledge" has social utility. And this social utility can be exploited by an enterprising mediator. A Picasso exhibit may draw some who are just curious; but what makes such an exhibit economically feasible or practical are those for whom "knowing about" and talking about Picasso and his paintings has social utility—i.e., those who can be expected to *use* the occasion as a basis for talking to each other, or in some other way having social currency. The daily or hourly repetition of the top ten popular tunes provides listeners with something they can use: it confirms their expectations and hence serves as a kind of identity ritual. Then there is "the news." For the most part, "the news" has to be what people expect; it has to provide assurance that what they beyond are talking about is what they should be talking about, because it is what "people" are talking about. Anything truly novel or "new" and unexpected has unknown social currency; perhaps none. Thus broadcasting or printing much that is really "new" or unexpected or unassessable in terms of its social currency would be an extremely high-risk venture, both for the broadcaster or editor, and for the consumer. Neither the economics nor the politics of the mass media can stand very much real "news." You can bet that the ABC, CBS, and NBC evening "news" will cover the same "news" in essentially the same order. This is due to no conscious conspiracy. The more people who get the same "news," even on different channels, the more assurance we can have as individuals that we really got "the news"—and that what we now "know" about what is going on is what we *need* to "know."

Examples are legion. The central theoretical issue, however, is this: The conventional ways in which people over time come to use places and people and ideas and things—including media and media fare—constitute a mutual constraint on both producer and consumer, both source and audience.[38] The producer is constrained to deploy the media and to produce that fare which people have a use for, when and where and how they have come to use the media and their fare. And users are reciprocally constrained by the ways in which particular personal and social "usefulnesses" are built into and out of the particular media and media fare available. This reciprocally-constraining system is never perfect, of course. The producer may misinterpret user interest or expectation. Or, the producer may be moved, for whatever reason, to produce something which he thinks people *ought* to have available. The producers of media fare do not live by bread alone, any more than do the consumers. Sometimes they simply experiment. These and other "imperfections" on the producer's side keep the system from being perfect. So, too, do users upset the inertia in the system. People are sometimes "obstinate."[39] They don't always react to media fare in the way even seasoned producers of that fare expect them to react. People may not always pay attention to what would be in their own best interest. Sometimes people will listen to what they "ought" to know about; and sometimes they won't. And, as consumers of the media and their fare, people are sometimes apparently just "fickle." Just when they seem to have taken a program or a feature or a new celebrity or some "current event" to their hearts, the affair may be over as quickly and as inexplicably as it started, and they begin to warm up to some new celebrity or some new cause or Social Issue[40] or some new feature. Even "Peanuts" no longer has the same appeal to the same people it once had, and "Star Trek" and the original "Laugh In" are now history. The "ecological crisis" has apparently given way to the "energy crisis" and this to the "Watergate crisis." Just as there are fashions in the way bathrooms are used, there are fashions in the usefulness of media fare. There are those people who don't know what they want in the fare of the media, simply because they are uncertain about the social currency it might have for them. Sometimes users don't go at all for the obvious. On other occasions they go overboard for the inobvious in what they buy or use. Who would have predicted the "hoola hoop" craze? Thus there are a great many imperfections in this reciprocally-constraining system, and this contributes to its continuous evolution and change. The mutual constraints which tend to "close" the system and to bring it into the perpetual equilibrium of perfect redundancy also provide for the dialectics of change. People want the security of the familiar and the routine and the predictable. But they also want the stimulation of the unfamiliar, the nonroutine, and the unpredictable. We want sameness; but we want some variety and change too—in our media fare as in other aspects of our lives.

The reaction of people to something truly novel cannot, of course, be predicted. And what is at work in the emergence or the decline of a current public fashion—whether in topical interests or clothes or media fare—is a set of variables so complex, so self-determining, that the particulars cannot be predicted. In the same way that the most accurate prediction we can make of tomorrow's weather is that it will be the same as today's, the most reliable prediction anyone can make about public tastes in media fare tomorrow is that they will be the same as today. This is why there is so much imitation and redundancy in programming, advertising, book publishing, songwriting, and so on. It is not that the producers conspire to present more of the same or similar media fare. It is that nothing succeeds like success. Except within very minor variations on already institutionalized themes, programs, formats, etc., the producers of media fare cannot predict what will appeal to consumers, and sometimes not even then. So when something seems to be "going," people get on the bandwagon, producer and consumer alike. An art exhibitor has some basis for calculating the appeal of a Renoir exhibit. He has no basis for predicting the public appeal of a totally unknown painter (unless, of course, there is already an audience institutionalized around the value of going only to exhibits of unknown painters, which happens). This is not "crassness" on the part of the exhibitor. He is constrained as much by the system as are those to whom he exhibits. People go to a Renoir exhibit because other

people go. They don't go to the exhibits of painters to which no one else goes. This is as true in those nations where the media and the arts are mainly tax-supported as it is in the U.S., where they are not. The exhibitor might be a philanthropist, however; he might undertake to exhibit the work of unknown painters simply because he believed it would be "good" for people to look at something different for a change. But if no one came, then no one else would come; and our altruistic exhibitor would thereby be jeopardizing the future possibilities of the very work he wanted to make known.

These are not trivial matters. All of this is in the nature of the conditions of everyday social life. These conditions are not different elsewhere simply because of a different political or economic suasion. The constraints of social institutionalization are real, and they are significant. *Any* sensed threat to an institutional relationship—any threat to the conventional uses (or non-uses) to which people put other people and the artifacts of their environment—is a threat not just to that relationship. It is a threat to the very existences of the people involved, sometimes minor, sometimes major. Every human existence hinges upon the conventional, institutionalized relationships that obtain between and among individuals in their environments over time. Without these, we could not have human existence as we know it. So when we speak of the institutionalization of, for example, a television star, we are not talking about whimsy. We are talking about the fundamental stuff of social life. And that is not trivial. In the same way that social order depends upon the reliable continuity of most of the people of that society, the reliable continuity of every individual depends upon social order. And the ways in which we institutionalize media fare as a part of that predictable social order is just as important to our existences as the conventional uses to which we put other people and the other artifacts of our environment.

What could be more traumatizing than to discover one day that everything one "knew" about what-is-going-on had no social currency at all, that what one "knew" seemed totally irrelevant to what everyone else was talking about, and that what everyone else was talking about seemed strange and without any personal relevance? The fact that this does not occur gives ample evidence of the underlying social processes at work. What has personal or social utility for us establishes real constraints on what it is feasible or possible for the producers of media fare to provide us. And what is provided places limits on what can be found in media fare having personal or social utility.

We create these mutually-constraining systems through our conventional uses of the media and media fare over time. The uses to which people put the media and media fare in their everyday personal and social activities serve to institutionalize particular media and particular media fare in particular ways. The time and the place and the manner of institutionalization of media and media fare can no more be predicted than can the time and place and manner of genetic mutation. The specifics of social evolution are as indeterminable as are the

specifics of biological evolution. In a totally controlled society, which could exist only hypothetically, the "controllers" might well concern themselves with the achievement of wanted "effects" and with the elimination of unwanted "effects" of the media and media fare. But in a free or "open" society, these are matters which emerge from the social behavior of people in the course of their everyday lives. They are not matters to be decided for them and imposed upon them.

Thus it is that in a free or "open" society the theoretical point of entry is that of the institutionalization of the uses to which people put the media and media fare.

The Dilemma

It would have been characteristic of social analysts until recently to seize upon the situation just described—the systemic constraints on producers and consumers of media fare that accrue from the institutionalization of particular media or media fare in particular ways—as a "problem" to be solved through "more" research or "better" social policy. But in recent years there has seemed to be an increased willingness to recognize that the human condition in its social context involves a number of basic paradoxes and dilemmas. To treat such dilemmas and paradoxes as mere engineering "problems" to be solved by the application of appropriate methods is both corrosive and destructive of humanity. Enlightened theory and research, and enlightened policy-making in these areas, requires recognition of the human dilemmas and human paradoxes of life in an "open" society, and calls for the kind of accommodation that does not destroy the humanity it is supposed to serve.

The basis of the dilemma created by the ways in which people institutionalize the media and media fare is identified by Paul Valery. Speaking of the works of artists and artisans, he distinguished between

> works which are *as it were created by their public,* in that they fulfill its expectations and are thus almost determined by knowledge of those expectations, and works which on the *contrary tend to create their own public.* [41]

The difficulty, of course, is that there is no reliable way to determine in advance which new works will in fact "create their own public." That publics do emerge to champion some new products, works of art, or media fare could hardly be denied. But the metaphor is misleading. Works do not "create" publics. It is publics—people—who in communication create the social worth or relevance or value of whatever works are made available to them. No product, no work of art, no media fare has intrinsic social worth, value, or relevance. These are qualities which are *attributed to them* by people. And these are the only qualities which have social consequences.

It is on this issue that the "practical-minded" and the "artistic-minded" are often set off against one another. Those whose minds run to the practicality or the feasibility of offering one kind of media fare rather than another are likely to think in terms of the public's interests or wants or needs, as evidenced by their past behavior. Those whose minds run to the ethestic or the idealistic issues involved are more likely to place these values above the risks involved.

But these seeming differences are not matters of "right" or "wrong." Historically, of course, both have been "right," and both have been "wrong" at one time or another. This is in the nature of the dilemma. If it had not been for those who thoroughly believed in the "intrinsic" worth of a new idea, there would have been little in the way of *human* history to write about. On the other hand, if it had not been for those who insisted upon the ultimate role that audiences and publics play in creating and maintaining the human and social *value* of new ideas and new human artifacts, there would have been little in the way of human *history* to write about.

Carpenter expresses the "idealist" view in this way:

> If you address yourself to an audience, you accept at the outset the basic premises that unite the audience. You put on the audience, repeating clichés familiar to it. But artists don't address themselves to audiences; they create audiences. The artist talks to himself out loud. If what he has to say is significant, others hear and are affected.[42]

But how can one *be* an "artist" except by having *some* audience which acknowledges him *as* an artist? Is it possible that anyone who simply calls himself an "artist" has thereby some way of "creating" audiences for his wares? Yes, Carpenter seems to be saying, *if* what that "artist" has to say is significant. But how does what one says become "significant" except through the belief of *some* audience? There have undoubtedly been a great many writers who believe their stuff is more "significant" than Hemingway's; and there are undoubtedly many aspiring actors and editors and political cartoonists who believe their work is more "significant" than anyone else's. But does the saying so or the believing so make it so?

To take the one position *or* the other—the "idealist" *or* the "practicalist" position—would be to do away with the mutual dependence of the producers and the consumers of media fare by mere rhetoric. Carpenter has an audience. It's easy for him to say he "created" it by saying something "significant." But what of all of the young scholars who don't agree with him yet don't have an audience?

Where so many alternatives are available that people must choose not only the media they prefer, but the mediators and the media fare that they prefer, anything new, if it is to be chosen or preferred by people in numbers at all, must be preferred at the cost of giving up a preference for something else. Carpenter's audience once "belonged" in part to some other artist or scholar. How is he to reconcile this? Is Jacqueline Susann to conclude that her work is more "significant" than that of most other writers because she has a larger audience? And on what basis do we, the "intellectuals," decide that it isn't?

The dilemma is simply that the producers of media fare have to give people what is familiar and comfortable and expected if they want to continue on as producers of media fare, whether they are operated commercially or by and for the State. Yet they must also give people variety, something novel. For their part, people must be able to find in media fare what they expect and therefore what is useful. Otherwise, they will have no use for the media and media fare. But they must also be able to find variety there, or they will turn somewhere else for it. But whether something new or different will have personal or social utility for people depends solely upon whether people use it as if it did have. Call it "irrationality" if you will. But in a free society, the producers of media fare can have predictability only at the cost of human and social evolution.

The "resolution" of this dilemma is not in producing *either* what people are used to *or* what they "should" have; *either* is self-defeating. Its "resolution" lies in accepting it as irresolvable and even in guarding and nurturing it as the underlying dialectic impelling all social change and evolution.

The Proliferation of Publics

The greater the variety of alternative media or media fare, the more audiences there will emerge. And, the more audiences or publics there are, the more alternative possibilities there are for the media and for media fare. But this differentiation is essentially from within. It is not unlike the literacy problem. Producing and distributing more different kinds of books will not necessarily increase the literacy of a society-at-large. But it will go hand in hand with a further differentiation of the existing book-reading public into several specialized audiences, with some attributing more "significance" or value or usefulness to biographies, others to fiction, others to documentaries, and so on. Or, to take another example: the more conflicting political points of view made available to a public, the more fragmented that public will likely become. Not all of the alternatives offered will "catch on," but those that do will be given the legitimacy of an audience, and that audience the security of having its differentiated beliefs confirmed and legitimized. What is measurable is that where the media and their fare are more heterogeneous, publics proliferate—and conversely. This raises some intriguing questions about the relationship between the rate of proliferation of publics and social order.

Media Alternatives and Social Order

The more real alternatives there are for people in a given society, the more internally differentiated that society will be. And the more differentiated publics there are in a society, the more possibilities there are for additional variety in ideas, things, tastes, fashions, etc. Where there may have been but one guiding ideology or world-view in earlier societies, one could be either for it or against it. Because he was not *for* the dominant world-view of his time, Galileo was presumed to be *against* it. Where there are alternative world-views espoused by different publics within the same society, one has some choice of which publics to subscribe to. When there was but one type of sword, one either liked it or did not. When a different kind of sword was introduced, there could be factions; there were undoubtedly fights and skirmishes between those who were convinced that the one was better than the other. When there was but one kind of music, or when there was but one music celebrity at a time, it was difficult to get into an argument about which was best; today one can overhear such arguments everywhere. In the early days of television, there was little talk about how "bad" it was; people even sat around watching the test pattern. We may suffer now in the U.S. the consequences of too many alternatives. There could not be differences of opinion if there were not real alternatives for people.

Perhaps what distresses some of the more "intellectual" critics of our present situation is the range of the alternatives, the scope of the choices becoming available to more and more people. Of course television could be "better." It could be "better" in France, too, and in Japan and England. But the question is, better *for whom?* We "intellectuals" *know* that a revered ballet is "better" television fare than a quiz show. We "intellectuals" *know* that a higher ratio of social documentaries to "escape" fare on television would raise social consciousness and improve the lot of people in the process. But we have no evidence of this. Is our dogma less irrational than any one else's? Contrary to current folklore—and this is generally how we deal with the popular media these days, from the current folklore about it—there is some evidence that there is more public affairs broadcasting on television in the U.S. than in England.[43] The B.B.C. may not be the end-all for everyone.

People seek the security of the familiar; but people also seek the stimulation of the novel. The normal individual needs the comfort of the expected; but he also needs the perturbation of the unexpected. We all need certainty. Couple this with the institutionalization of the things we use and the people we see and the talk we engage in every day, and we have that certainty. But we also need variety. Couple this with the technological inventiveness and the affluence of a society such as that of the U.S., and we have that variety, whether in can openers, home music amplifiers, automobiles, spectacles, or television fare.

The more real alternatives there are for people in mass media fare, the more the society becomes differentiated. Yet the more differentiated the society becomes, the more utility there is in the fare of the mass media as a basis for social integration on another level. Another paradox. It is not unlike the process of socialization itself, through that process, we mold new members into cogs that fit the existing social machinery. But through that same process we also necessarily foster and nurture their individuality. The apparent need that people have to differentiate themselves into smaller communities having interests, values, tastes, beliefs, etc., different from other such communities has led in the past to a specialization of the media. *Life,* in attempting to be *something* to *everyone,* failed, as had many other such magazines in the years since World War II. While most of the general "mass" circulation magazines have declined and disappeared, a great many new specialized periodicals have emerged. As such specialization increases, there is a parallel increase in the need for something which would contribute to communication *between* the increasingly specialized or differentiated audiences. Certain media fare—such as "the news," as already suggested—can be used in this way.

In his recent book, *World Communication: Threat or Promise?,* Colin Cherry raises the issue in this way: threat *or* promise?[44] In free societies, if unimpeded by well-intentioned but misguided policy-making, the continuing increase in alternative media and media fare is *both,* both threat *and* promise. It has been both since the first troubadour wandered into a remote village.

And this raises some intriguing questions about the ultimate compatibility of *mass* media and democracy. In his essay *On Liberty,* John Stuart Mill wrote that "The individual must be protected . . . against the tyranny of the prevailing opinion and feelings. . . ." To the extent there are many specialized worlds, not one general one, the individual would thus be protected. But if government policy requires that all television programming, for example, as well as all stations, be "balanced," how are we to maintain our separate worlds?[45]

An approach such as this raises a great many such questions. They cannot all be answered here, if at all. The challenge is that we must learn to think both more substantively and creatively about these issues. Hopefully the approach outlined here makes some small contribution to the possibilities for doing so.

Notes and References

1. Thomas S. Kuhn, *The Structure of Scientific Revolutions* (University of Chicago Press, 1962, 1970).
2. For example, P. F. Lazarsfeld, B. Berelson, and Helen Gaudet, *The People's Choice* (New York: Duell, Sloan and Pierce, 1944); P. F. Lazarsfeld and F. N. Stanton (eds.), *Communications Research, 1948–1949* (New York: Harper, 1949); Wilbur Schramm (ed.), *Mass Communica-*

tions (University of Illinois Press, 1949); and the work of Carl I. Hovland and his associates in the Yale Communication and Attitude Change Program, which had its inception in the W.W. II work of Hovland, A. A. Lumsdaine, and F. D. Sheffield, reported in *Experiments on Mass Communication* (Princeton University Press, 1949).

3. Melvin L. DeFleur, *Theories of Mass Communication,* 2nd ed. (New York: David McKay, 1970), p. 118.

4. *Ibid.,* p. 119.

5. For three of a great many views on this condition of Western man, cf. Allen Wheelis, *The End of the Modern Age* (New York: Basic Books, 1971); Gunther S. Stent, *The Coming of the Golden Age: A View of the End of Progress* (Garden City, N.Y.: Natural History Press, 1969); and Lewis Mumford, *The Myth of the Machine: Technics and Human Development* (New York: Harcourt, Brace & World, 1966).

6. By Walter Weiss, pp. 77–195 in Vol. V of *The Handbook of Social Psychology,* G. Lindzey and E. Aronson, eds., (Reading, Mass.: Addison-Wesley, 1969).

7. Shirley A. Star and Helen M. Hughes, "Report on an Educational Campaign: the Cincinnati Plan for the United Nations," *American Journal of Sociology,* 55:1 (1950) pp. 389–400.

8. Karl R. Popper, *Conjectures and Refutations: The Growth of Scientific Knowledge* (2nd ed.), (New York: Basic Books, 1965).

9. Denis McQuail, *Towards a Sociology of Mass Communications* (London: Collier-MacMillan, 1969), ch. 4 on "new directions."

10. *Op. cit.,* ch. 7 on "contemporary theories."

11. Harold A. Innis, *The Bias of Communication* (University of Toronto Press, 1951).

12. Harold Mendelsohn, *Mass Entertainment* (New Haven: College and University Press, 1966).

13. E. Katz, "Mass Communication Research and the Study of Culture," *Studies in Public Communication,* 2 (1959) pp. 1–6.

14. William Stephenson, *The Play Theory of Mass Communication* (University of Chicago Press, 1967).

15. Marten Brouwer, "Prolegomena to a Theory of Mass Communication," in Lee Thayer (ed.), *Communication: Concepts and Perspectives* (New York: Spartan Books, 1967), pp. 227–239.

16. Walter Lippmann, *Public Opinion* (New York: Harcourt, Brace, 1922).

17. Marshall McLuhan, *The Gutenberg Galaxy* (University of Toronto Press, 1962).

18. E.g., W. Schramm, "The Nature of Communication between Humans," in *The Process and Effects of Mass Communication* (rev. ed.), W. Schramm and D. F. Roberts (eds.) (University of Illinois Press, 1971).

19. It seems impossible to spike this bit of rumor-become-dogma. Cf. R. A. Bauer, "The Obstinate Audience," *American Psychologist,* 19 (1964), pp. 319–28; E. Katz and P. F. Lazarsfeld, *Personal Influence: The Part Played by People in the Flow of Mass Communications* (New York: Free Press, 1964); and Lee Thayer, *Communication and Communication Systems* (Homewood, Ill.: Irwin, 1968).

20. See the Cover Story, " Pop Records: Moguls, Money and Monsters," *Time,* February 12, 1973.
21. These competencies may derive broadly from the specific cultures and subcultures within which one has been socialized to live and think and know and believe. But these competencies are generative processes; they are not, as they are frequently treated in popular psychology, entities.
22. In *The Passionate State of Mind* (New York: Harper, 1954), Eric Hoffer says, "Propaganda does not deceive people; it merely helps them to deceive themselves."
23. The full title is *Human Understanding: The Collective Use and Evolution of Concepts* (Princeton University Press, 1972).
24. On Languages as media, see Marshall McLuhan, "Myth and Mass Media," in H. A. Murray (ed.), *Myth and Mythmaking* (Boston: Beacon Press, 1968). On the "languages" of the media, see E. Carpenter, "The New Languages," in E. Carpenter and M. McLuhan (eds.), *Explorations in Communication* (Boston: Beacon Press, 1960).
25. See Paul Bouissac, "Poetics in the Lion's Den: The Circus Act as a Text," *Modern Language Notes,* 86:6 (December) 1971.
26. This was the gist of Katz's paper on mass communication research in 1959 (see note 13), and others have argued in this direction, with apparently little or no "effect". In response to the question of what makes a book sell, Charles Darwin replied to Samuel Butler, "Getting talked about is what makes a book sell."
27. This is of course true of all human inventions and artifacts. The wheel as such had no social effects; it was and is the uses to which wheels are put that have had social and human consequences.
28. In *The Art of Conjecture* (New York: Basic Books, 1967).
29. On the relevance of the concept of covenant for this kind of inquiry, see J. F. A. Taylor, *The Masks of Society: An Inquiry into the Covenants of Civilization* (New York: Appleton-Century-Crofts, 1966).
30. For a view of the role of one kind of fare—literature—in this regard, see ch. 5, "Literature and Society," of Leo Lowenthal, *Literature, Popular Culture, and Society* (Englewood Cliffs, N.J.: Prentice-Hall, 1961).
31. See, e.g., J. Campbell, *Myths to Live By* (New York: Viking, 1972); J. G. Frazer, *The Golden Bough* (New York: Macmillan, 1922); O. E. Klapp, *Heroes, Villains, and Fools* (Englewood Cliffs, N.J.: Prentice-Hall, 1962). For a contemporary analysis of the "mythic" function of mass entertainment, *c.f.* E. Morin, *The Stars* (New York: Grove Press, 1960).
32. Alan W. Watts, *Myth and Ritual in Christianity* (London: Macmillan, 1954).
33. *Cf.* Claude Lévi-Strauss, "The Structural Study of Myth," in T. A. Sebeok (ed.), *Myth: A Symposium* (Indiana University Press, 1955); and Roland Barthes, *Mythologies,* Trans. Annette Lavers (New York: Hill & Wang, 1972). For a general overview of the "Structuralist" approach, see Richard T. DeGeorge, *Structuralists: From Marx to Lévi-*

Strauss (New York: Anchor Books, 1972). *Cf.* Mircea Eliade, *Myth and Reality* (New York: Harper, 1963).

34. E.g., R. C. Schmidt, "The Mythic Structure of Television Programming," Meeting of the International Communication Association, Montreal, April 1973.

35. Donald W. Fiske and Salvatore R. Maddi, *Functions of Varied Experience* (Homewood, Ill.: Dorsey, 1961), p. 13. If it seems paradoxical that people need both sameness and variety in some dialectical mixture, then it may be.

36. One might compare this with the concepts of *communication-pleasure* and *communication-pain* suggested by the psychiatrist T. A. Szasz in *Pain and Pleasure* (New York: Basic Books, 1957), and extrapolated by William Stephenson in *The Play Theory of Mass Communication* (University of Chicago Press, 1967); but I believe there is more than just "pain" and "pleasure" involved.

37. See the references cited in note 36 for a discussion of these terms.

38. In "The Communicator and the Audience," *Journal of Conflict Resolution*, 2:1 (1958), pp. 67–77, Raymond Bauer proposes, on the basis of experimental evidence, that (a) images of the audience affect the communicator, and (b) users commit sources to a position.

39. *Cf.* R. A. Bauer, "The Obstinate Audience," *loc. cit.*

40. On the phenomenon of Social Issues in general, with the issue of our ecology as the exemplar, see L. Thayer "Man's Ecology, Ecology's Man," *Main Currents in Modern Thought,* 27:3 (January-February 1971), pp. 71–78.

41. *Oeuvres, I* (Paris: Gallimard, Bibliotheque de la Pleiada), p. 1442.

42. Edmund Carpenter, *They Became What They Beheld* (N.Y.: Outertridge and Dienstfrey, 1970), in the "Foreword." Carpenter's philosophy can be contrasted with that of Konrad Lorenz, in *On Aggression* (New York: Bantam, 1962):

> If his contemporaries pay attention to a teacher or even read his books, it can safely be assumed that he is not an intellectual giant (p. 266);

or that of Jonathan Swift, in Thoughts on Various Subjects:

> When a true genius appears in the world, you may know him by his sign, that the dunces are all in confederacy against him.

43. E.g., Karen Possner, "A Comparison of a Week of Television Programming in New York and London," University of Iowa, School of Journalism, (unpublished ms., 1972).

44. (London: Wiley-Interscience, 1971).

45. On the necessity of isolating populations to optimize evolutionary health and vigor, see Garrett Hardin, *Nature and Man's Fate* (New York: Rinehart, 1959). A "global village" as a criterion for the species reflects the hubris and the myopia of technologism.

CHAPTER IV

Counterpoint:
Moeller and Thayer

In the two preceding chapters, Leslie Moeller and Lee Thayer presented quite divergent views of the mass communication phenomenon, its nature and its uses. Since it was our intent that these two chapters form the core of the section of this book entitled "Dialogue," we sought to extend the concept by inviting a rejoinder from each author to the work of the other. Again, as with their principal chapters, the approaches of the two contributors differ.

Moeller's response focuses upon his interpretation of Thayer's original chapter as a "uses-and-gratifications" explanation of the mass communication process (which Moeller points out is something editors have known, taken for granted and made use of for a century), and then expands his discussion to an exploration of the "needs" of the mass media user.

In a contrasting style, Thayer's commentary sticks more closely to Moeller's original chapter, raising questions that challenge the underlying assumptions of Moeller's presentation ("there is no such thing as a human "need" simply "to know" . . .), as well as exploring a number of fundamental issues which he believes Moeller avoided.

A Critique of Thayer's Mass Media and Mass Communication
LESLIE G. MOELLER

Professor Thayer's *uses-and-gratifications* approach to understanding the mass communication phenomenon and the relationship of the audience to the content of mass media seems both logical and sound. It is especially important that the topic be explicated from this point of view because editors for at least a century have paid very high allegiance to the uses-and-gratifications concept. Their allegiance to this principle has in fact been so taken for granted that it is very seldom spoken or written about by scholars in our field. Indeed, if an editor does not take into account the manner in which his product is used by the audience and the manner in which it gratifies the needs of an audience, that editor does not very long have a product to produce (at least if he derives his income from the audience or advertisers in order to continue operations).

At the same time that mass communication practitioners have rather much taken the principle for granted, researchers have been somewhat neglectful in considering the approach.

Even so, Katz, Gurevitch and Haas, in their monumental work "On the Use of Mass Media for Important Things," do trace the history of over 30 years of research by Cantril, Herzog, Warner, Henry, Waples, and Riley and Riley, as well as more current studies by Blumler and McQuail, Emmett, BBC Audience Research, and some half dozen other researchers. The Katz-Gurevitch-Haas compilation, done in Israel, has one major weakness when viewed from an American perspective: it does not include magazines among the mass media examined (it is devoted to radio, television, newspapers, books, and film). From the point of view of our own society, the omission is especially interesting considering the increasing number of specialized magazines which are developing and already exist apparently because they do produce gratification on the part of the reader.

This same study developed a list of possible mass media audience needs, and then surveyed 1,500 adult respondents to discover the relative importance of those needs. The researchers reported that the group of eight items endorsed by 70 percent or more of the respondents were dominated "by what might be described as 'collectivity-oriented' needs, pertaining to the state, the nation (or the national tradition), and the family." The need selected as "very important" by 90 percent of the sample was "to feel pride that we have a state." Lowest on the list of mass media related needs was "to escape everyday reality," which was rated as "very important" by only 16 percent of the total sample.

Some interesting additional findings hold implications for the central issue of uses-and-gratifications under discussion here. The research suggested that television is the most diffuse medium in the sense that its users apply its content to a wide range of functions, while newspapers and movies are viewed as having more specific applications. Conversely, for individuals indicating that matters of state and society are more important to them, newspapers are the most important medium. Wrote the researchers, "altogether the centrality of the newspaper for knowledge and integration in the socio-political arena cannot be overstated." As for needs having to do with "self," knowing oneself is best served by books; enjoying oneself is associated with films, television and books; while the newspaper "contributes to a self-regulation and self-confidence."

The researchers conclude with the observation that "it should be noted that media-related needs are not, by and large, generated by the media. Most pre-date the emergence of the media and, properly, ought to be viewed within the wider range of human needs. As such, they have always been, and remain, satisfied in a variety of ways, most quite unrelated to the mass media. The surprising thing is to realize the extent and range of the media's encroachment on the 'older' ways of satisfying social and psychological needs." The findings of Katz, Gurevitch and Haas simply underscore my earlier contention that the notion of uses and gratifications is implicit in the functions performed by mass media editors.

In a recent attempt to analyze the future of the daily newspaper, I used a somewhat different approach than did Thayer to the whole matter of uses and gratifications. I posited what I call *elements of need* on the part of the citizen when he considers the mass media. I have suggested that the individual wants most of the following elements, in varying mixes and intensities, with different needs operating more strongly than others at different times (and clearly several of these elements overlap):

1. The citizen wants a satisfactory report of the state of the world; this does not necessarily mean accurate, or complete, or fair, or adequate. The "satisfaction" is in terms of each individual's own mix of needs.
2. The individual needs adequate news of the *changes* in the world and a picture of the rate of change, along with sufficient continuing material to make clear the elements of stability.
3. The citizen needs a sufficient noting and description of the problems of the world, with an estimate of magnitude and immediacy, and needs to know that progress is being made toward improving at least some of the problem situations.
4. In general, media content should be "relevant," an overworked word which I have defined as "useful" or "instrumental," i.e., being applicable to near-future personal problem-coping efforts, or having direct meaning for the life of the individual and those close to him.
5. Media content should be interesting, reasonably easy to comprehend, and relatively pleasurable.
6. Increasingly, the citizen will want aid from the mass media in facing demands on him for added education or re-education to new activities.
7. The individual needs an adequate guide to buying goods and services, a process which seems to become more complex with each passing day.
8. Many citizens today face increasingly more leisure time, and the attendant question of what to do with that time. They will want to feel that such time is not being "wasted." Entertainment can help fill the void, but something more than entertainment is wanted.

9. The individual needs a friend, a "resource," a someone "who helps me" in facing the complexities of the world (which helps explain the impact of "Action Line" or "Got a Problem" or "Dear Abby" programs and columns.)
10. In a more general way, the citizen expects the mass media to contribute to making a good society, and that the media ought be more directly concerned with this activity than is usually the case.

Thayer's skillful discussion of institutionalization is another instance of a factor which the profession has not only taken into account, but has taken for granted for almost as long as the mass media have existed. News processors *know* that readers of a print medium, for example, want to be able to locate the same material in the same place in their publication day after day. News people know that even slight variations will cause enough difficulty for readers so that in most publications they are consciously held to a minimum.

Changes in nature of content are again subject to the same "slow change" rule. Most users of the mass media are rather well accustomed to the nature of the content of their media and, while they may talk about the need for change, they aren't always so enthusiastic about it when it happens in the media product to which they attend.

On the other side of this issue, however, users do change the nature of the product, and the managers of the media hunt out the needs of their audiences.

In the early days of television, most of the owners of television sets were in the upper socio-economic classes, with above average education, and above average cultural backgrounds. Those were the days, then, when it was possible to have programs such as "Playhouse 90" on national network television. But as audiences became larger, and as more and more people in lower socio-economic levels (with the usually lower educational and cultural backgrounds) came into the audience, it was no longer feasible for networks to present original and occasionally off-beat productions of this type. The audience attracted by such presentations was no longer large enough to retain a major share of the market to obtain the all-essential advertising.

Instead, the networks shifted to content which was more suitable to the existing audience, introducing the situation comedy, detectives series, westerns, series involving violence, and soap operas. These new programs were not only closer to the general needs of the larger audience, but the audience knew with more certainty what sort of media product they would receive, and ran less risk of being exposed to presentations that were overly-intellectual.

Considering problems for the media in matching the needs of their audiences, the current situation of daily newspapers provides a poignant example. It was noted at a recent convention of circulation managers that circulation of U.S. daily newspapers had fallen off 3.6

percent. It was further observed that during the past five years the ratio of daily newspapers to households in the U.S. declined from 1.0 to .89 for daily papers, and from .80 to .74 for Sunday papers, confirming the fact that a growing number of households no longer buy a daily paper, and an even larger number buy no Sunday paper.

The vice-president for marketing for the *Philadelphia Bulletin* explained the problem this way: "The key to success in our business is the ability to attract and hold the interest of the newspaper reader, and today's reader, or potential reader, is a very different person from the one who bought our newspapers only a short time ago, and so is the competition for his and her time and attention."

He went on to say that in years ahead, because of the complexity of the new reader, "the need for greater specialization will grow at a rapid rate. As it does, one of the most basic new dimensions with which newspapers will be confronted will be the need to identify specific groups within the potential newspaper audience, and find ways, on a daily basis, to present special content intensely designed to serve the particular requirements of particular readers."

In spite of Thayer's protestations to the contrary, the mass media must be economically solvent in order to fulfill their social responsibility. To that end, I am again reminded of the pertinence of a comment to me by two executives of a major firm specializing in locating executive personnel for daily newspapers: the greatest current demand from daily newspapers is for persons who have high skill and capability in marketing. This translates, in terms of modern mass media management as determining the needs of the potential audience, designing a product that will suit those needs, and making the resulting product available in such a manner that it will be convenient for the customer to buy and use.

A Critique of Moeller's The Big Four Mass Media

LEE THAYER

No one could have done a better job of writing this paper than Professor Moeller; what he has revealed here is but the tip of the iceberg of his vast knowledge of such matters.

It is, indeed, difficult to point to anything at all wrong with what he says, since he says so little of moment, and says that so guardedly (or, perhaps, as they say in the trade, so "objectively"). Nor should he be brought up short for what he does not say. Nevertheless, I believe it is mainly in what he does not say that most of the meatier and more controversial issues lie.

The major shortcomings I see in Professor Moeller's chapter are these—first, the assumptions which underlie his whole posture; and secondly, the fundamental issues which he avoids.

As to the first, Professor Moeller hypostatizes the media— something which any cub reporter should get cuffed for doing, in spite of the fact that he might have to go to the dictionary to learn that hypostatization means attributing to abstractions (such as "the media") human characteristics they could not have. How can "the media" as such have "been in favor of" anything at all? Perhaps the publishers and the editors and the reporters were or were not in favor of something. But "the media"?

But there is more here than meets the eye—a whole syndrome, nicely captured in Professor Moeller's posture, a whole host of assumptions that deserve questioning; all adding up to an apparent detachment that veils an underlying, irremedial bias, and one which leads him to an undue whitewashing of "the media." For example, Professor Moeller points to the fact that ever-larger amounts of capital are required to "gain entry" to the media, and hints that such a situation might have an effect on the "content" made available to the "society." Without question, *any* way of organizing, *any* way of supporting, *any* way of censoring or controlling the "media" will affect the "content." What's hidden here is the inference that there is some way of organizing the media which would *not* affect the "content." What's implied is that we're being deprived because "the media" are big business; that we're soon to be disadvantaged by big business in this aspect of our lives much as we have been disadvantaged compared to other people of the world in food, housing, health care, etc.

And still more, even though Professor Moeller speaks as if he were "merely" reporting, he is at least nicely demonstrating that there is no such thing as "merely" reporting. His almost trivial discussion of the "economics" of "the media," for example. Aside from the fact that his "big four" media exclude the record industry, which is larger than the television industry, and aside from the fact that he seems to favor less concentration but more government protection as a monopoly (the softness of his manner here may obscure his "eat-your-cake-and-have-it-too" attitude), and aside from the fact that he must have missed Katz's point completely when he suggests that "the media" have attracted people by their "increased efficiency and lowered per-unit cost" ("economic man" redux), Professor Moeller reveals a remarkable bias in just this: Is the *ownership* of the media more or less widely distributed in the U.S. than elsewhere—say in France and Canada? He seems to be pointing to powerful cartels and the evils they may bring down upon us. Yet what more powerful cartel is there than a government "owned" and operated television station? Do you find Public Radio responsive to *your* needs because it is paid for with your tax money?

It would be easy to accuse Professor Moeller of naivete. But he is not naive. He is a man with a mission, a purpose, a goal, a motive, a bias. Like a good reporter, however, he glosses it.

And this, largely, in what he does not say—though I was amused by his comment about "the public" backing the "the press" on the "Watergate affair." Now I assume that a careful researcher and reporter such as Professor Moeller has data to this effect; can one find it anywhere, except in the newspapers? Not so amusing is that he may believe the intense feeling against the war in Vietnam was at least fired by "the media." Well, *if* so, and that's a big if, by what prerogative? And that old

saw about the "marketing function" brought this to mind—if country roads were improved and paved because they were "farm-to-market" roads, should they therefore be condemned by those who would use them for some other purposes? Or, better, should those who have other uses for them demand that parallel roads be constructed for *their* use?

Professor Moeller refers to the "ritual" use of the media as "mundane," thereby implying, we must assume, that the functions he believes to be important are grandiose. A reasonable assumption; I think they are grandiose, and I think they represent a non-empirical, irrational approach to the study of the media in society.

Let us consider his choice of the Hutchins Commission's report as providing the appropriate criteria for evaluating media performance. "Still very pertinent" is the only rationale he offers for selecting that Commission's criteria rather than dozens of others. But, then, if the purpose was actually that of setting of paper tigers to purr at or windmills to tilt at, he probably couldn't have made a better choice.

As he says, some of the words are a little abstract—like "the goals and values of the society." Or, "the day's events." (Private fantasy: the morning newspaper consists of nothing but a "true, comprehensive, and intelligent" photograph of the sunrise; the evening paper nothing but a . . . and so on. Event of the day: A newsreel of people watching Walter Cronkite.)

More here, too, than meets the eye. Suppose there were a reporter or editor or other "gatekeeper" out there in the media jungle who was "truthful, comprehensive, and intelligent"; he would still be seeing the world in and through himself, and that's what he would report. I have no doubt that Professor Moeller is himself "truthful, comprehensive, and intelligent"; would that compensate for clinging to an old journalistic concept of "objectivity"—that the less one knows about anything at all, the more "objectively" he can report it?

And where, in all of these grandiose words, is the guy who pays the bills? My criteria are much more earthy: I want the paper delivered on time, in a readable state; I want to know the scores of yesterday's

games (and here is a place where inaccuracies *can* cost customers); I want the front page to be on the front and the ads to be where they belong, my favorite comic strips not to be "delayed in the mail," etc.

And, Professor Moeller may think that being able to talk about what is being talked about is minor; but it seems major to most people I know who, when the morning paper didn't come, were greeted at the commuter stop with: "Hey, what d'ya think of that absolutely fantastic thing that happened at the track yesterday?" What *do* people talk about, anyway?

Let us not hide behind "needs," either. People do not have a need to know anything except insofar as it serves their purposes in some way. There is no such thing as a human "need" simply "to know" what is going on around the world—except as those tidbits may become social coin. Did people have a "need" to know about "The War of the Worlds" before it was broadcast? The relationship between the distribution of knowledge and social structure and social order is a great deal more pertinent to any discussion of the functions of the media than are the Hutchins Commission's "ideals." (But take a look at my own chapter in this book on such matters as these, and judge for yourself.)

Professor Moeller is enamored of the "leadership-in-social-change function." The media have, he says, an obligation to work . . . for the adoption of important social changes considered to be of crucial import. By *whom?* The fallacy here is in assuming that there is more mentality in the collective media than there is in the individuals who work for them. Beyond this, do reporters and cameramen have any special training to equip them for this self-appointed Moses role? Ask Professor Moeller, who, in his own institution, was long opposed to any training or education of future journalists which went much beyond the sheer techniques of the trade. Journalism schools are notoriously conservative, backward, and resistant to change. There has been a classical and binding tradition therein that teaching how to prepare and produce and distribute messages is enough. It is not likely that such programs are going to attract or produce those individuals who will be capable of performing the "leadership-in-social-change-function" that Professor Moeller speaks about. (Could this be why most of the leaders of the industry did not in fact come from journalism schools, and perhaps never will, in part because of the lack of real leaders-in-charge at the heads of those schools?)

But let's be fair: *If* the media had "presented and clarified the goals and values of this society" adequately since 1776, would we be caught with our collective pants down as often as we have been? Where were all of our media savants when the energy crisis was developing? Where are they now, when the next resource crisis is likely not be be fuel, but water?

If the media had "projected a representative picture of the constituent groups in the society," why have we often been so surprised to discover those we never knew existed; and whatever happened to the "silent majority" and who speaks for it as an endangered species?

If the media have always provided a "forum for the exchange of comment and criticism," why are the relationships between groups and nations more stressed and polarized than every before?

If the media generally always provide "a truthful, comprehensive, and intelligent account of the day's events," why is it that, judging from "the news," 75 to 90 percent of the day's "events" take place in government, and most of the rest is mere civilian catastrophe?

The Commission, from whence Professor Moeller drew his criteria for evaluating media performance, referred to the media as "perhaps the most powerful educational instrument there is." Okay. Since there has been a general decrease in overall intelligence and literacy in our society in the past 50 years, how well would you say the media had fulfilled *that* responsibility? And since more and more of our citizens suffer from disabling functional illiteracies, shall we also commend the media for that?

But perhaps this is not fair. There is no way to assess media performance on the basis of such abstract and "grandiose" criteria without equivocating. But perhaps that is just the reason Professor Moeller selected them.

And now, to what Professor Moeller did not tell you.

One of the networks was accused of hiring actors and rehearsing them to enact an embattled beach landing, so that they could scoop the other networks with "on-the-scene" film of the Bay of Pigs landing. The same network was accused of using film of a South American child suffering from malnutrition at the opening of a *documentary* on hunger *in the U.S.* The Chairman of that network later received his industry's highest and most prestigious award—not, one would presume, for condoning these little everyday tricks of newsmakers, but apparently for refusing to comply with a federal government request for information. Now, if the government officials had been up-to-date, they would have obtained the information they wanted surreptitiously, and paid the informer—as newspaper officials might have done. But, they did not, and were denied freedom of access to "needed" information while, at the same time, being lobbied by the same industry for legislation to insure freedom of access to all information, except that deemed "by the media" to be crucial to *their* competitive position in the industry and their continued economic viability (Professor Moeller alludes to this).

Having no more than noted such matters, here is the point: the various levels of members of the media comprise fraternities of their own, from whence they draw their guiding principles. What the network chairman was recognized for was preserving the power and integrity of the fraternity—*whatever* the gains or losses to the society at large. So that "all the news that's fit to print" can be translated, "that content and style and format which will serve to maintain our position in the industry." And "truthfulness and comprehensiveness" may translate "what we can get by with on this side of the law but within the bounds of plausibility" or, "what the yokels out there have come to expect."

What Professor Moeller didn't tell you was that various media agencies may even sponsor research on what people want, but those who run the papers and the stations don't want to know. What Professor Moeller didn't tell you was that the management of the *Washington Post* was miffed at the administration (pre-Watergate) because of some FCC ratings regarding *Post*-owned TV stations in Florida. Can we take the sheer relentlessness of the *Post's* management in this instance—and almost alone—to be typical of media performance in putting the "country's" interests before "their" own?

What Professor Moeller didn't tell you is that the new adversary stance of the media vis-à-vis the government may be causing us more problems than it solves. Or, in sum, that there are always two sides to the coin, and that things are never so simple as they seem. As a good reporter, he had a weightier obligation.

He should have told you that our deepest cultural myths—not our everyday fashions but our deepest cultural myths, the ideas by which we ultimately define ourselves as human, today as ever in human history—are carried in the entertainment we consume. He spoke of "entertainment" both slightly and disparagingly, and of "the news" almost reverently. What are we to make of this demeaning objectivization of human life?

He should have told you that no reporter can be any more truthful, comprehensive, or intelligent than his readers or viewers, that there is no credibility where there is no credulity, and that, therefore, it is impossible to evaluate the performance of "the media" without simultaneously evaluating the performance of their consumers, *viz.,* the whole matter of the effects of violence on TV. If Gandhi had watched American television, would he had been converted to violent aggression? Was Hitler the kind of fellow he was because he watched too much TV?

The media aren't going to be any better than their consumers. That's because, as the wise man said, "A word to the wise ain't sufficient if he isn't wise."

CHAPTER V

In Search of Alternatives

In many respects, neither the view of Moeller nor Thayer occupies center position in contemporary thinking about mass communication, although together they serve well to highlight the range of differences among current conceptualizations of the phenomenon. In considering both the nature and the significance of the variance between these two mass communication frameworks, it might prove useful to place the debate in a broader context of the sort suggested by Thomas Kuhn in his book, *The Structure of Scientific Revolutions.*[1]

The developmental history of scientific thought, writes Kuhn, is characterized by a recurring cycle of paradigm emergence, acceptance, competition, and rejection. During most periods, the majority of scholars working in a particular field share and support a common paradigm and a common understanding of the class of events which they study. Within the cycle, new paradigms are advanced, generally toward the end of obviating inadequacies noted in the traditional and more popular framework. Should such a new alternative construct—initially accepted and advocated by only a few scholars—vie successfully, gain currency and ultimately replace its predecessor, the cycle is completed and begins anew.

From a number of aspects, the Moeller and Thayer positions can be viewed as representatives of competing paradigms, and their dialogue as an important transitional stage in the evolution of mass communication theory. As Kuhn notes:[2]

. . . proponents of competing paradigms will often disagree about the list of problems that any candidate for a paradigm must resolve. Their standards or their definitions of science are not the same. Must a theory of motion explain the cause of the attractive forces between particles of matter or may it simply note the existence of such forces? Newton's dynamics was widely rejected because, unlike both Aristotle's and Descartes' theories, it implied the latter answer to the question. . . . More is involved, however, than the incommensurability of standards. Since new paradigms are born from old ones, they ordinarily incorporate much of the vocabulary and apparatus . . . that the traditional paradigm had previously employed. But they seldom employ these borrowed elements in quite the same way. Within the new paradigm, old terms, concepts, and experiments fall into new relationships one with the other. The inevitable result is what we must call, though the term is not quite right, a misunderstanding between the two competing schools.

The sort of incompatibilities to which Kuhn refers emerge rather dramatically when one compares the pervasive media-centered paradigm summarized by Moeller with the functional, recipient-centered construct presented by Thayer. The "big four" approach, emphasizing the mass media as a causal force, certainly has been the more persistent and traditional one in both scholarly and popular writings about mass communication, and has served as the organizing framework around which most textbooks used in the field have been built.

But there is some evidence that the classical paradigm may be in transition, and we pick up what appear to be subtle differences in the ways some scholars are beginning to talk about mass communication. Recent writings, among them those of Schramm, DeFleur, and Mc-Quail, have placed increasingly less emphasis on the cause-and-effect orientation which has long dominated mass communication theory. While we cannot help but be encouraged by efforts to question and explore alternatives to the cause and effect paradigm, much of the work so far seems only to have magnified the conceptual schizophrenia which currently characterizes the field.

Take for example Schramm's revision of his book, *The Process and Effects of Mass Communication.*[3] In updating how the field has progressed since his earlier volume was published, Schramm and Roberts point out the inadequacy of stimulus-response psychology and social theory categorizations as bases for the study of communication. They declare that we have passed beyond the "bullet theory" or "hypodermic needle" model of mass media effects (where media messages were thought to have direct effects upon the receiver). Schramm and Roberts write:[4]

It [Bullet Theory] did not square with the facts. The audience, when it was hit by the Bullet, refused to fall over. Sometimes the Bullet had an effect that was completely unintended.

The audience, they note, was for too long undervalued and plays a much more active role in mass communication than was previously presumed. And finally, they instruct, communication must be looked at in terms of systems models, mutual causality, and interactive relationships.

As we noted earlier, this is a much different way of talking about the process than has been true in the past. But genuinely new ways of thinking require something more than simply a new rhetoric, a difficulty Schramm and Roberts clearly do not overcome. The progress they chronicle does not appear integrated conceptually even throughout their own work. Immediately following their acknowledgement and embracement of a more dynamic and systemic concept of the communication process, they re-establish the centrality of the source-message-receiver model of communication, and write:[5]

> It is no longer necessary to defend the idea that a message has a life of its own, separate from both the sender and receiver. If anyone questions this, let him remember how he feels when he has put a letter into the mailbox and wishes he could recall it to make a change. But it is out of his control, just as though he were a general who had sent his army into battle without him and had to wait . . . to learn [the result] of the battle.

One is almost tempted to add, "and whether or not the bullets hit their targets." It is indeed hard to rid ourselves of the notion that communication is something people do to each other with messages. There appears little of systems notions, mutual causality, or what one might call transactional about Schramm's notion of the "unleashed message." It is, however, hard to interpret that particular passage other than that the mailed message is going to cause something the sender now wishes it wouldn't cause. That the sender's second thoughts have more to do with communication than does the message now enroute to its receiver doesn't enter Schramm's explication of the process. The juxtaposition of these two paragraphs in the Schramm and Roberts book serves to underscore the ambiguity necessarily associated with the transitional phase of the cycle discussed by Kuhn.

One finds the same sort of problem in the prolific and controversial work of Marshall McLuhan, who advanced the reasonably viable concept of media as extensions of man's sensory apparatus. On the one hand, McLuhan made popular phrases such as "we shape our tools and thereafter our tools shape us," which in rather poetic terms suggests a reciprocal causality between man and media, yet elsewhere writes about the effects of media on man, invoking the classical stimulus-response model.

Yet another example of the dilemma is seen in DeFleur's attempts to wrestle with the problem of meaning in communication messages. What transpires in the communication act, he writes[6]

. . . is not actually a "transfer" of meaning. In the communicative act there is no essence, spirit, or invisible "something" that leaves the central nervous system of one person and travels to that of another. Such a concept is unnecessary and muddies the waters of legitimate inquiry into the nature of human communication. . . .

As mass communication texts go, DeFleur's statement appears to represent fairly enlightened movement away from the "bullet theory," although David Berlo made the same point more than 17 years ago with his now well-worn incantation: "meanings are in people, not in messages."[7] It would appear, however, that Berlo's contribution was both too significant for, and too far ahead of its time. And while DeFleur echoes the Berlo observation—as have many others—the reverberations prove short-lived as he proceeds to unfold his explanation "for achieving isomorphism in meaning." He writes:[8]

> But if the communication act is not a "transfer of meaning," then how does communication occur? A convenient way of answering this question is that it takes place through the operation of a particular set of components in a theoretical system, the consequence of which is that there is *isomorphism* between the internal responses (meanings) to a given set of symbols on the part of both sender and receiver.

It's not that meanings are in words, DeFleur argues, but that people simply understand them in an identical manner. His thesis is that humans learn relationships between particular words and particular "real world" objects and events. Through continued usage, he claims, these significant symbols become conventionalized. Once we have established identity between the significant symbol and that for which it stands, he goes on, we can respond to the symbol (or set of symbols) by internally experiencing the object or event. In essence, we generate the same feelings and behaviors upon hearing certain symbols that we would toward the objects or events those symbols represent. Communication between humans, he continues, takes place because we have all learned the same responses to the same significant symbols. Therefore, he claims, it is not the words that transmit the meaning, but the fact that we internally experience the same thing upon hearing certain significant symbols that, as DeFleur puts it, "gets meaning coordinated" between interactants.

While DeFleur's message-centered theory seems useful for explaining a single message exchange event, it seems less than adequate for explaining the dynamics by which meanings are created, conventionalized, misunderstood and ultimately changed, all of which seem critical to the basic phenomenon he wishes to explain. At the least,

albeit indirect. DeFleur's attempts can be viewed as yet another voice
added to the chorus of frustration, reconfirming disconcertion with the
classical model, and exemplifying difficulties of proposing an internally
consistent and proactive alternative. The model developed by DeFleur
to illustrate his concept graphically,[9] is indicative of this larger problem.

Like Schramm's, the DeFleur model (labeled "The Components
for a General System for Achieving Isomorphism of Meaning") reverts
to a mechanistic linear presentation with a source, who selects "appropriate significant symbols (message) with which to express the internal
responses (meanings) the communicator wishes to present to his audience." The message then moves sequentially through a transmitter,
channel, receiver, and destination, and the significant symbols are appropriately decoded. For communication to take place, according to
DeFleur, the receiver will have meanings for the significant symbols

that are "isomorphic" with those of the source. Essentially, DeFleur has simply recomposed a model offered by Schramm some twenty-two years ago in his first edition of *The Process and Effects of Mass Communication.* [10]

So long as we continue to conceive of the communication process in terms of mechanistic models, regardless of what new terminology we adopt to talk about such models, we are struck with the so-called "Bullet Theory" of communication whether we want to be or not.

Many of these same concerns have been expressed by Denis McQuail, who mounts an extensive and meticulous critique of contemporary communication research and scholarship in his book, *Towards a Sociology of Mass Communication.* [11] Like Thayer earlier in this volume, McQuail calls for greater focus upon the uses to which people put media products, agreeing that most current analyses describe the mass media more in terms of what they do to people, rather than what people do with media products.

There exists now a growing pool of scholars and researchers pursuing the so-called "uses and gratifications" approach to understanding mass media-related behavior. While the undergirding concept of the uses and gratifications approach is not a new one, it has taken several years for the framework to gain significant momentum. Like with so much of behavioral research, it is possible to delve back into early studies and demonstrate how it is that such work was really dealing with current and emerging thought in the field. But it is the more direct appeals of scholars like Katz,[12] Davison,[13] and Berlo,[14] all writing in 1959, and the general emergence of the so-called "receiver-orientation" notion in the sixties, that should be credited with giving thrust to the uses and gratification framework.

It was Katz's contention that mass media content would be attended to only if an individual saw it as useful, and that such selectivity is determined by values, interests, association and roles. He suggested that interpretation of mass media content had more to do with what the individual receiver brought to the interface than did the media products themselves.

Jumping to a more generic level, Davison, like Thayer, linked communication to the environment, postulating that all human behavior results from attempts to satisfy needs; that such needs are met by either altering or conforming to the environment; that needs will vary in importance to the individual, and that communication will likewise vary in potency as a tool for achieving those needs. In the context of an article on effects of communication written in 1959, Davison's observations clearly had to be on the cutting edge. Perhaps the only, although major, difference between this statement and Thayer's position centers on the concept of communication. While Davison views communication as a tool for achieving needs, Thayer would view the entire process itself—that is the altering of and conforming to the environment, as well as the creation (or naming) of "needs" and the "satisfactions" thereof—as the fundamental process of communication. It is, indeed, this very position that separates Thayer from the "uses and gratifications" school of thought.

The conceptual underpinnings of the uses and gratifications approach hold that:

1. The social environment exerts certain pressures on both individuals and groups within the society, and that
2. such pressures create needs, which
3. initiate behaviors directed toward satisfying those needs,
4. including use of mass media content.

Referring to this particular formulation, McQuail writes:[15]

> The application of this frame of reference involves the taking account of needs, motives, value orientation and subjective interpretation of a situation on the part of the individual actor (or collectively). "Uses and gratifications" studies have more or less implicitly involved such an approach with an emphasis on the generation of such "needs" by the environment which then result in particular uses of the mass media.

So long as those currently enamored of the uses and gratifications approach, as presently interpreted, understand its limitations as a potentially general theory of mass communication, and further understand it as merely a subset of a more powerful and generic construct of the process of human communication, it perhaps represents one of the more productive paths yet followed by mass communication scholars and media researchers. Its advocates seem to best reflect the shift toward a functional, recipient-oriented paradigm discussed by Thayer. Even so, there is some evidence that this framework will be as slow in growth and impact as its predecessors, as witnessed in the concluding remarks of the McQuail book.

Groups and organizations monitoring media coverage of their activities, he writes, may well acquire information that has either been changed or suppressed by their own institutional sources. He further observes that the mass media "compete with the communication networks of other institutional orders and these may need to change or adapt as a result."[16] There remains in McQuail's comments, we believe, a continuing implicit assumption regarding the centrality of the "big four" as a causative force in society, which is not reflective of the systems concept he calls for so often throughout his volume. Secondly, there is a reluctance to view "the communication networks of other institutional orders" in themselves as legitimate mass communication enterprises. Again, we suspect, part of the reason is to be found in the continual confounding of mass media and mass communication.

Perhaps we have said little more in the foregoing than traditions of the past die hard, even when we work with zeal and diligence to leave them behind. In the haste to move beyond the inadequacies of previous frameworks, it may be important to simply note, after Kuhn, that conceptual traditions are sort of a mixed blessing:[17]

> In the development of any science, the first received paradigm is usually felt to account quite·successfully for most of the observations and experiments easily accessible to that science's practitioners. Further development, therefore, ordinarily calls for the construction of elaborate equipment, [and] the development of an esoteric vocabulary and skills. . . .

This sort of professionalization of a discipline, notes Kuhn, can lead in two quite opposite directions: First, in those areas to which the paradigm directs the attention of scholars within a discipline, it leads to the amassment of detailed information and to increased precision in the observation-theory matching process which might not be achieved in any other way; secondly, professionalization built around an initial paradigm leads also to "an immense restriction of the scientist's vision and to considerable resistance to paradigm change."

If these same dynamics apply to mass communication theory, and there is no reason to believe they do not, then the media-centered tradition of the "big four" as powerful causative agents in our environment has been for us such a mixed blessing. And as we have benefited in a variety of ways from the richness of detail the paradigm has afforded us in particular areas, so may we suffer the difficulties of dislodging ourselves from a world view that has so totally engulfed us for the past 50 years.

At any rate, it is precisely this problem that the remainder of this book attempts to address; to kick out, as it were, some of the panels of the box we have built around our thinking. The first two chapters in Part II explore some of the more generic issues regarding human communication in general, and mass communication as a special instance of that process. The remaining chapters, we believe, will provide some interesting insights into a number of institutions whose functions, audience concerns, and decision-making processes are strikingly similar to those of the big four mass media, and whose roles may well be equally significant.

Notes and References

1. T. S. Kuhn, (Chicago: The University of Chicago Press, 2d. ed., 1970).
2. *Ibid.,* p. 149.
3. W. Schramm and D. Roberts, (Urbana: University of Illinois Press, 2d. ed., 1971).
4. *Ibid.,* p. 9.
5. *Ibid.,* p. 15.
6. M. DeFleur, *Theories of Mass Communication* (New York: David McKay Company, 2d. ed., 1970), p. 91.

7. D. Berlo, *The Process of Communication* (New York: Holt, Rinehart and Winston, 1960), p. 214.
8. DeFleur, *op. cit.,* p. 91.
9. *Ibid.,* p. 92.
10. W. Schramm, (Urbana: University of Illinois Press, 1st ed., 1961).
11. D. McQuail, (London: Collier-Macmillan, 1969).
12. E. Katz, "Mass Communications Research and the Study of Culture," *Studies in Public Communication,* 2, (1959), pp. 1–6.
13. W. Davison, "On the Effects of Mass Communication," *Public Opinion Quarterly,* 24, (1959), pp. 343–60.
14. Berlo, *op. cit.*
15. McQuail, *op. cit.,* p. 90.
16. *Ibid.,* pp. 92–93.
17. Kuhn, *op. cit.,* p. 65.

PART TWO
ALTERNATIVES

CHAPTER VI

Notes Toward a Reformulation

The way one thinks about mass communication must, or should, inevitably grow out of and reflect how one conceives of human communication and human behavior in general. Our goal in this chapter will be to provide a summary of our view of human communication, its role in human behavior, and the implications of that understanding for a reconceptualization of mass communication and mass communication institutions. The view we develop here is built upon a series of empirically-derived propositions about all living things, applied in the following summary to humans and human communication systems:

1. All living systems are structural and functional units which maintain themselves (grow, change and deteriorate) only through interactions with their environment. Man, as are other forms of plant and animal life, is an instance of a living system.

2. Interactions between living systems and the environment are subsumed under two essential and fundamental life processes: a) the consumption and transformation of matter into energy, which may be termed physiological metabolism; and b) the acquisition and transformation of environment-data into information, which may be termed information metabolism, or communication.

3. Thus, communication is viewed as one of the two essential life processes of all living systems.

4. Communication is continual. For living systems there are no "breakdowns in communication"; there is no option not to be in communication with the environment.

5. Human communication is a special instance of communication, and is transactional and symbolic in nature.

6. For the human, communication is the process by which an individual creates and relates to his environment; it is those internal processes through which he senses and makes sense of, adopts and adapts to his environment.
7. For humans, the environment is largely symbolic.
8. To an increasing extent, the symbolic environment is defined, diffused, reified and perpetuated through mass communication institutions.

The Nature of Human Communication

The foregoing propositions imply a view of human communication derived from man's unique symbol-using capacities. While humans are not the only living organisms that process information about their environment (nor can they be said to be the only animals who utilize language), humans alone have the capacity for creating, storing, retrieving, and diffusing information and—through symbols—for attaching significance to the entirety of their physical and social environments, as well as to themselves. This ability, peculiar to man, has given rise to a dimension unique to human existence—a *communicational environment*. The communicational environment is composed of *symbolic realities*—anything that has or might be said, thought, or imagined—cast in the form of knowledge, order, culture, and all else that we know as organized society.

Given thrust by an increasingly sophisticated technology, man's communicational environment presents him a reality with which he must cope and to which he must adapt in the same ways he has had to deal with his physical environment. For modern man, the communicational environment is perhaps as formidable and filled with pitfalls as was primitive man's physical environment. In adapting to his physical world primitive man could, at the least, rely upon his senses to verify his reality and weigh the consequences of his behavior vis-à-vis that reality. But the symbolic realities man has created and sustains through interaction with other humans do not afford that same kind of direct validation. Man's beliefs and values, laws and morals, politics and economics, and the many epistemological and social collectivities upon which his existence has come to depend, have no reality beyond what he has or can say or think or imagine about them. This communicational environment, purposely and mutually created and maintained through social communication, has become as significant in determining man's behavior as his physical environment once was.

The study of communication, then, is the study of symbol or message-related behavior. It is essentially the examination of the role of symbols, symbolization, and symbol internalization in the creation, maintenance and change of all individual and social organization. For understanding these processes, it seems essential to distinguish between three aspects of human communication: intrapersonal communication, social (interpersonal) communication, and mass communication.

Intrapersonal Communication

The notion of communication involving the metabolism of information dictates the necessity for some sort of transformation, a change of information from one state to another. For living systems, that exchange is between the organism and the environment. In human systems, that basic process will be referred to as *intrapersonal communication,* and includes the concept of the individual adapting to both the physical and communicational environments, and adapting both the physical and communicational environments to individual needs. In both instances, the transformation involves the conversion of *environment-data* (the "raw stuff" of a process reality) into *information*. In developing a distinction between these two concepts, we begin by regarding environment-data as factual, as that which exists. What we comprehend (or invent) about the form and significance of these environment-data, we refer to as information. Information is extracted from the environment through inference; it is only information *about* environment-data—an abstraction that makes environment-data functionally useful to the individual toward some present or future end. What is important to note is that we fashion our behavioral responses to our environment not upon environment-data, but upon our personal conceptual surrogate for environment-data, i.e., information.

The essence of intrapersonal communication, then, is the ongoing dynamic process of man-environment co-determination—man striving to organize his environment, and the environment shaping human behavior through the regularity of occurrence of certain patterns and sequences. Regarding this fundamental process, O. J. Harvey wrote, "One's concepts or system of meaning serves as a transformer through which impinging events are coded and translated into psychological significance."[1] Without such an "internal mediating system," writes Harvey, the environment would be largely irrelevant to the individual save reactions to the physical impingements it places upon him. Harvey, as have others, stresses two important features of such definitional frameworks (or symbolic realities): First, they are personal in nature, geared to individual utility, and as such necessarily prevent "a 1:1 correspondence between input and behavioral outcomes"; secondly, without them, "the individual, both in self structure and biological being, would be doomed to extinction." The impellent in the process of creating such symbolic realities, or definitional frameworks, stems from two uniquely human capabilities identified by Alfred Korzybski—*self-reflexiveness* and *time-binding*.[2]

Self-Reflexiveness Man not only takes into account certain aspects of his environment but, through his capacity for self-reflexiveness, can conceive of himself in relationship to that which he takes into account. The implications of this capacity are obvious. The ways in which man senses and informs himself of the environment, his ways of thinking, seeing, and creating information, are largely a consequence of how he

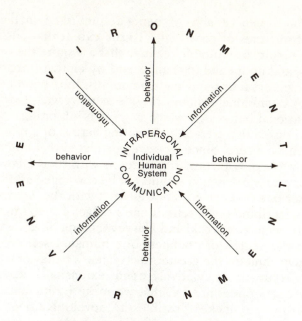

Intrapersonal communication describes the process of individual adapting to both the physical and communicational environments, and adapting both the physical and communicational environments to individual needs. In both instances, the transformation involves the conversion of *environment-data* into *information,* upon which subsequent behaviors are based.

has organized himself with and how he has been organized by the environment—including the communicational environment. Concomitantly, that which he takes into account both alters and elaborates what he can take into account. This capability of man to view himself as a "self," as part of and apart from his environment, is the core of the communication process. For not only can man transform environment-data into information, but he can and does create information about information, a characteristic Korzybski referred to as the "process of abstracting." Not all definitional frameworks resulting from this process are, however, "equally adequate to all environments or task demands," claims Harvey.

In point of fact, the central theme of Korzybski's work is built around the notion that the self-reflexive process of abstracting can be either growth-inducing or growth-inhibiting. To the extent that human exchanges with the environment do effect an alteration and an elaboration of one's abilities to perceive and control that which is around him, one exhibits what Korzybski labels "extensional behavior," a proactive form of behavior that maximizes one's opportunities for adapting the environment toward one's own ends. Referring to a complex definitional framework similar to Korzybski's "extensional orientation," Harvey says it "demands that the system or standard of meaning applied to it must be multi-dimensional, open to modification from environmental feedback, and even capable of being relinquished in favor of other shadings or qualities of construal." To the extent that one's process of abstracting results in symbolic realities that are quite the opposite, i.e., fixed, rigid, and unopened to change, and which therefore unduly color subsequent observations and understandings, thus preventing elaboration of one's definitional framework, one exhibits what Korzybski refers to as "intensional behavior," which is growth-inhibiting.

The distinction we are highlighting here is of considerably more than academic concern. Since we have postulated that humans, as living systems, survive only through interactions with their environment, the two notions under discussion should not be construed as discrete binary states (either one does or does not interact with the environment), but as ways of describing the extent of one's range of such interactions. Put another way, what Korzybski and Harvey (among others) suggest is that the greater the degree of openness of a human system to interactions with the environment, the greater that system's behavioral effectiveness in that environment. If relatively open, extensional, and elaborative, self-reflexiveness undergirds all that we mean by human progress and cultural advance. It makes possible the development of our cultural institutions and of our sciences. If relatively unopen, intensional, and non-elaborative, self-reflexiveness gives impetus to inadequate "informationing," to dysfunctional "mapping-of" and "mapping-into" the environment. Thus, the nature of the individual's capacity for self-reflexiveness operationally defines his communicational competency. If one's abilities to comprehend his environment are "impaired" through a reasonably fixed, static process of abstracting, his ways of seeing, thinking, and creating information from environment-data will be non-elaborative, and thus limit one's ability to complexify both that which he takes into account (develop alternative understandings of and multiple meanings for the same environment-data set) and his capacity to adapt the environment to meet his needs.

Time-Binding Korzybski classified living systems in terms of what they could *do,* as opposed to what they *are,* itself a basic contribution to understanding human communication as an operational rather than philosophical discipline. He classified plants as "chemical-binders," because they convert solar energy into organic chemical energy. Animals, while possessing chemical-binding characteristics, he wrote, move from place to place and are, thus, also "space-binders." Man, said Korzybski, while both a chemical- and a space-binder, is also a *time-binder.* Man's ability to abstract from and symbolize his environment, to store, and at some future time, retrieve those symbols, permit him to bind time.

At the intrapersonal level of communication, the notions of self-reflexiveness and time-binding are inextricably interwoven. Together they serve the function of "memory" and "past experience." It is principally through time-binding that man both creates and discovers the patterns and sequences of his environment (physical and communicational) and gives names to those patterns. It is through self-reflexiveness that the interrelationships among those patterns and their significance to the "self" are created. Through self-reflexiveness, humans self-determine ends, invent means to achieve those ends, and monitor their "progress" by assessing current state-of-affairs vis-à-vis intended state-of-affairs. Since man invents, confirms, and maintains information in conjunction with other humans, he also time-binds in a longer range cultural and social sense by providing information and elaborated symbolic realities for as yet non-existent generations.

Intrapersonal and Social Interdependence

Pragmatically, of course, it is simply not possible to talk about the basic process of intrapersonal communication in the absence of some concept of social communication. While, conceptually, language may not be a requirement for intrapersonal communication (it is a consequence of social communication), we would have to conceive of primitive man living in total isolation from other humans in order to comprehend intrapersonal communication operating in its "pure" form. At the same time, one necessarily develops an inadequate and misleading understanding of social communication and its functions without first comprehending the nature and consequence of the underlying phenomenon of intrapersonal communication. As we noted earlier, between-person communication is fundamentally the process of two living systems organizing with one another toward some end, and in so

Through social communication, humans mutually shape and are shaped by each other, resulting in the creation of symbolic realities which serve to maintain the communicational environment. It is through this process that the world as we know it is defined, labeled, and categorized, our understandings of it shared and validated, and our behavior toward it and toward one another regularized and regulated.

doing generating a set of symbolic realities which will permit each (or either) the attainment of that end. The fact that the environment-data being taken into account in such an encounter are other human systems and/or information (transformed environment-data) produced by other humans is of no consequence; the basic processes of co-determination and mutual adaptation remain unchanged. What is important to understand is that information created or behaviorally manifested by one human system becomes environment-data for the other with whom he is intercommunicating, and, as such, must then be transformed (re-created) by the second, thus emerging as information about information.

Understanding the implications of this particular notion is a crucial prerequisite to any significant reconceptualization of mass communication theory.

Social Communication

The process of social or interpersonal communication depends upon and takes its existence from the individual level of intrapersonal communication. Unlike the basic process of which it is an extension, however, social communication cannot occur in the absence of some shared symbol system or language. Language is that interfacing tool which permits man to create, store, retrieve and share information with other humans. It is through the process of social communication that man, in conjunction with his fellows, creates his symbolic realities and maintains his communicational environment. Through social communication humans mutually shape and are shaped by each other, resulting in communized knowledge and understandings. It is through social communication that the world as we know it is defined, labeled, and categorized, our understanding of it shared and validated, and our behavior toward it and toward one another is regularized and regulated. Through time-binding and self-reflexive elaboration, symbolic realities ultimately take the form of social structures, cultures, knowledge and other institutions which, in turn, control humans and are used by humans to control other humans.

In a similar vein, Peter Berger writes:

Society is a dialectic phenomenon in that it is a human product, and nothing but a human product, and yet continuously acts back upon its producer. Society is a product of man. It has no other being except that which is bestowed upon it by human activity and consciousness. There can be no social reality apart from man. Yet it may also be stated that man is a product of society. . . . The two statements . . . are not contradictory. They rather reflect the inherently dialectic character of the societal phenomenon. Only if this character is recognized will society be understood in terms that are adequate to its empirical reality.[3]

More than 55 years ago, Walter Lippmann offered us substantially the same observations. Man proceeds through his world, wrote Lippmann, by inserting between himself and his environment, a *pseudo-environment.*

To that pseudo-environment his behavior is a response. But because it *is* behavior, the consequences, if they are acts, operate not in the pseudo environment where the behavior is stimulated, but in the real environment where action eventuates. . . . We shall assume that what each man does is based not on direct and certain knowledge, but on pictures made by himself or given to him. . . . The way in which the world is imagined determines at any particular moment what men will do.
. . . The very fact that men theorize at all is proof that their pseudo-environments, their interior representations of the world, are a determining element in thought, feeling and action. For if the connection between reality and human response were direct and immediate, rather than indirect and inferred, indecision and failure would be unknown. . . .[4]

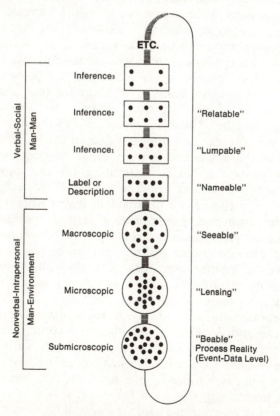

Korzybski's structural differential (or process of abstracting) schematic also serves to depict both the distinction and relationship between the concepts of intrapersonal communication and social communication.

Korzybski's structural differential, originally developed as a means of schematizing the self-reflexive process of abstracting discussed earlier, will serve equally well to graphically tie together the notions under discussion both here and in the preceding section. The version employed here was adapted and modified by Johnson,[5] which he called, simply, the process of abstracting.

In short, the "non-verbal" levels delineated on the Johnson diagram coincide with the individual, intrapersonal level of communication discussed earlier. The sub-microscopic level represents what Johnson termed the "process reality" and what we have been referring to as environment-data, that which we regard as factual. The macroscopic level represents the individual human system equipped with its neurological sensors through which it interacts with the environment. The relationship between these two levels is displayed in two significant ways: First, the fewer number of dots at the macroscopic level indicating both a limited and abstracted transformation of environment-data; secondly, the closed circle on the macroscopic level representing a finite set of possible observations within the limits of human neurological systems, as well as the limitations imposed by the individual's definitional framework for taking environment-data into account. The microscopic level simply acknowledges man's technological capabilities for devising extensions of the neural system which increase the range of his senses (e.g., telescope, electronic sensors, radar, etc.). In lieu of an extended presentation of Korzybski's theoretical construct, one further observation seems pertinent. Johnson was fond of calling the submicroscopic level, the "beable level," stressing it represented that which *might exist* in a process reality to account for that which we are only partially able to observe at the "upper" two non-verbal levels of abstracting. His label, "beable," clearly places the individual's concept of the sub-microscopic environment-data in the inferential class.

All of that contained in the "verbal" level of the schematic represents the process of social communication, the source of the communicational environment and the processes whereby our symbolic realities are constructed and maintained. It was Korzybski's notion that man abstracts from reality only to the extent his senses will permit him. What man then recreates is not reality, but a conception or an abstraction of (information about) reality, since his senses limit receptivity to certain kinds of environment-data. Korzybski, however, was more interested in intercommunication, the ways in which man symbolizes (names) his information about reality, and the ways in which he with his fellows elaborate and institutionalize those data. Korzybski was aware that man can and does create for himself a communicational environment comprised of symbolic realities, verbal surrogates of "non-verbal" environment-data. One of his most often quoted observations is, "Whatever you say a thing *is*, it is not." He was equally aware, as his process of abstracting schematic indicates, that man could further talk about anything that he had said or had talked about (he could make inferences about inferences). Indeed, as we noted earlier, it is this process that has permitted man to create all his "higher order" systems such as science, religion, economics, and culture itself. But the central thrust of Korzybski's writings was his overriding concern that man seemed unaware that his symbolic realities were of a different order than the environment-data from which they were created.

Putting aside the "hygienic" and prescriptive dimensions of Korzybski's work, it is difficult to dismiss his basic concern for the consequences to man of using his symbolic realities as the basic mechanism of survival. The root of that concern must be traced to the ways in which man conceives of the products of intercommunication. The dilemma is that the more successful humans are in social communication, the higher and wider the level of intersubjective agreement regarding a mutually created symbolic artifact, the stronger the illusion of reality that artifact accrues. Thus it is that "beauty," "freedom," "communism," "right," and "wrong" become intractable "truths." What this prevailing view fails to come to grips with was best expressed by Johnson: "There is no right or wrong in nature." Environment-data are. It is only through human communication—intrapersonal and social—that they become problematical. Humans, for example, experience hope and joy, despair and misery, all with no substantial change in their environment-data. And what is more, humans will experience opposing responses given the same set of environment-data. They may also, unlike other living systems, suffer great anguish and physical pain by simply anticipating some probable (or even improbable) future state of affairs.

Because social communication is a uniquely human process, it is an inescapable conclusion that our human problems, in so far as they are person-person problems, are a function of the extent to which we fall victim to our socially created symbolic realities. The basic problem is that man acts not on the basis of environment-data, but on the basis of his symbolic realities. While such behavior may produce a desirable state of affairs in his communicational environment, it might very well prove detrimental to his physical environment. It is thus we view the ironies of the purposeful destruction of immense quantities of food toward the end of preserving an "economic reality," while millions upon millions of humans suffer disabling malnutrition; and of the confiscation and destruction of the homes and livelihoods of whole populations of persons in order to ensure their right to live lives of "self-determination" and "freedom"; and of the pursuit of better and more sophisticated technology in the name of "progress," which requires plundering and polluting the natural environment to accomplish. But perhaps an even greater concern is man's ability to further create symbolic realities to justify those he already uncritically pursues. One concern of late is that because there has been such wide-spread discussion of the problems of environmental pollution, there has arisen an attendant illusion that there must be "those" who are looking after it for us as well. This situation, coupled with the unswerving belief that technology will ultimately be perfected to offset the increasing rate of environmental pollution has, in the eyes of some, resulted in permitting the individual citizen to feel relieved of personal responsibility for the problem.

Mass Communication

The by-product of social communication is a series of symbol sets which, if they are to become symbolic realities and part of the communicational environment, must be widely shared and intersubjectively subscribed to within a larger social framework. An obvious prerequisite for achieving this condition is the creation, diffusion, reification and maintenance of symbol sets appropriate to the establishment of the symbolic reality. That function is served when overlapping multi-person systems (or networks) become widely interconnected by a given set of symbols, ultimately forming a much broader suprasystem and an increasingly widened sharing of the emerging symbolic reality. These symbolic realities become, then, part of the total communicational environment where they again must be viewed as environment-data for individuals in the system. This dynamic relationship between intrapersonal and social communication provides us with the most generic definition of mass communication.

It, therefore, functions by:

1. providing a source of socially organized environment-data, which
2. stimulate social interaction by giving people a focal point around which social communication can take place within and between multi-person systems (networks), through which
3. significant symbolic realities are socially constructed, nurtured, diffused, and homogenized, thereby
4. developing a communication environment through which people establish, maintain and alter relationships, and evolve a sense of identity in terms of self, community, time and place.

From the vantage point of social organization, this process seems as fundamental and necessary to the multi-person system (social network, society, culture) as is the process of information metabolism to the individual human system. For as the individual system's ultimate survival is contingent upon its ability to organize with the environment-data, so the multi-person system's continued existence is based upon its ability to coordinate and sustain its communicational environment. From the individual perspective, mass communication, as a source of environment-data, is a functional prerequisite to adaptation to both the physical and communicational environments and forms the basis of socialization and the essence of enculturation. From the social perspective, mass communication functions to perpetuate epistemic order, social organization, and the variety of collectives that constitute the bulk of the environment of civilized humans. It is that process through which we have created and agreed to a language, established and submitted to some code of law, developed and operated some form of exchanging and distributing resources, defined and respected some hierarchical order of relationships, performed and avoided and judged human behaviors, and come to understand that eating peas with a knife is boorish.

Writes Sir Geoffrey Vickers:

> I am impressed by the fundamental nature of this process. Insofar as I can be regarded as human, it is because I was claimed at birth as a member of a communicative network, which programmed me for participation in itself.[6]

What man can become, therefore, is greatly influenced by what he communicationally has been, and he will be limited (or enabled) to see and to understand what his symbolic realities permit him to see and understand. And while the human capacity for creating symbolic realities has most certainly freed man from the bondage of his physical environment, it is also clear that same capacity holds greater potential for determining man's future and ultimate survival than perhaps his physical environment ever offered.

Mass Communication Institutions

Man is an organizer. He has a compulsion—is in fact required—to make sense of and bring order to his environment. As Peter Berger and Thomas Luckman[7] have noted, social order is a human product, neither given in man's environment nor dictated by man's biological structure. Since man lives in an open and unstructured process reality, he must provide himself with a stable environment in which to conduct his affairs. It is from this human imperative that man creates and produces his social order, which exists so long as man continues to produce and maintain it. The social construction of reality and order occurs, as we have stated, through the processes of intrapersonal and social communication. The process through which those symbolic realities and consequently the communicational environment are inter-subjectified and thus maintained, is what we have identified as the mass communication phenomenon, a *function* necessarily endemic to any social organization.

Historically, however, man has always sought to capture and preserve—in the name of efficiency, effectiveness, and/or predictability of outcomes—such basic functions by institutionalizing them, by inventing structures to house them. In short, man the organizer must not only bring order (and thus control) to his physical environment, but to his communicational environment as well. Regarding the development of institutions, Berger and Luckman suggest:

> All human activity is subject to habitualization. Any action that is repeated frequently becomes cast into a pattern which can be reproduced with an economy of effort and which, *ipso facto,* is apprehended by its performer *as* that pattern.[8]

Habitualized actions, they further suggest, become embedded in human behavior, provide the psychological gain of narrowing choices, and free the individual from the "burden" of repetitive decision-making each time that object-action situation is reiterated. Further describing the process, they write:

> Institutionalization occurs whenever there is a reciprocal typification of habitualized actions by types of actors. Put differently, any such typification is an institution. What must be stressed is the reciprocity of institutional typifications and the typicality of not only the actions but also the actors in institutions. The typifications of habitualized actions that constitute institutions are always shared ones.[9]

A mass communication institution, then, is a *structural-functional* unit, operating in a one-to-many mode, which has as its goal the purposeful diffusion of information into and with the intent of exerting control over the communicational environment, and thus controlling the behavior of individuals vis-à-vis that environment toward some end. Mass communication institutions at once evolve from and are a response to the mass communication function. They exist so long as they serve as viable structures for giving currency to and providing maintenance of symbolic realities crucial to the social systems in which they operate. In this sense, mass communication institutions are not only themselves products of the process of institutionalization, but are, as well, instruments necessary to the effectuation of the process of institutionalization.

Implications

The juxtaposition of these two concepts, mass communication and mass communication institutions, as we have reformulated them, lend considerably greater power and scope to our ways of thinking about and studying mass communication. As that process which serves as a prerequisite to reality construction, to creating a shared communicational environment, and to establishing and maintaining viable social organization, it is clear the mass communication function has existed as long as humans have lived together in any collective form. And given that man from his beginning has sought to harness and exert control over some aspect of his environment and the behaviors of his fellows in it, we may also assume that mass communication institutions—however crude and elementary—have also been with us throughout man's interactive history. That we know so little historically about either can perhaps be explained by the continuing tendency for contemporary scholars to link the beginnings of mass communication to the development of one or another technological innovation. Most media books trace the early history of mass communication to innovations such as the invention of paper or the development of moveable type or the discovery of electricity, focusing almost exclusively on the development of means of passing along the "news." In large measure, that same organizing concept continues to characterize the current definition of mass communication. It is precisely this conceptualization, however, that has led a generation of scholars to embrace the mythology of the "big four," unwittingly imposing an intellectually constraining framework upon the field of study.

By our definition, *any* institution that *purposively* disseminates information—i.e., some form of constructed or "packaged" environment-data—into the communicational environment which is either designed or functions to shape individual construction of environment-data toward the maintenance or construction of any given symbolic reality, serves the mass communication functions and is a mass communication institution. The nature of that information need not be and in most cases is not "news" as currently and popularly defined. Additionally, it makes little difference whether distribution takes the form of multiple "messages" distributed to large numbers (or "masses") of individuals, or whether large numbers of people are exposed to an individual message, since either functions to provide a basis for reality creation and social homogenization, and both fulfill the one-to-many mode of a mass communication institution.

Our framework further suggests that the content of a message is perhaps less important than its effectiveness in stimulating the relational function of the mass communication phenomenon. At the same time, if the content of the message, or if the form of delivery itself, is not supported by the communicational environment—the medium or subject matter is no longer a salient or widely shared symbolic reality—the potency of the disseminating mass communication institution is proportionately reduced. Content, then, can be appropriately viewed as a product of mass communication institutions and the catalyst of the mass communication process. In support of this view, several years ago Kaarl Nordenstreng tentatively reported "that perhaps the basic motivation for media use is just an unarticulated need for social contact."[10] Within the context of his 1969 treatise on mass communication, McQuail likewise stated, "It now makes sense to regard a moderate degree of exposure to mass media as at least a mark, and possibly a requirement, of membership of modern society."[11] It is likely that neither Nordenstreng nor McQuail grasped the full significance of those observations at the time they were made, for despite their insightfulness, neither writer fully pursued the implications of those findings, nor was there the slightest suggestion that either viewed the "mass media" as anything other than the "big four." While the importance of television, radio, newspapers, and magazines as sources of organized environment-data is undeniable, definitions which view mass communication as synonymous with these media—and not as a fundamental and endemic social phenomenon—unjustifiably preclude consideration of numerous other mass communication institutions which are both structurally and functionally analogous to the big four.

Our reformulation of this classical definition makes relevant the study of a number of institutions heretofore not seriously considered "legitimate" mass communication institutions, and yet whose mode of operation and ultimate survival most assuredly depend upon both attraction and maintenance of large audiences and upon remaining viable as sources of socially relevant symbolic realities. The school, the church, the museum, the recording industry, to name only a few, serve the mass communication function and must also be considered mass communication institutions. More than 700 million visits to the nation's some 6,000 museums are recorded annually; the Chicago Museum of Science and Industry alone draws an audience in excess of 3-million persons each year. More than 600,000 persons attended Broadway theatrical performances last season, and more than 100 million attended a church, temple or synagogue of which they are a registered member. The list of organizations and statistics goes on, including fraternal orders, labor unions, political parties, professional associations, nationally organized youth groups, all of whom play a major role in contributing to and shaping the communicational environment, and seek to influence the individual's response to that environment toward some end.

Life-Cycle of Mass Communication Institutions

The number and form of such structures cannot be fixed, because as old ones collapse and die, new ones rise to take their place. A logical extension of our own definition of mass communication institutions is that they are structures developed to fill pre-existent functions. The development and growth of these structures is such, however, that they are not always—or perhaps do not remain—isomorphic with the functions they purport to institutionalize. This is true because such institutions themselves are human organizations, and are endowed with and accrue a set of symbolic realities of their own. And when the maintenance and preservation of those comparatively esoteric and internal symbolic realities are permitted to overshadow the functional performance of a mass communication institution, it will move toward extinction. There are, then, always a large number of co-existing and competing mass communication institutions, and in numbers far greater than acknowledged in our traditional understanding of what constitutes the mass media. The life-cycle of such institutions forms a characteristic pattern that moves thusly:

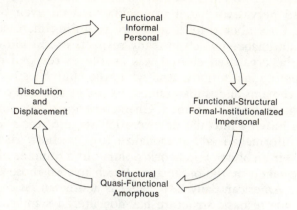

Functional
Informal
Personal

Functional-Structural
Formal-Institutionalized
Impersonal

Structural
Quasi-Functional
Amorphous

Dissolution
and
Displacement

LIFE-CYCLE OF MASS COMMUNICATION INSTITUTIONS

This pattern, of course, does not represent an original observation; it is common to every organized human endeavor. With respect to mass communication institutions, it simply states that when a functional interpersonal or social network seeks successfully to widen its influence upon the communicational environment beyond its network boundaries, and toward its own ends, it becomes a mass communication institution. It will remain such so long as it viably performs its initial function, or acquires another which is supported by the communicational environment. If not, then its energies will be more and more consumed in efforts to preserve and maintain its structure.

The duration of the cycle varies markedly from institution to institution, dependent upon technological developments, the socially attached relevance of symbolic realities specific to the institution, the social use of competing mass communication institutions for performing the same functions, the adaptability of the institutional structure to challenge and change, and a variety of other potentially related but as yet unresearched contributing factors.

There are, quite obviously, a number of historical and current examples of the operation of this life-cycle among mass communication institutions. For example, in his chapter on religion appearing later in this volume, James Hitchcock writes "that until at least the 18th century the churches were probably the major organs of mass communication, the only agencies able to convey messages regularly to the majority of the population." The rise and fall of the Christian church as a dominant mass communication institution provides a classic example of the life-cycle diagram presented above, as it moved from an informal, highly personalized, functional way of life, to a rigorously rule-laden, highly ritualized and institutionalized, impersonal hierarchial structure. As the latter, the organized church at one time exercised virtual control over the creation and maintenance of the individual's communicational environment. As Hitchcock points out, the church's authority was at one time so pervasive that it was acknowledged even by those who violated it. Encumbered by a structure requiring increasingly greater internal maintenance (which in many respects overshadowed its initial function), the organized church was unable to respond to challenges from competing institutions. And while the church's structure, for the most part, remains and is maintained, its use as a source of homogenizing symbolic realities has waned. Characteristic of mass communication institutions moving into the deterioration stage of their life-cycles are efforts to informalize and personalize, to, in short, recycle and re-establish their viability. Hitchcock points out a number of such efforts being undertaken by the organized church toward those ends.

The American daily newspaper is another mass communication institution whose basic structure has not altered significantly over the past 75 years. Since 1950, however, daily newspaper circulation has fallen off sharply relative to the nation's population growth, and in 1975 suffered an actual loss of 1.2 million in daily circulation. In 1970, an average of 1.2 newspapers were delivered to U.S. homes daily (itself a shrunken figure over better times); in 1975; that figure fell to below less than one (0.8) paper per home per day. In addition, a number of research studies have noted a declining correlation between newspaper editorially-advocated positions and reader behavior (e.g., endorsement of political candidates for whom readers then vote), and instances of newspaper-initiated events of societal import (viz. "Watergate"), although still dramatic, have become the exception rather than the accepted. In short, there are gathering signs that the institution of the daily press is no longer functioning as extensively as it once did as an homogenizing agent in our society. Further, the daily newspaper's response to challenges from other mass communication institutions has been less than formidable, although the predictable pattern of attempting to "re-personalize" its product is evidenced through increased use of reader opinion in so-called "op-ed" pages, and the establishment of regional and/or neighborhood editions aimed at more indentifiable subsets of a newspaper's more general audience. But, both of interest to and in support of the life-cycle notion, the strongest response of the newspaper industry to competitive inroads has been to strengthen and maintain its structure. Recent trade publications of the industry have focused on the fact that in spite of losses in both circulation and advertising linage, newspapers have increased their income and profits by raising costs to both consumer and advertiser. Others have invested large sums in researching and changing the physical appearance of their publications. In spite of forecasts by market analysts and exhortations by newspaper executives that current trends in the industry must be reversed, the ultimate survival of the institution rests upon its continued relevance to the individual, and the groups to which he belongs, as a source of maintenance of the communicational environment. (A continuing criticism of the daily newspaper industry is that reporters report and editors edit more for their fellow journalists than they do for their readers.) It should be clear, at least from our frame of reference, that simply maintaining the structure of a mass communication institution is not likely to have any necessary relationship to either maintaining or restoring the initial function which gave rise to that institution.

The Role of Technology

Interestingly enough, for many mass communication institutions whose use is no longer as central as it once was to the homogenization of social units, technological innovations are blamed for their fall from dominance. Hitchcock will later cite the introduction of mass printing as contributing to the loss of the church's influence. Newspapers and commercial radio, among others, place the blame for their waning influence on television. To be sure, technological innovations have and will continue to play a central role in the rise and fall of mass communication institutions. But we are not at the same time willing to concede that technology alone will ensure, in any predictable fashion, the growth and ultimate role of any mass communication institution, particularly in our society where faddish preoccupation with gadgetry has made technology itself a higher order mass communication institution. To that end, we believe it is as imperative to maintain a distinction between technology and the mass communication institutions which employ technology as a means of distributing their products, as it is to distinguish mass communication institutions from the mass communication phenomenon. A brief look at two technologies sharing generally the same life span may illustrate the point.

The history of the mass communication institutions employing television as a medium is, within a few years, nearly isomorphic with the availability of the technology. Television is both a relatively young and, technologically, a relatively unsophisticated medium. It was first made available to the public (on a limited basis) in 1939, and became widely accessible around 1947. Today, most electronic engineers would agree that the full potential of the technology is yet to be recognized. But while the technology may be relatively new, the current major controllers of the medium—commercial television networks and stations—pre-date considerably wide-scale public use of television. From its inception, the new medium was literally swallowed by then existing mass communication institutions, commercial radio network and radio station owners, who imposed upon it a variety of pre-existing structural filigree. And so commercial television was born to the inheritance of commercial radio's peculiarities, its precise and often frantic time format, its interruptive schedule of advertising "spots," its star system, its often unfathomable and influential rating system, and innumerable other institutional trappings that seem to defy any necessary functional referent with respect to the new medium.

What the potential uses of the technology of television might be is a question which, in a very real sense, has never been fully addressed. While very few seem to be questioning whether or not the medium of television will remain with us, considerably more than a few have raised the possibility that the mass communication institutions which have thus far attached themselves to the technology may not have an equally guaranteed future. Such speculation in the midst of commercial television's current dominant role in the mass communication process might seem somewhat untenable, but, as we have pointed out, while the medium itself is yet developing, its primary institutional users are not. At least one key to assessing the prospects for the networks' continued domination of television lies in determining the current state of the relationship between their functional performance and their efforts directed toward structural survival suggested by the life-cycle concept presented earlier. In addition, we should at least note some rather striking successes of alternative uses of television technology. There is a burgeoning popularity for electronic games played on the home television screen. This innovation has already been followed up by similar pre-programmed teaching-learning devices geared for use by younger children employing their television sets. And a number of entrepreneurs have for some time been seeking low-cost technology that will allow the television owner access to a wide range of non-network fare through the use of video cassettes, played through his own set and at his own convenience. Pay cable television continues to make dramatic gains in many areas of the country, offering yet another use of existing home-owned units.

Pursuing the relationship between technology and the development of mass communication institutions, we most note—even if we cannot yet account for—the mercurial growth of citizens band radio. Both the technology and the enabling legislation for the use of citizens band radio roughly parallels that of television. Unlike television, however, the medium lay fallow for a considerable number of years attracting only a handful of users. It has been only during the past few years that the public has found use for the technology on a wide-scale basis. By the end of 1976, there were in excess of 30-million CB sets in operation in the United States. The Federal Communications Commission projects the eventual issuance of more than 60 million Class D (CB band) licenses, and expects both the number of units in operation and the number of persons using CB (a single license can cover multiple users) to be considerably higher than that. In point of fact, the federal government's control mechanisms for citizens band radio were so overrun, that in mid-1976 they were forced to institute on-site-of-purchase temporary licensing procedures to preserve some semblance of order among users of the medium.

The manifestations of citizens band radio serving the functions of the mass communication process are legion. CB jargon has penetrated American slang to a considerable degree; a CB dictionary of slang terminology employed by users of the medium was posted on the best seller list. Several hit records, television programs and movie scripts have been written in response to the broad impact of citizens band radio use. A major New York City radio station mounted a contest designed to lure the 10 percent of its automobile commuter audience, lost to CB, back to commercial radio. And more recently, the FCC, yielding to pressure from citizens band enthusiasts complaining of saturation usage in many heavily populated areas, expanded the number of available CB channels from 23 to 40.

The example of CB radio affords us a number of interesting observations. It is perhaps the first medium with relatively broad dissemination capabilities whose "programming" rests in the hands of its audience. The parameters placed upon CB radio through the Federal Communications Commission are not overly restrictive and, for the most part, have been liberally interpreted by most CB users. In terms of availability, one can today own and operate a citizens band radio station for considerably less than it costs to own a television set or a stereo record player, or for roughly the cost of what one pays annually to subscribe to a daily newspaper.

In classical mass communication terms the medium is used to convey news and information, to provide warnings of and prescriptions for appropriate responses to impending danger, and to entertain. The audience is relatively large, heterogeneous, and anonymous. The nature of the communication experience can be characterized as public, rapid, and offering content designed for immediate consumption.[12] But what should be more intriguing to the student of mass communication is that these networks, quite the opposite of commercial media, function with a minimum of structure and a maximum of individual participation. Citizens band radio is currently, in terms of the life-cycle model, functional, informal, and personal. It has, to a limited degree, begun to evolve its own rules of operation beyond those prescribed by the FCC. It is difficult to imagine at this point just how citizens band broadcasting might become more highly institutionalized, but charting its evolution ought to be the sort of problem which is of central interest to serious students of mass communication.

Notes and References

1. O. J. Harvey, *Motivational and Social Research* (New York: The Ronald Press Company, 1963), p. 3.
2. A. Korzybski, *Science and Sanity,* 3rd ed. (Lakeville, Conn.: Aristotelian Library Publishing Company, 1948; 1st ed. New York: Dutton, 1933).
3. P. L. Berger, *The Sacred Canopy* (Garden City, N.Y.: Doubleday & Company, 1969), p. 3.
4. W. Lippmann, *Public Opinion* (New York: Macmillan Company, 1922).
5. W. Johnson, *People in Quandaries* (New York: Harper & Brothers, 1946), p. 135. The diagram used here was adapted by R. W. Budd, "General Semantics: An Approach to Human Communication," in

R. W. Budd and B. D. Ruben, *Approaches to Human Communication* (New York: Spartan Books, 1972), p. 111.

6. G. Vickers, "The Multivalued Choice," in L. Thayer (Ed.), *Communication Concepts and Perspectives* (New York, Spartan Books, 1967), p. 272.

7. P. Berger and T. Luckmann, *The Social Construction of Reality* (New York: Doubleday, 1967).

8. *Ibid.*, p. 53.

9. *Ibid.*, p. 54.

10. K. Nordenstreng, "Comments on 'Gratification Research' in Broadcasting," *Public Opinion Quarterly,* 34, 130–132 (1970).

11. D. McQuail, *Towards a Sociology of Mass Communication* (London: Collier-Macmillan, 1969).

12. C. F. J. Campbell and J. Mickelson, "Organic Communication Systems: Speculations on the Study, Birth, Life, and Death of Communication Systems," in B. D. Ruben and J. Y. Kim, *General Systems Theory and Mass Communication* (Rochelle Park, N.J.: Hayden Book Company, 1975), pp. 222–236.

CHAPTER VII

Extending the

Concept

It has not been our intention in the preceding chapter, nor in this volume, to minimize the role or function of the traditional big four mass communication institutions in the mass communication process. We have, rather, attempted to develop a framework which places these more commonly studied mass media in a broadened context of mass communication. In so doing, we have sought to provide a fresh and substantially more generic conceptualization of both mass communication and mass communication institutions. Our basic notion has been that the one-to-many model which distinguishes mass communication institutions can be applied with validity and utility to a number of public enterprises in which communication with mass audiences is not only the organization's prime function, but is in fact its sole means of survival.

This extended view of what constitutes a mass communication institution includes, then, a number of activities seldom, if ever, regarded as germane to mass communication study. Among them are architecture, religion, popular art, politics, libraries, museums, legitimate theater, restaurants, the fashion industry, to mention only a few. In the chapters that follow, eight such institutions are examined at some depth by active professionals who, by virtue of their positions, serve the mass communication functions through the institutions over which they preside or to which they contribute.

There are a number of useful ways to approach the study of these alternative mass communication institutions. The dynamics of organized religion, the museum, or the library, for example, may be examined to determine the extent to which each conforms to our definition of a mass communication institution, and in what ways each serves the functions of the mass communication process. From the narratives presented by each of the practitioners in the following chapters, to what extent can the institution represented be characterized by and located at some point on the life-cycle model presented earlier? Does there appear to be a logical relationship between the institution's life-cycle status and the extent to which it appears to be contributing to the communicational environment? In terms of the functions being served by the particular mass communication institution under discussion, one might explore the relative relationship between its content dimensions and its relational or linking function, both of which are essential to the creation and maintenance of symbolic realities.

At a somewhat different level of analysis, it may be useful to compare and contrast the operating dynamics of one institution with those of others—most especially with the traditional mass media. For while the message units and delivery systems employed by each of these "alternative" mass communication institutions may differ markedly in kind, the decision-making processes related to "message" design and "audience" analysis are often virtually identical. Within the traditional mass media, for example, professionals engage in a number of complex decision-making processes in the preparation and distribution of media fare. Such processes typically include problem-naming in terms of identifying the subject matter and the scope of its context. Data collection includes interviewing, first-hand observation, and secondary background research. Processing of raw information continues through writing, filming, photographing, and taping. Subsequent alteration and shaping occurs in editing, rewriting, layout and composition, time sequencing, and selection of additional materials. The manufactured information is finally published or broadcast, and thereby diffused to audience members who further alter its characteristics as they shape it to their own needs and appetites.

The set of decisions and process-dynamics described as characteristic of the preparation of traditional mass media fare can be understood as one instance of the transformation of information that is characteristic of all mass communication institutions. In Figure 7.1 we have provided a generalized model of the operational processes involved in the transformation of information, which may be usefully applied in the analysis of any mass communication institution. It is most important that this model be viewed not as a model of the process of communication, but as a description of the operational procedures engaged in by mass communication institutions in packaging and disseminating information. In any case, we present it here only as an organizing framework from which to inquire into the similarities and differences between and among the institutions described in the following chapters.

For example, the processes of problem-naming, interviewing, observation, and secondary research in developing popular mass media offerings may be viewed generally as *information acquisition*. These same deliberative and surveillance activities characterize as well the functions performed by a museum curator, a political campaign strategist, or a

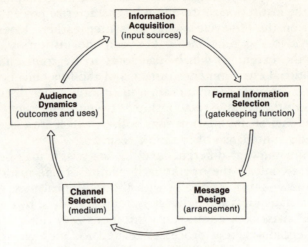

OPERATIONAL PROCEDURES IN
PACKAGING AND DISSEMINATING INFORMATION

professional librarian. Waissman and Fox, in their chapter on legitimate theater, provide us with an excellent description of a producer's activities in searching for new material. Soleri shares with us the more artistic and philosophical—although nonetheless pragmatic—concerns of the master architect in his quest to acquire information relevant to his purposes.

Similarly, *formal information selection* is the more general category which encompasses what is popularly known as editing. This is the crucial process of selecting from all the data gathered, what will be packaged for dissemination and what will be left out. Further, the editing function entails giving some shape to that selected information. From the more generalized framework of information selection, one may ask, for example how museum curators select from available artifacts those which are appropriate or essential to present to their audiences. Vincent Sardi, in his presentation on restaurants, gives considerable attention to the editing of his famous New York City establishment and it is this same important editing activity that makes one library distinctly different from another, or one newspaper unlike another, although both have essentially the same pool of information from which to select.

Closely related to information selection is *message design*. Among the popular media, this category includes such activities as layout and design for the print media, or establishing a controlling framework and format with appropriate continuity for the broadcast media. Understandably, there is a strong relationship between the information selection and message design operations, with each affecting the other to a considerable degree. The concept of message design is as much art as it is mastery of technology. The orchestration of the bits and pieces that combine to make Sardi's a unique establishment requires every bit the precision and "feel" for the audience as is necessary to successfully direct and produce a television documentary or to design and layout the pages of *Better Homes and Gardens.* And the mix of artifacts and exhibits in the Chicago Museum of Science and Industry is perhaps as critical as the skillful mix of news and features that create a weekly *Time* magazine or a daily *Washington Post* newspaper.

Channel selection may or may not be a major concern for a mass communication institution. For the popular big four, it generally is not, since each is wedded to an existing technology. There have been some interesting variations attempted among the popular mass media, however, like adapting the magazine format to television, or the "newspaper of the air" sometimes touted by commercial radio. Picture magazines, such as the now defunct *Look* and *Life,* could have been thought of as printed versions of television (although both pre-dated television and perhaps became victims of wide-scale adoption of that medium). The strength of many alternative mass communication institutions is that they can and do draw heavily on several technologies. Because this is so, decision-making regarding channel selection adds a degree of complexity not always faced by the producers and editors of the popular media. The museum curator, to continue the example, must not only look to the appropriate content mix, but concern himself with media mix as well—including how and when to introduce audience control over, as well as interaction with, both medium and content. The architect, on the other hand, must interface his concepts and audience with an entirely different class of media decisions.

For any mass communication institution, ultimate survival depends upon the nature of the final product, and more importantly, on the uses to which the audience member puts the product. *Audience dynamics* focus upon the accuracy of assumptions made by decision-makers regarding the nature of the audience as well as the wisdom of the options exercised in the other categories of the process. While mass communication institutions can control the nature of their packaged products, it is, in the end, the audience that will determine the viability of that product in the communicational environment, and provide the ultimate basis for explaining why some restaurants flourish while others die in rapid succession, or why one political or religious institution succeeds while others fail. Each of these instances—among others—may have profound implications for comprehending the fate of *Life, Look,* and *The Saturday Evening Post,* or help to shed light on the trend of deterioration among American daily newspapers.

In our presentation of this model of mass communication institution information processing, we have, for sake of example, broken it into isolated parts. It is our hope that in using the model as a means of working through the remaining chapters, it will suggest a more dynamic and interactive process leading to some fairly complex questions about both the phenomenon and institutions of mass communication. For example, the nature of the relationship between medium and message, so much in contention in the works of Marshall McLuhan, can be placed in an interesting perspective when one considers the relationship of these two information components, not only in the context of the traditional media, but in, say, the context of architecture. For another, the information transformation processes which take place between when a "news story" is reported up until it is read or heard and discussed, compares in some rather interesting ways to the dynamics by which a piece of art is transformed from essentially a personal image to mass information. And the political strategist whose understanding of the importance of audience dynamics in the political process means "winning is the only thing," sheds interesting light on the economic interdependencies that require the simultaneous marketability of a news program to both corporate and mass audiences.

Of course, the point of the analytic comparisons we advance is to broaden and redefine one's thinking about the nature of mass communication and mass communication institutions. If one believes, as we suggested earlier, that no small part of man's future course will be determined by the functions performed by our institutions of mass communication and, equally, the manner in which we respond to those performances, then it behooves us to carve out the broadest and most comprehensive understanding of that phenomenon as is possible. The kind of thinking and scholarship that has for so many years viewed the big four mass media as synonymous with mass communication, has severely restricted our understanding of the mass communication phenomenon. In response to this limited and constraining view, we offer a unique perspective on the mass communication process and mass communication institutions. With the framework presented in the previous chapter, and the potentially new perspectives provided in the eight subsequent chapters, we hope to facilitate the sort of conceptual reevaluation, reformulation, and refinement referred to by Thomas Kuhn earlier in this volume.

COMMENTARY
Libraries and Museums:
Organizing and Distributing Knowledge

Perhaps the easiest place to begin extending the concept is with institutions which, by their nature, readily conform with even the most classical definition of mass communication. Two such enterprises are the public library and the museum. One need not be an analogical wizard to understand that the role of a museum curator or a library director and that of a newspaper editor, for example, are virtually the same. All three are concerned with the selection, processing and dissemination of information; the institutions served by all three perform the teacher-watcher-forum function, and all three are in the entertainment business. Like the "big four" mass media described by Moeller earlier, both the library and the museum are highly dependent upon audience acceptance and continued support. And most assuredly, the art of editing the contents of either of these institutions requires the same set of generic skills and decision-making processes employed by big four media editors.

But lest we miss the point here, our goal is not to make traditional mass media out of these two or any of the other institutions presented in this section of the book. To reiterate, what we are examining here are structural-functional units or enterprises, operating in the one-to-many mode, which purposely diffuse information into the environment toward some end. If that activity results in providing organized environment-data which stimulates multi-person network interaction and creation of widely shared symbolic realities, we are viewing the contribution of a mass communication institution in service of the mass communication function.

The two alternative mass communication institutions explored in this section are of particular interest, because they both deal with the organization and distribution of knowledge—a function commonly linked with the big four mass media. Viewing the total knowledge/information economy,[1] however, the "big four" not only do not have the market cornered, but fall considerably short of sharing even a controlling interest. Among the numerous other contributors, in addition to libraries and museums, are filmmakers, book publishers, educational institutions (public, private, universities, technical, trade, etc), data processing institutions, research agencies (government, industrial, private), professional associations, to name only a few.

The notion of a communication economy, advanced so well by Alfred Smith,[2] provides a useful perspective for reading the following two chapters. Smith maintains that the wealth of nations and the basis of their power is no longer usefully measured in terms of traditional resources—land, labor, capital and commodities. "Today our primary resource is information. Today knowledge is the primary wealth of nations and the prime base of their power. Today the way we trade messages and allocate information is our communication economy," Smith observed. Recent U.S. government policy moves urging the restriction of the international flow of knowledge, in one instance nuclear information and in another computer related knowledge, support the soundness of Smith's predictions.

The increasing centrality of the role of knowledge in our society must be considered a given. This simple fact alone underscores the importance of developing a broader understanding of mass communication as the study of sources of that knowledge. It is thus that an extensive look at the public library and museum, as representatives of such knowledge sources, find their way into a book about mass communication. Both institutions are, in effect, vast warehouses of informational artifacts which form the basis of knowledge. Their combined resources, both artifactual and human, account for a significant share of the communication economy. Perhaps the main reason they have not been so considered is that, to date, both these institutions have viewed themselves in reactive rather than proactive roles.

As *repositories* of knowledge, they have waited for their audiences to come to them in a rather self-selected manner. The major role of public libraries and museums has been, simply, the organization and distribution of knowledge. They have not, as institutions, taken fullest advantage of their potential to also create and market knowledge (although their organizational function, at some lower level, is in effect a means of creating knowledge). Museums perhaps to a greater extent than libraries are more involved in the knowledge creation process, since their function often involves bringing meaning to artifacts which are not of themselves self-explanatory. A moon rock, for example, might well be viewed as simply another rock without the appropriate captioning, context and display. Elaborate dioramas or entire rooms are frequently designed to provide a context for a single artifact or a small collection of items. Captions, or verbal descriptions of items in a museum are of course critical. Such explanations, by nature, advance some theory of the history and activity of humankind, not to mention the fact that without them a trip through a museum would be reasonably meaningless. One is most taken by this notion visiting a museum in a country where he or she does not speak the language. What one is able to "see" under those conditions is considerably limited.

In reading the next two chapters, one becomes aware of the enormous potential of our knowledge warehouses and senses early signs of their awakening to that potential. The case study of the Rochester Public Library presented in Chapter VIII provides only a brief view of the possibilities for the future of such institutions. This sort of innovation, coupled with present and anticipated information storage-retrieval-distribution technology, sets up the real likelihood that our knowledge warehouses, such as libraries and museums, will become the next major mass media of our society. Information specialist Edwin Parker has also forecast the development of some sort of mass information distribution system.[3] The new medium, says Parker, should be developed along the lines of a public utility, or, as he calls it, a "public information utility." He speculates such a system, employing a variety of computer storage and retrieval components, could be developed on a local basis, and yet have national network potential (in the manner of those now existing in commercial broadcasting). The information utility could, at least initially, employ existing cable television and broadcast facilities modified to carry two-way communication, thus making the medium responsive to subscriber informational needs upon demand. Speculating about the technological shape of such a system, Parker writes:

> This new communication medium can be described as looking like a combination of a television set and a typewriter, functioning like a combination of a newspaper and a library, and permitting a communication network that is something of a combination of a telephone and telegraph system. It has one radical new property that previous mass media lack: what is transmitted over the communication channel is controlled more directly by the receiver than the sender of the message.[4]

Parker maintains that among the advantages of such a system are:

1. increased amounts of information available to the public, and increased efficiency of the medium since everything need not be distributed to everyone in the audience
2. greater variety in the ways information packages can be constructed
3. individual receiver selection of information (both in content and timing) as opposed to source control of information selection, packaging and transmission
4. improved "feedback" capability (since the individual subscriber can "talk" to the system) currently lacking in the public media
5. greater convenience to the user than offered by current information-giving institutions.

While it would be possible, as Parker does, to continue this speculative cycle about present and future technologies, it will not be the mechanics that will ultimately shape (nor should they) the future of either the library's or museum's participation in such a system. Librarians, for example, have been employing computers for years, but have only succeeded in streamlining *the existing system* (which has served only to harden the shape of the prototypical library), rather than developing new concepts of interfacing their vast warehouses of information with their audiences. At the same time, there is nothing in what Parker says that many libraries and museums aren't, however crude the form, already doing. In point of fact, the activities of the more proactive units, such as the Rochester Public Library and the Chicago Museum of Science and Industry, seem to closely parallel, in both structure and intent, the speculations of the futurists.

The critical point of consideration for those in the business of organizing and distributing knowledge, however, lies with Parker's observation that the new medium of which he speaks will draw its content primarily from materials prepared for other media—newspapers, magazines, and other print forms—until packages specifically designed for the new technology are available. It should be obvious that in this area, libraries and museums, as well as many other similar archives, already have an enormous edge over such institutions as a result of their meticulous systems of knowledge categorization and storage. The age-old problem of the library in particular has been it stores far more information than it is capable of retrieving. While the new technology forecast by Parker would seem well suited to the solution of this problem, the strategies for bringing these vast warehouses of knowledge to their fullest utility must evolve from new ways of conceiving of their function in society, rather than through the mere application of new technology. To ignore these vast and untapped resources as possible sources of input for a new mass information medium simply because our traditional modes of classifying legitimate mass communication media have not heretofore included them, seems to us to be not only unfortunate, but absurd. The emergence of the "communication economy" coupled with Parker's prognostication of a "public information utility" raise a number of socio-political issues which should be central to the study of mass communication. Some of these were alluded to by Parker:

> The development of a new technology for the storage, manipulation, and distribution of information raises significant social and political implications because the actual or potential redistribution of information threatens the existing distribution of power in society. That is not to say that there is a complete one-to-one correspondence between information and power. Nevertheless, information and information processing capacity does contribute a significant correlate of power such that, other things being equal, improved information services to different segments of the population are likely to increase their political power, if only by permitting them to find out where and how to best apply such political pressure as they can mobilize.[5]

Speculation about the future of mass communication in our society, by scholars and practitioners alike, has been both too limited and too conservative, and, without a significant redefinition of the field, in danger of being too late as well.

Notes and References

1. A. G. Smith, "The Cost of Communication," presidential address, International Communication Association, 1974. Abstracted as "The Primary Resource," in *Journal of Communication,* 25, 15–20 (1975).
2. *Ibid.*
3. E. B. Parker, "Information Utilities and Mass Communication," in H. Sackman and Norman Nie, *The Information Utility and Social Choice* (Montvale, N.J.: AFIPS Press, 1970).
4. *Ibid.,* p. 53.
5. *Ibid.,* p. 51.

CHAPTER VIII

Libraries:
Relics or Precursors?

David Davidson and Richard W. Budd

Central to the history of civilized people and the development and growth of societies has been man's ability to time-bind; to preserve the knowledge of the past and the present so it might be utilized by generations of the future. Accordingly, man has always provided some mechanism, whether by design or default, for storing informational artifacts marking his time and place of existence. Such archives have taken a variety of forms, ranging from simple burial sites to elaborate structures specifically designed for such future-oriented storage.

Libraries, in one form or another, developed almost simultaneously with the invention of systematic forms of writing and the discovery of methods of keeping written records. While most of these early libraries were quite likely private archives and employed cumbersome methods for storing equally cumbersome records (clay tablets, papyrus scrolls), they nonetheless established the function of collecting and storing records for future retrieval and reference. The most important library of early Western civilization was established at Alexandria in Egypt in the third century B.C.[1] The library at Alexandria not only gathered the largest collection of documents for its time, but coupled the notion of storage with scholarship and research, attracting scholars from all over the known world.

The concept of a public library was given impetus by and flourished under the Roman Empire. The libraries of Rome were both publicly owned and open to use by anyone who could read.[2] With the collapse of Rome and the onset of the "dark ages," libraries again became the private property of the rich and of esoteric groups, primarily the church through monasteries, and universities. The development and spread of moveable type, dating from 1450, of course gave immense thrust to book manufacturing. And while libraries were somewhat con-

servative about accepting the printed volume over the more familiar manuscript, books eventually altered permanently the concept of the library:

> Printed books were plentiful enough to be loaned for use outside the library walls, and hence the public circulating library became a possibility. The typical 16th century library became the oblong room with books around the wall, and with tables for readers in the center, or perhaps display cases for historical objects. The library room came to have stipulated times for opening, with a librarian or keeper on duty. With books in larger numbers, new methods of classification and arrangement had to be devised and various experiments were made in this direction . . . [and] something in way of a catalog or finding list was usually available. A beginning had been made toward the modern library.[3]

The Prototype American Public Library*

History, as a search for origins, can be very satisfying because it gives us a sense of linkage with the past. It can also, however, give us valuable insights into the structure and function of modern day institutions, and often outline where and why change may be warranted. To put this whole problem in perspective, it might be well to consider briefly the historical development of the public library in the United States, particularly during the period when the institution was given much of its current shape and structure. Reviewing that period will develop the view that the American public library is a consequence of urbanization which necessarily resulted from rapid and extensive industrialization.

The application of energy to the production of goods in the United States caused many far-reaching changes, not just in that it forced people to come together around the sources of power, creating vast population centers. That change alone was revolutionary. But this spatial change interacted with the social conditions of the period to create a new and fundamentally different way of living than had ever before been experienced by mankind. Greer summarizes the most striking changes in American life since the middle of the 19th century as:

1. increasing use of non-human resources of energy, translated through machines into human values
2. the increasing span of the organizational networks in which man and machines are integrated for productive and distributive purposes

* The authors express their appreciation to Dr. Ralph Blasingame and to Mary Jo Lynch, both of Rutgers University Graduate School of Library Service, for their significant contributions to this section.

3. a resulting increase in the amount of productivity for each human participant.[4]

The population centers formed during the early phases of industrialization, while varying in many respects one from the other, became the foci of a culture in which new and specific achievement norms developed from a changed occupational structure, one depending upon the acquisition and utilization of specialized knowledge. Along with the fundamental changes in expectations placed upon the individual and upon society, a new kind of social system and class system emerged based upon individual achievement. The new system required the individual to gain skills and, in many instances, bodies of knowledge for which he previously had little or no use.

The nature and extent of changes brought about by the industrial movement and its attendant urbanization affected the total society. The drain of persons from rural to urban areas, the development of an entirely new job structure based on individual achievement rather than on primary group achievement, the massive changes in rural life generally brought on by the application of power to the processes of agriculture, and a host of other factors resulted in changes of an extent and nature not previously undergone by mankind. In this context, the urbanization of our society included not only persons living in the largest cities, but those living in the most rural of environments. To a considerable degree, the urban condition—or urbane way of life—has established for all of us views of what education is required and what opportunities we ought to be able to have as individuals, no matter where we are geographically located.

The pace and complex demands of the urban-industrial society developed:

1. a need for different kinds of socializing institutions than had existed in the past
2. an economy that could both cater to and support such institutions
3. a type of leadership (previously unknown in our society) that could ensure continuity of support at a reasonable level from the public purse for such institutions.

The public library was one such socializing institution, and its growth can be viewed not so much as a continued development from colonial beginnings to the present, but rather as a specific response to major spatial and social developments growing from that particular time in our nation's history.

The Inheritance of Industrialization

The public library produced by this industrialized society took its characteristics from the times (the mid- to late-19th century), and inevitably:

1. Became a local agency, in the sense that pressure for the creation and support of the agency came from the population center of location, not from the state or national government.
2. Took on the characteristics of municipal government of the time, governed by a board or commission which had substantial autonomy and was largely divorced from "politics." A substantial degree of isolation from public policy and the public pulse resulted.
3. In terms of public policy, became a bureaucratic organization conceptualized as having one or several goals, each of them sub-divided so that means could be independently devised to meet them, and goals were usually stated in terms of efficiency. This view assumed performance could be controlled centrally and that individuals within the organization would substitute judgments of superiors for their own. The prototype library, consistent with the times, tended toward authoritarian rather than participative management, a style inherent in the bureaucratic form. This sense of authoritarianism and isolationism resulted in little or no continuous reporting of the library's activities to the public.
4. Had little or no capability for or interest in self-study. It was assumed, given certain material inputs and good will, the end result would be a service provided in the interest of the public.
5. Dictated that the central library occupy a position of great importance in this early public library structure. Here were lodged the persons with the greatest knowledge and authority about libraries and librarianship; here most decisions were made

about materials to be bought for all points in the system. The building was typically monumental, reflecting its Olympian posture in all matters. Here too, because of centralization of resources, it was most clear the organization needed certain "normative" activities. By this is meant the regularization of decisions with respect to acquisitions, from what sources, how they should be organized for use, preserved, withdrawn, etc. It was also generally felt the more "serious" works in the central library's collection were of greater importance than the works of fiction and popular non-fiction often found in branch libraries.

6. Attracted a large number of vigorous, talented individuals to leadership positions, who sought to train personnel to work in the agency, so as to produce the best service at the lowest cost. The idea that persons should be continuously trained to assume leadership positions was largely set aside or perhaps not even considered. In addition, persons attracted to this new and interesting agency, if they had formal education beyond high school at all, were graduates of a "classical" system of education and, consequently, unfamiliar with the sciences, technology, and the social sciences.

7. While locally supported, without so much as moral support from higher levels of government normally, held itself apart from surrounding rural areas, as its source of funding indicated it should.

8. Was conceived of as both a support for serious study and as a supplier of printed materials for general reading. Its twin orientation toward building and preserving collections of "meaningful works" and its desire to serve the masses were, in many ways, in competition; its goals were internally contradictory. To make matters worse, the library's isolation from various segments of the community left it with only vague, general views of what audience was to be served in what subject areas and at what level. These contrasting goals frequently resulted in internally competitive programs, often rationalized by persons responsible for policy making in terms of "rounded collections," or "general public," or other phraseology which could be interpreted to indicate that these competing goals were, in fact, complementary and mutually supportive.

9. Owing little allegiance to any political faction, the prototype library board held itself separate from politics and accounted to the public only in gross terms. In turn, the public, though generally sympathetic to the library (as well as they could understand the institution), gave relatively little allegiance to their library unless it was in some fashion threatened. At the same time, relations between the local governmental unit and the library were ordinarily neither very clear nor very strong.

Some Consequences of the Prototype

The result of these and a variety of other forces operating during the rapid industrialization and social revolution of the period was the emergence of a public library that was predominantly a local agency, reasonably autonomous and isolated, and bureaucratic in form. As a local agency, libraries are limited in both resources and potential for diverse development within the local context. Their fortunes rise and fall, both economically and politically, with the local climate. The bureaucratic form of administration has necessarily resulted in strong centralization, an autocratic form of management employing a narrowly (but popularly) defined operational criterion of efficiency, frequently proving counterproductive to the library's more (altruistic) community goals. Perhaps the most significant manifestation of the library's autonomy has been its isolation, particularly from the very audience it is designed to serve. Without sufficient input from its publics and having developed no effective mechanisms for self-study and renewal, library administrators and personnel have been left with the development of internal criteria for their operations, thus establishing a classical one-way model of communication. Such a model is common to a tightly organized bureaucracy with fairly static leadership. Goal-setting and evaluations of achievement take on an incestuous character, and need no outside validation of their viability. Based on the notion of classical scholarship, libraries set out building their collections, reinforced by their assumption that such collections were providing a public service in the public good. Yet another consequence of this policy was the confusion surrounding the kind of audience the library was serving, a confusion that was inevitably reflected in the collections developed by most libraries of the time.

This concept of the prototype library, then, has had an enormous effect upon all aspects of librarianship. Thousands upon thousands of public libraries have been created in the image of the prototype,

many of them still operating in very much the same manner as they did then. A good number of libraries were brought into being in places which neither had the need, the economy, nor the civic leadership required to support the creation of such an institution. The prototype has, in addition, substantially perpetuated itself by strongly influencing libraries of other types—most principally and most visibly, college and research libraries.

The organizational structure of the prototype American public library would not appear to differ greatly from a great many public and private agencies or businesses which developed during the same time period. In fact, one would be surprised if there were strong structural differences between organizations developing in common socio-economic circumstances.

The hierarchical structure alluded to above was, of course, developed in response to the conventional economic thinking of the time. While a consideration of the economic assumptions underlying the hierarchical structure is outside the scope of this chapter, it should be noted that the structure was primarily developed and adopted by organizations concerned with the production of goods rather than services.

Before one evaluates the "prototype" public library with its obvious parochial tendencies and its institutional elitism, it ought to be recognized that what constitutes a contemporary definition for a "public" agency may not have been appropriate in the historical context.

From time immemorial, libraries have been archives. Their primary, if not sole, purpose has been to preserve the past for use by the present and the present for use by the future. If one ignores the somewhat egotistical assumptions underlying such a task we find that at the pragmatic level, libraries are warehouses. They are places where we keep stuff so we can find it when we need it. In this context, the development of the prototype library may not be as inappropriate as it might seem at first glance.

It may also be enlightening to note that paralleling the hierarchical organization of the *people* who work in the institution (the prototype) we find the same organizing principle being used to rationalize the *archives*. The Dewey Decimal System invented by Melvil Dewey and introduced between 1870 and 1880 became, by the early 1900s, the single most pervasive taxonomy for organizing library archives in the United States. The Dewey Decimal System is, of course, hierarchical in nature. It begins by dividing all recorded knowledge into ten major classes and then continually subdividing these classes in a fashion that makes it possible to make finer and finer distinctions between the documents being classified. Beside providing a code for each document for warehousing purposes, the Dewey number represents a symbolic code which describes in some detail the intellectual contents of the item.

In summary, then, it might be argued that the prototype library, with its attendant schemes for codifying the archives may have been quite satisfactory in the context of the society in which it was developed.

In practice, however, the prototype library with its inward focus upon its organization and its archives has become more than somewhat dysfunctional. One could argue, for example, that most of the contemporary sterotypes about public libraries are a consequence of the ways in which the library chose to organize itself. Most of us carry images of the institution which evoke the "Silence" sign, or of "Marian the Librarian," or austere but imposing buildings guarded by lions or eagles or oversized concrete urns. In terms of utility, our stereotype calls up feelings of frustration based upon experiences of being unable to find exactly what we want.

The fact that these stereotypes may not be totally true is unimportant here. They are generally shared by most contemporary Americans and, as such, suggest rather strongly that a major barrier to interaction exists between the institution and its potential audience.

There is a contemporary American more which says barriers to communication ought be erased. It should be noted that as long as the library has as its goal the building and maintenance of the archives, barriers between the institution and a too large public audience are functional. If the library doesn't have to actively deal with an audience, it can devote its people and material resources to building and maintaining the archive.

The point is, of course, that libraries can no longer afford to ignore their audience.

The Contemporary Picture

The metaphor for the prototype library was the industrial organizational development of the United States from 1800 until about 1950. The focus of most American organizations was on the production of goods. The strong trend since 1950 toward the provision of services rather than the production of goods is obvious, even to the most naive observer of American economic life.

A somewhat more subtle trend involves an emerging concept of the economics of information. The growing proportion of our GNP devoted to the production and dissemination of information has been documented by Fritz Machlup.[5] It would appear from both the scholarly analysis of contemporary society and from some rather obvious surface observations that the so-called post-industrial society may be characterized as the "Age of Information." While it might seem overly poetic to say that information and knowledge are replacing water, steam, coal and oil as sources of energy (and power), as a society we are behaving as if this were true. This societal belief in the primacy of information and knowledge is manifested in environments as divergent as the growth of continuing education, concern over the "effects" of mass media, government secrecy and record-keeping, interlocking computer systems, the American Telephone Company as "Ma Bell," and continuing interest in the cost of shares in IBM or Xerox.

It would appear to be a given fact that in today's complex interactive society, the individual—at all levels—needs to know more about what is going on, if not to get ahead, merely to survive.

Such a situation would seem to argue that the public libraries would be institutions of primary importance to a society that suffers from the paradox of acute information need and, at the same time, information richness. After all, taken as a group, no one knows more about existing sources of information than professional librarians, and no one has greater access to larger archives of data. Further, in a society undergoing strong economic oscillations, public libraries remain free and open to the population at large. In spite of all this, it is clear that public libraries are not particularly important to most Americans.

While there no doubt are a myriad of contributing factors to the library's lack of salience in an information-oriented society, the major factor finds its genesis in the organization itself. Libraries were developed as archival institutions rather than as information-processing agencies. Archives can afford to ignore their audience as long as the archive is in and of itself important to that audience. But public archives (libraries) decreased in importance to the communities supporting them as other competing factors became increasingly relevant. The social and economic phenomenon of urbanization which created giant metropolitan areas and made possible the great public libraries of New York, Chicago, Baltimore and other American cities no longer exists. That process, in effect, has been reversed, leaving in its wake what is euphemistically known as urban blight. It is difficult to justify continuing expenditures on public libraries given the often severe and competing problems of housing, unemployment, welfare, education, and essential city services which dominate the agenda of contemporary city governments.

In this context one might realistically ask why we have urban public libraries at all. Since public institutions normally face extinction unless they can prove their viability and value to the community, we must conclude that libraries must be doing something right.[6] Part of what they are doing right is serving their traditional literate book-oriented clientele. This is the relatively constant twenty percent of the American population that view themselves as public library users. Of greater interest here is the rather drastic change in orientation beginning to manifest itself among some of the country's leading libraries.

The Public Library as Information Processor

Most institutions or organizations which fulfill their goals or find themselves with goals which are no longer important either change their goals or go out of business. When a polio vaccine was discovered, the March of Dimes switched to other crippling diseases which strike children. "New Deal" agencies like the C.C.C. and the N.R.A. went out of existence when the depression ended. The trend among more successful libraries would seem to be somewhat different. Rather than shifting their goal from the archival function to something different, these institutions seem to be attempting to create an audience for existing archives and existing technical expertise developed around those archives. The most promising recent change in organizational focus is based on the assumption that while information is important to the public at large, the library and its methods for distributing that information are not.

The key to making the library salient is tied to making the professional staff active information agents or intermediaries between the archive and the individual in society who has a specific information need. This strategy for redefining the librarian as information agent has the advantage of maximally using the librarian's technical expertise in information collection, information retrieval, and information abstraction or distillation.

While these technical skills have always existed in the profession, the librarian is now required to become communicationally active and, more important, communicationally *interactive* in order to ascertain the specific information needs of individual clients and client groups.

The Public Library as Communicator

Libraries communicate books. Using the more contemporary abstraction, libraries communicate information. The archival role requires the institution gather, store, and in some fashion, disseminate information in a manner which makes it available to anyone interested in obtaining that information. It is the manner and mechanisms of that distribution process that perhaps best characterize the problems librarians are struggling with in arriving at a contemporary and viable operational philosophy that will ensure their continued social relevance. The dividing line of that intellectual debate, outlined in some detail by

Hanks and Schmidt[7] in a recent journal article, slices between the notions of the library as a reactive institution meeting informational needs initiated by users, and the library as a proactive, client-centered (in a collective sense) information disseminating institution.

The former of the two positions (and they are by no means mutually exclusive) is, of course, the more traditional one, the one to which most library schools educate future librarians—that of responding to demands for specific information about specific questions. The institution and its people are "designed" to carry out this function quite well. Library methodology and structural devices have been developed and refined—like the card catalogs and computerized availability lists—to allow individuals seeking information to find much of it on their own. In this sort of environment, the audience is capable of, in a sense, creating its own messages, by selecting from an informational universe which has been pre-codified. The information one can acquire is both limited by what is available in the library's collection, and by the manner in which the information has been coded by the institution.

In terms of the traditional activities of public libraries, then, we would classify them as *responsive* communication systems—that is, the system is designed to respond to specific but unknown questions and to provide messages the system itself does not create. The responsive system requires that the communication interaction be initiated by the receiver rather than the sender. The library becomes the medium of exchange, the (albeit a passive one) channel in the communication process. Research and development in librarianship, then, revolves around doing it better. Ideally, the professional librarian would survey his/her audience, determine what information that audience needs now and in the future, select from the informational environment that data appropriate to the perceived needs of the audience, and codify it for retrieval. Much of what the librarian is concerned with in performing this function involves the creation of meta-messages—messages about messages (card catalogs and other indexing devices) which enable the user to retrieve the specific information he seeks.

One of the consequences of being a responsive system is that if no one asks the system to respond, it runs the risk of going out of business. For public libraries, this particular consequence has been of considerable concern in recent years. The library has been substantially challenged by other media for public attention, many of which require less effort on the part of the public in terms of gaining access and understanding output. Further, the library, because of its past history mentioned above, continues in competition with other municipal agencies for dwindling shares of budget dollars.

On intellectual grounds, those arguing for renovation of library systems point out that the traditional organization has lost relevancy in terms of current demands for and use of information and, indeed, reinforces the notion that much of the public library's audience is defecting to other sources of information. Hanks and Schmidt write, "The traditional paradigm reinforces conservatism in the face of change."[8]

They argue that the library must become less passive, more client-oriented and its services more attuned to various local constituencies.

It would, of course, be misleading to characterize the entire library profession as traditionally bound to the passive model of service, and not to recognize the fact that several libraries are well out in front of their critics in developing new concepts of librarianship. The trend toward a proactive role on the part of more successful libraries is exemplified by a high level of development of the responsive system, as well as by an expanded view of what constitutes an archive and the uses to which it can be put. Increasing the efficiency of a responsive system, however, must be viewed simply as a necessary move to preserve the institution's existing client group (audience). Establishing the role of a proactive information agency requires creation of new audiences. Independent of the difficulties of bringing about change within the organization itself are the difficulties inherent in getting the public at large to perceive the library in its new role as active supplier of pertinent information. Exemplary of one such effort is the Rochester, New York, Public Library.[9]

Forging a New Image

At first glance, the Rochester Public Library would appear a typical city library system in a reasonably typical middle-sized city (approximately 500,000 people) in upstate New York. A closer look, however, reveals a network of substantial complexity.

The Rochester Public Library has a main branch plus 14 other neighborhood branches. This network exists within a larger system called the Monroe County system, which includes the 35 libraries in Monroe County. The Monroe County system, in turn, is part of a larger formal system called the Pioneer Library System, which includes the libraries of five upstate New York counties. Linkages among these as well as other similar systems provide a library cardholder with potential access to 150 libraries in 14 counties. The member libraries in these systems sponsor an ongoing information campaign to make users aware of the ease of access to library service anywhere in the 14-county area. (Maps provided in the publicity flyers not only locate the libraries but even detail which buildings are accessible by wheelchair.)

At a more fundamental level, this organization can be viewed as a sophisticated attempt to provide service to a varigated environment of rural and city dwellers alike, to blue collar workers and technicians, to commuters and stay-at-homes as well. In effect, the system reflects an awareness that diverse populations are not often meaningfully distinguished by public boundaries, such as city or county lines. Here, as in many other such alliances, is an attempt to strike some balance between local control of public institutions and system efficiency in financial terms, as well as a pragmatic solution to the old problem of generating an organization of sufficient size to carry real political clout.

While the main branch of the Rochester Public Library has become the nucleus of this extended system, its centrality is a function of its activist leadership rather than being the bureaucratic center of the system which characterized the prototypical "main library" discussed earlier. In short, then, the Rochester Public Library is the major component in a large, complex, interlocking network serving a sizeable, heterogeneous audience which shares only geographic proximity. The fundamental dimensions of this client group are suggested by the activities of the system's consultant roles. One of the advantages of such a network is that special expertise may be utilized in a shared format when none of the individual components alone could afford such an array of experts. An examination of these activities should suggest what the system thinks its goals are and how best to achieve them.

1. *Adult Services, Young Adult Services and Children's Services.* These three general categories are traditional in the library profession. They reflect the long-standing view that specific age groups require specific and different library and/or information services.

2. *Outreach Services.* This expertise group is relatively new in the profession. Outreach people are concerned with client groups who don't utilize the institution but whom the library thinks it can serve. In general these "non-client" clients fall into two groups. The first group consists of the socially and culturally disadvantaged. The second group is composed of the physically disadvantaged, persons who cannot come to the library.

3. *Audio-Visual Services.* These service areas indicate awareness on the part of the library that there are informational needs existent which require media other than the book for appropriate transmission. These consultants are concerned with the problems of collection, storage and dissemination of non-print media.

4. *Building Services, Public Relations and Training Coordination.* These roles are lumped together here because they are not specifically concerned with particular audiences or clients. The training coordinator fills an internal educational role for staff development. The building services role is a specialized one concerned with the construction and utilization of facilities.

The public relations department deals with disseminating information about the library rather than information from the library.

The Audience

As noted earlier, one of the keys to unlocking the immense potential of the public library as a potent mass medium of force, lies in how the profession itself views its function vis-a-vis its audience. Given the characteristics of libraries, data regarding its responsive posture with its audience is quite easy to come by. On that dimension alone, the following statistics will give some feeling for the Monroe County Library system within a single year.

Activity	Total Persons
Book Circulation (4,406,484 volumes)	1,809,504
Gallery Attendance	21,806
Copies Made*	144,829
Reference & Readers Advisory**	207,140
Films Circulated (43,396 16mm. prints)	1,020,050
Total Persons	3,203,329

* reflects an addition to book circulation, normally materials (e.g., journals) which do not circulate, but have information user needs.
** individuals to whom information is provided directly upon request without providing user directly with document. Approximately one-third of such requests are received by phone.

The data presented above is particularly revealing when it is recognized that all of the persons tabulated in each category initiated the information exchange by making a request of the system, and that the population of the five-county system having access to the Monroe County Library system is less than 1,000,000 persons. It should be noted also that the Monroe County Library system is composed of only 35 (although the largest) libraries out of the total 150 in the five-county system. It should be further noted that responsive audience contact occurs in a number of areas other than those suggested above. While no circulation figures are available, the size of the collections (noted parenthetically) associated with each of the media listed below may suggest actual usage figures: 8 mm. reel-to-reel, cassette, and loop films (3,300); framed prints, framed art work reproductions ready for hanging (2,800); sculpture reproductions (220); recordings, popular and classical music and spoken word instructional LPs (25,000); audio tapes, reel and cassette (1,250); slides, art, history, travel and science (11,000); and film strips, both sound and silent (300).

On the basis of this crude data, it would appear that the library can document at least four specific transactions per year for every man, woman and child in the available audience. While it will be argued that the reactive role played by the library in these instances does not qualify it as a communication source in the traditional sense, it should be recognized that a prerequisite to such transactions requires the construction of a massive collection of potential messages that will bring users to the institution. It seems clear, then, that the Monroe County system has had at least a modicum of success in responding to the information demands of the community it serves.

The Proactive Library

In today's world, it is reasonable to assume that public institutions will not survive without broad-based community support. This is particularly true of libraries which are perceived as producing "nonessential" services in the context of a goods-oriented society. If, however, we are indeed entering the "Age of Information," as was suggested earlier, the institution of the library could be strategically poised to become the next major mass medium in our society. It is perhaps this understanding of the potential of the institution that has propelled future-oriented librarians into the proactive mode of dealing with their vast archives of latent information. To be sure, the more basic dimension of "survival" has been an addition (and frequently a primary) motivating factor. Survival of the institution is currently particularly salient to urban areas where the audience "responded to" no longer lives in the city where the major resources of the library are located. This clearly is a consideration for the Rochester Public Library system.

As a responsive system, the public library finds it reasonably easy to perform its functions because, through years of experience, librarians have come to know well the composition of their audience. They are the people who repetitively use the library's services—high school students writing term papers, older persons tracing geneologies, mystery story buffs and, in metropolitan areas, local businessmen. That, of course, does not represent all or nearly all of the categories of users; it simply says that the responsive audience is that easily identifiable and that the institution traditionally deals many times with relatively few different individuals.

The notion of generating an audience, however, is quite a different matter, requiring an entire set of skills which traditionally have not been part of the librarian's training or repertoire. The beginnings made in Rochester rest upon the assumption that in an increasingly complexified world, the necessity for making decisions based on information rather than on intuition becomes likewise increasingly more important. The management of that institution further asserts that no one else is better prepared to handle the technical dimensions of information selection, codification and dissemination than the professional librarian. While Rochester's initial efforts at becoming an active purveyor of information perhaps do not qualify its program the label of "the new prototype," they are powerfully suggestive of the kind of expanded role libraries can play in their communities.

Some of the programs currently being pursued by Rochester and the Monroe County system:

1. *Operation Bullseye* is a program that came about because the library was able to recognize its own limitations of expertise in reviewing a very wide range of potential archival materials. The library decided to use the skills of experts in the community to review new informational sources. The operation involves sending new titles to appropriate persons in the vicinity for review and analysis. The program not only broadens considerably the library's input of expert advice, but the reviewers benefit by being kept up to date on new materials available to them in their particular fields. The program has the potential of developing into a mutually beneficial two-way flow of communication which provides both parties to the transaction valuable new inputs.

2. *Books to People* is another program totally initiated by the library and holds great potential for establishing local libraries as fully functioning media operations. The library continuously monitors announcements of community activities and organizational meetings. Once a topic for a meeting or an organization's particular goals are determined, the library searches its archives for all materials pertinent to that topic or organizational interest. A librarian then attends the meeting bringing the collected books and materials, pre-checked out and ready for distribution. The books and other materials are returned to the library by mail.

3. *The Pied Piper and the Little Red Wagon* is an attempt to recapture the library's audience of children which typically disappears during the summer months. It is, in essence, an extension of the Books to People program. Children's librarians become "Pied Pipers" and the Books to People becomes a "Little Red Wagon" filled with children's books. Routes are established throughout the area and the procession goes out into neighborhoods, stopping at specific places and at regular times for a story hour and book checkout and return.

4. A direct spin-off of this notion became known as the *Beach Program,* started by a young adults librarian who, having virtually no clients during the summer vacation period, filled a station wagon with books and went to the beach. The librarian not only found the young adult audience, but retired persons and day campers as well. The program now provides books and materials to three separate client groups, but also carries full equipment for presenting a film program for the day campers in case of inclement weather.

While it may be argued that the major share of these activities are primarily designed to entertain rather than inform, the activity has performed the major and more important function of joining the librarian's expertise with the archives on the one hand and the consumer on the other—and has initiated a concept that is destined to grow in sophistication and impactfulness. Coupling the librarian's training to distill complex bodies of information into bare essentials with a philosophy that believes such energies should be focused on providing people with information they need, has resulted in the establishment of the Urban Information Center. While the Center is still in its developmental stages, the kinds of problems it has undertaken give only the slightest insight into what will be possible in the not too distant future. The Urban Information Center program has begun by attempting to survey and meet the needs of some of the more obvious urban issues, which in turn has helped the library to identify and interact with a number of previously unserviced client groups.

As a result of these interactions the library has compiled and maintains a continual update on the full range of health and social services offered by agencies in the community. This directory is available at all 35 libraries in Monroe County, including the Biblioteca Manuel Alonso, which serves Spanish-speaking residents. More important than compiling and maintaining the directory is the active problem analysis and referral service provided by the library's Center. Leaflets in both English and Spanish are distributed throughout the community, calling the attention of the residents to this service.

While the directory and referral system may appear to be redundant with existing social service agencies, the reality is quite different. Social agencies are divided along governmental lines, not client lines. The library's directory is unique because it ignores these divisions and focuses on the kind of service offered. The directory is a kind of subject classification of agencies. Its uniqueness and currency is attested to by the fact that many social service agencies buy copies from the library for their own use in referring clients to appropriate sources of help.

While these referral systems are designed to serve the urban poor, a nontraditional audience for the library, these services are not limited to "new" audiences. The library also maintains a free employment service for individuals 55 and over; GROW (Gaining Resources for Older Workers) had more than 300 placements in 1973. This service facility recognizes that the elderly and the unemployed have traditionally used the library as a place to go.

The second area of technical expertise that the Rochester library utilizes proactively is the abstracting and indexing prowess of librarians. Library professionals are trained to reduce complex bodies of information so the contents may be represented in symbolic or real language shorthand. Dewey decimal numbers, subject heading catalogs and abstracting services are all examples of the familiar end result of this process.

In Rochester, the library has turned these skills to assist in understanding complex areas of legislation. Voting regulations and social welfare legislation, like income tax forms, tend to be written in "legalese." They are incomprehensible to the people who most need to understand them. In response to the informational needs in the areas of voting rights and food stamps, for example, the library produced and distributed flyers which made available to the public the basic information necessary to use this legislation as intended. Unlike most library public documents, this information was available not only at library buildings, but at barbershops, beauty parlors, supermarkets, bars, churches, and meeting halls of all kinds where the persons in need of the information might normally collect.

A more sophisticated example of the same kind of pragmatic application of the librarian's skills to community problems involved charter reform in the Rochester city government. The report of the municipal study committee, like most reports of its genesis, was ponderous, excrutiatingly long and incomprehensible. The public library staff reorganized the report around its central issues—both pro and con—and the resulting summary was more concise and readable than the original. In addition, its new form increased the possibility that the individual voter could better weigh the complex series of arguments necessary to reach a more rational and informed decision about how to vote.

In summary, the Rochester Public Library (and the Monroe County system) provide a strong example of a unit committed to reestablishing the institution's relevancy in the community. But more than that, it could represent the birth pangs of a potentially new and powerful medium—the transition of the library from the prototype archival-responsive system to a proactive information processing and disseminating system. Even in its present form, it has demonstrated that to be both powerful and effective, a mass medium will not succumb to the scatter-shot "to-whom-it-may-concern" model of message distribution.

The Rochester experience has shown the library can, perhaps to a greater extent than any other contemporary medium, identify and service audience segments in a highly focused and economical fashion. The extent to which the library profession and those responsible for the training of future professionals are prepared to meet and fulfill the enormous potential that is quite naturally inherent in the library structure is problematical. What seems unquestionably clear, however, is that the sooner the library profession finds a new and creative means of unlocking and increasing the availability of the vast stores of information residing in our public libraries, the more influential the institution will become in fashioning the future of our society.

Notes and References

1. Elmer D. Johnson, *Communication,* 4th ed., (Metuchen, N.J.: Scarecrow Press, 1973), pp. 32–33.
2. *Ibid,* p. 35.
3. *Ibid,* p. 82.
4. Scott Greer, *The Emerging City* (New York: Free Press of Glencoe, 1962), p. 4.
5. Fritz Machlup, *The Production and Distribution of Knowledge in the United States,* (Princeton: Princeton University Press, 1962).
6. J. B. L. Hefferlin, *Dynamics of Academic Reform* (San Francisco: Jossey-Bass Press, 1969).

7. Gardner Hanks and C. James Schmidt, "An Alternative Model of a Profession for Libraries," *College and Research Libraries,* 36:3 (May, 1975), pp. 175–187.

8. *Ibid.,* p. 175.

9. The Rochester Public Library was selected because of its reputation both as an excellent library as well as an atypical one. Recognition must be made of the extraordinary leadership provided by the library's director, Harold Hacker, and our thanks for his invaluable assistance in the preparation of this chapter.

CHAPTER IX

The Transmission of Cultural Heritage: Museums

Victor J. Danilov

More than 700-million people visit America's approximately 6,000 museums each year in search of culture, knowledge, and/or entertainment. They represent a cross-section of humanity in terms of age, sex, ethnic, social, economic, and geographical backgrounds.

The International Council of Museums has defined a museum as "a permanent establishment administered in the public interest, with a view to conserve, study, exploit by various means, and basically, to exhibit, for the pleasure and education of the public, objects of cultural value."

There are many types of museums, with history, art, natural history, and applied science institutions being the most common and influential. It is possible to find museums for almost any special interest, including automobiles, dolls, trains, stamps, rocks, and steam engines.

Every museum is different in content, yet all are alike in that they provide a channel for disseminating information in one or more forms about their specialty.

History of the Museum

The word "museum" comes from the Greek word "Mouseion," meaning "temple of the Muses," or a place to study. The Muses were the nine goddesses of the arts and sciences in Greek mythology.

The first institution called a museum really was a form of university, founded some 2,200 years ago in Alexandria, Egypt, by Ptolemy I, a Macedonian general who conquered the country about 300 B.C. Actually, museums as we know them did not develop until hundreds of years later. They grew out of the private collections of noblemen and wealthy individuals during the Renaissance between 1300 and 1500 A.D.

The Ashmolean Museum at Oxford University in England was among these early museums. It was established by the university in 1683, being based primarily on the antiquities collected by Elias Ashmole. The oldest of the great national museums is the British Museum, which started with the collections of three scholars in 1759. Located in London, it preserves and interprets the history of man.

The first museum in the United States was founded in Charleston, South Carolina, in 1773 by the Charles-Town Library Society. The founding minutes indicate that the natural history and historical museum, now known as the Charleston Museum, was created at least partially to show the intellectual independence of the Colonies.

During the next century, historical and natural science museums sprouted across the continent, appearing even in frontier towns between New York and San Francisco. They generally were offshoots of historical societies, academies of science and colleges.

The historical societies and science academies originally organized libraries and collections for the benefit of their members, but some collections became so large and burdensome that they later were institutionalized as public museums. Museums of natural history were developed as laboratories—to show the wonders of God's creation—by denominational colleges in the early 19th century. However, these college museums diminished in importance after the publication of Darwin's "Origin of Species" in 1859.

The first American art museum was the Walters Gallery of Art founded in 1858 in Baltimore. It was followed by the Albright Art Gallery in Buffalo, New York, in 1862, the Corcoran Gallery of Art in Washington, the Metropolitan Museum of Art in New York in 1869, and the Museum of Fine Arts in Boston in 1870. Most of the early art museums arose from the private collections or benefactions of wealthy individuals.

The foundation for the modern museum—the so-called "public museum"—was laid about 1870 with the formation of a corporation having as its principal purpose the operation of a museum—and having a broader purpose of public service than was characteristic of most of its predecessors. Until this time, museums were created by and for special-interest groups.

The museum movement was spurred by the development of art as a major museum subject and by the introduction of the concept of public museums. Among the museums organized as independent corporations and opened to the public at this time were the Metropolitan Museum of Art and the American Museum of Natural History in New York, the Museum of Fine Arts in Boston, the Pennsylvania Museum of Art in Philadelphia, and the Art Institute of Chicago.

It also was during this period that state and municipal museums made an appearance. The state museums developed from natural resource surveys of the states, and were assigned the cataloging and storing of collections for reference purposes. Among the early state museums were the New York State Museum, organized in 1836; Il-

linois State Museum, 1851; Washington State Museum, 1880; Nebraska State Museum, 1891; and New Jersey State Museum, 1895. The municipal museum, which is owned by and operated as a department of city government, was conceived as an equitable means of providing sufficient funds to operate a community museum. Early municipal museums included the Public Museum of the City of Milwaukee, founded in 1857, and the Park Museum in Providence, established in 1894.

The American applied science museum did not appear until 1933, when the Museum of Science and Industry was opened in Chicago. It was quickly followed by the Franklin Institute Science Museum in Philadelphia and the New York Museum of Science and Industry. The Chicago museum was inspired by the Deutsches Museum in Munich, which was the first museum to make use of visitor-participation exhibit techniques and to place emphasis on the principles and applications of contemporary science. All of the prior museums dealing with science and industry—such as the Conservatoire des Arts et Metiers in Paris, established in 1799, and the Science Museum in London, opened in 1857—were confined to collecting and preserving historic machines, instruments, and other such objects.

In recent years, a number of special-purpose museums have been launched to fill community needs not being satisfied adequately by established museums. In Atlanta, for instance, the DeKalb County School System founded the Fernbank Science Center in 1965 to serve as a 65-acre outdoor nature laboratory for school children. The Anacostia Neighborhood Museum was opened in Washington, D.C., in 1967 by the Smithsonian Institution as an inner city museum and cultural arts center.

It has been said that the purpose of museums is to acquire, preserve, and use objects. For many years, museums were concerned almost entirely with the collecting and preserving of "things" considered to be of cultural value. Fortunately, the emphasis has shifted to the dynamic function of use.

Contemporary Museums

Within the last century, museums have become instruments of public education or uplifting. They have sought to enlighten the average person in art, history, or science. In the process, they have become institutions for the public rather than the elite.

This educational role has been formalized at many museums with the offering of courses, lectures, demonstrations, workshops, conferences, and guided tours. Some institutions have full-time staffs organizing educational programs and working with the school systems.

At the same time, museums have been re-examining their exhibit techniques for communicating with the public. They gradually are moving away from static exhibit approaches, with the long rows of "don't touch" panels, paintings, and cases, to more dynamic exhibit methods. The applied science museums have pioneered in visitor-participation devices that involve the public and audio-visual techniques that dramatize the presentations. They also have placed greater stress on contemporary subject matter exhibits, rather than concentrating on the past.

Community pressures have affected the offerings of existing museums and resulted in the founding of new institutions with museum characteristics. Museums have been called upon to assist in educating the public on drugs, pollution, energy, mass transportation, housing, and other problems afflicting society.

Museums also have recognized the importance of telling their stories to the general public through news releases, publications, radio-television programs, motion pictures, circulating exhibits, and other

such public relations techniques. Most of these activities are designed to inform the public about new attractions, to report on research findings, to raise funds for operation or expansion, to perform an educational function, and to attract members, volunteers, and the public to the museum.

Functions of Museums

The objectives of museums differ almost as much as the content of museums. However, their overarching purposes might be summarized as follows:

1. To transmit the cultural heritage.
2. To serve as repositories for historic objects.
3. To contribute to new knowledge through research.
4. To educate and guide the public.
5. To reflect contemporary society and point the way to the future.
6. To entertain and serve as a diversion.
7. To disseminate information about the museum.

The manner in which these functions are fulfilled varies somewhat from one type of museum to another and even among museums of a similar nature. A brief consideration of the different types of museums helps explain why.

Historical Museums Institutions that concentrate on the history of a geographical area, specialized field, or period of time are the oldest and most numerous of museums. They are operated by historical

societies, universities, governments, associations, companies, and special-interest groups. The emphasis is on the collection and preservation of objects from the past that are considered to be of historical value. In general, historical museums are static in nature and are limited in their use of visitor-participation techniques because of the rarity, value, and fragility of historic objects that must be protected.

Art Museums Art museums have proliferated greatly in the last generation. In addition to the traditional art museum that collects, preserves, and displays art treasures, primarily from the past, new museums have developed that specialize in modern, decorative, graphic, primitive, cultural, and other types of art. These museums also are hampered in their public communication efforts by the nature of their collections, which usually are invaluable works of art that cannot be touched by the visiting public and frequently require a special background or guided tour to be fully appreciated.

Natural History Museums At one time, a "science" museum was a natural history museum, sometimes called a natural science museum. But this no longer is the case. Many different types of science museums abound today. As the name implies, a natural history museum is concerned with the history and study of nature. Typical exhibits deal with fossils, mammals, birds, reptiles, insects, minerals, gems, the origin and structure of life, and the biology and cultures of man. Because of the nature of the materials, most of the objects are exhibited behind glass—in rows of cases or as part of life-sized dioramas. As a result, visitor involvement is difficult. Extensive research is carried on by the professional staffs of many of the natural history museums. The field expeditions and their findings and films frequently provide the basis for better museum communication.

Applied Science Museums Applied science museums also are known as science and technology centers or museums of science and industry. They emphasize the physical sciences, engineering, and sometimes the life sciences. Founded primarily for mass science education, applied science museums seek to further public understanding of the principles of science and their application in society and industry. Unlike the natural history museums, they usually do not have extensive collections, professional curators, or engage in substantial research. Most of their exhibits are designed specifically for public interaction and education, and sometimes are sponsored by companies, trade associations, government agencies, professional societies, universities, and other outside groups.

Other Museums In addition to these four principal types of broadbased museums, there are many specialty institutions that could be classified as museums. They include planetariums (sometimes found

at applied science or natural history museums), railroad museums, automobile museums, aquariums, naval museums, pioneer villages, lapidary museums, children's museums, black cultural centers, aircraft museums, and even old castles and ships. In most instances, these museums simply display their historic, artistic, or scientific collections. But there are exceptions. For example, some planetariums have elaborate "sky shows" and accompanying exhibits, some transportation museums offer rides on old-time vehicles, and some nature centers have biking and riding trails and various films, lectures, and courses.

Audiences

To survive, a museum must find effective ways to convey its messages through exhibits, educational activities, special programs, and a wide range of public relations activities. Auctions, calendars of events, conferences, seminars, workshops, educational courses, ethnic programs, fund-raising letters, member reduced-fare excursions, membership campaigns, and mobile exhibit vans are but a few examples of the techniques used to reach the audience.

And, of course that audience does not simply consist of museum goers, but members, volunteers, employees, contributors, school officials, students, business leaders, scientists, government officials, taxpayers, minority groups, and the general public as well.

Museums are very much in the people business. They move in many different directions at the same time as they seek to educate the public, raise funds, enroll members, assist schools, train volunteers, open exhibits, offer special programs, conduct research and more.

The Museum of Science and Industry: A Case Study

An examination of the evolution of the American applied science museum movement shows how one type of museum evolves a sense of purpose and utilizes various approaches to reaching their publics.

A Brief History

The story begins with the founding of the Museum of Science and Industry in Chicago. In 1911, Julius Rosenwald, a Chicago businessman and philanthropist, and his family were vacationing in Munich, Germany. It was there that Rosenwald's eight-year-old son, William, became fascinated by a new type of museum filled with machines that could be activated and other ingenious devices.

By pushing a button, working a lever, or depositing a coin, it was possible to generate static electricity, move the pistons in a cutaway engine, or examine the effect of an x-ray machine. The approach was a dramatic departure from the traditional museum collecting and preserving original objects from the past.

This unique museum bore the unwieldy name of "The German Museum for the Preservation of the Mysterious Past in Natural Science and History of Engineering," but was commonly known simply as the Deutsches Museum. It was founded in 1903 under the leadership of Dr. Oskar von Miller, a leading German electrical engineer, who successfully argued that working sectioned models and visitor-participation devices were a much more effective way to illustrate scientific, engineering, and industrial history and principles.

Rosenwald, who was head of Sears, Roebuck and Co., went to the Munich museum to find out what was so intriguing about the place. He was impressed with what he saw and came away feeling that the United States should have such an exciting museum. But it was not until 1921 that he had an opportunity to pursue the project. At that time, Chicago was debating what to do with a deteriorating classic Greek structure that was the Palace of Fine Arts at the World's Columbian Exposition in 1893.

In a letter to Samuel Insull, then president of the influential Commercial Club of Chicago, Rosenwald wrote: "I have long felt that Chicago should have as one of its important institutions for public usefulness a great Industrial Museum or Exhibition, in which might be housed, for permanent display, machinery and working models illustrative of as many as possible of the mechanical processes of production and of manufacture."

He explained the advantages as follows: "In an industrial center like Chicago there ought to be a permanent exhibit of this character, for the entertainment and instruction of the people; a place where workers in technical trades, students, engineers, and scientists might have an opportunity to enlarge their vision; to gain better understanding of their own problems by contact with actual machinery, and by quiet examination in leisure hours of working models of apparatus; or, perhaps, to make new contributions to the world's welfare through helpful inventions. The stimulating influence of such an exhibit upon the growing youth of the city need only to be mentioned."

Rosenwald urged that the abandoned and decaying Palace of Fine Arts be rebuilt and converted into the nation's first contemporary museum of science, technology, and industry. He offered to contribute $1-million to the cause. The Commercial Club endorsed the idea and the South Park District raised $5-million through a bond issue to restore the building.

The museum was incorporated in 1926, but did not open until 1933 and the rebuilding was not completed until 1940. Meanwhile, Rosenwald contributed some $7-million to the project. As fate would have it, he failed to see his dream come true. He died the year before the museum opened.

Rosenwald stubbornly resisted efforts to name the museum after him. He threatened to withdraw all financial support if his name was used, saying that it was a peoples' museum that should not be a testimonial to anyone and that it eventually would have to be self-supporting.

That was how the Museum of Science and Industry came into being in Chicago, and how the modern science/technology museum movement received its start in the United States. Today, there are more than 20 American museums dedicated to explaining scientific and technological principles and their applications in society and industry.

In the 40 years since the opening of the Chicago museum, applied science museums have become among the most popular attractions in their communities. Approximately 15-million people visit these scientific and industrial showcases each year. Visitor involvement still remains the key to their popularity, although the exhibits and programs have been greatly expanded and improved.

In the early years, American museum officials traveled to Europe to study and adapt the ideas of such pioneering science and technical museums as the Deutsches Museum in Munich, the Science Museum in London, the Conservatoire National des Arts et Metiers in Paris, and the Technisches Museum fur Industrie und Gewerbe in Vienna. Now, representatives of museums from throughout the world come to the United States to see and learn about new exhibit and operating approaches.

Goals

As any tour of applied science museums will show, a striking difference exists between European and American museums. Unlike most European museums, science/technology museums in North America normally:

1. Emphasize the present and future, rather than the past.
2. Use historic objects only as a frame of reference.
3. Focus on scientific principles and technological applications.
4. Make extensive use of visitor-participation and demonstration techniques.
5. Conduct educational programs for children and adults.
6. Work closely with the schools, the community, and industry.
7. Operate independent of the government.
8. Present numerous special exhibits and programs in response to timely local, regional, and national needs.
9. Are dedicated to the belief that museum-going can be enjoyable.
10. Serve as the focal point of many community activities.

In other words, America's science museums are "living" institutions. They constantly change and seek to bring science to the masses. Rather than being primarily storehouses for historic instruments, machines, and vehicles from the past, they are basically community centers for personal-involvement science education.

In 1973, the American applied science museums joined forces in an effort to further public understanding and appreciation of science and technology. Twenty-five museums that emphasize contemporary science and visitor-participation techniques have become members of the newly formed Association of Science-Technology Centers.

The association was formed to provide a mechanism for sharing resources, exhibits, and ideas, as well as to facilitate joint programs of common interest to the museums. The move resulted from two years of discussions among personnel from museums that are concerned primarily with the physical and life sciences and engineering and that focus largely on the basic principles of science and their applications in everyday life and industry.

These museums feature modern three-dimensional exhibits that explain principles, describe applications, and frequently point out future trends. Instead of having a "hands-off" policy, science museums design most of their exhibits to involve the visiting public.

America's science/technology museums are convinced there is no substitute for actually touching, operating, or manipulating a computer, an antique car, a laser, a locomotive, or any of the thousands of other objects found in their exhibit halls. Virtually every exhibit has a button to push, a crank to turn, a lever to lift, or a phone to use.

The Chicago Museum

The Museum of Science and Industry in Chicago has the largest attendance and greatest array of exhibits of all U.S. science museums. More than 3-million people visit the museum every year to see the 75 major exhibit halls with some 2,000 exhibit units on such diverse subjects as communications, mathematics, steelmaking, food, petroleum, chemicals, automobiles, photography, agriculture, electricity, aviation, natural gas, trains, nuclear energy, medicine, hardwoods, music, physics, machinery, computers, and space exploration.

The museum probably is best known for its operating full-scale coal mine, captured German U-505 submarine, chick-hatching incubators, actual Apollo 8 spacecraft that circled the moon, 16-foot walk-through heart, full-sized 747 jetliner, "Picturephone" line to Disneyland (a two-way TV-phone), and a spectacular new circus exhibit with 22,000 hand-carved figurines and a 30-foot-high motion picture screen.

As part of an industrial participation plan, some 50 companies, trade associations, health organizations, universities, and federal agencies present exhibits at the Chicago museum. They include such organizations as American Telephone and Telegraph Company, Eastman Kodak Company, General Motors Corporation, International Business Machines Corporation, Sears, Roebuck and Company, American Iron and Steel Institute, American Cancer Society, Atomic Energy Commission, and National Aeronautics and Space Administration.

Among the new innovative programs at the Chicago museum are a "Science Playhouse" series in which science is taught through theatrical techniques; a "Working for a Better Environment" program to show how the public can help fight environmental blight; a "Black Esthetics" festival and special theater programs for the Spanish-speaking to introduce minorities to the Museum; a "Children's Science

Book Fair" to interest youngsters in reading about science; and traveling exhibits on the interaction of art and science and the design contributions of R. Buckminster Fuller.

Other Applied Science Centers

Other large American applied science museums are the California Museum of Science and Industry in Los Angeles, which is operated by the State of California; the Franklin Institute Science Museum in Philadelphia, which traces its ancestry to 1824; and the Museum of Science in Boston, which is a combination physical science-natural history museum.

One of the continent's newest science museums is the Ontario Science Centre in Toronto, which was established in 1969, as part of Ontario's centennial observance. It is located in a glittering new building and incorporates many of the best features of the older American science-technology museums.

Another new facility is the Technological Museum in Mexico City. It was founded in 1970, by Mexico's Comision Federal de Electricidad and is rather heavily oriented toward electricity, although its exhibits are being broadened to encompass other phases of the physical sciences.

The Lawrence Hall of Science, operated by the University of California, occupies a relatively new building on a hill overlooking the Berkeley campus. Opened in 1968, as a memorial to Dr. Ernest O. Lawrence, Nobel laureate and inventor of the cyclotron, the structure is a comprehensive science education center. In addition to serving the general public, the Lawrence Hall of Science is deeply involved in developing new science curricula and teaching techniques and in training science teachers.

Four of the science/technology museums are located in buildings left over from world's fairs. Chicago's Museum of Science and Industry is housed in a 14-acre classic Greek structure from the 1893 Columbian World's Exposition. The Exploratorium in San Francisco is located in the Palace of Fine Arts from the 1915 Panama-Pacific International Exhibition. In New York, the Hall of Science occupies the former science pavillion at the 1964–65 World's Fair. The Pacific Science Center uses the U.S. Science Exhibit complex from the 1962 Seattle World's Fair.

In general, applied science museums are independent not-for-profit institutions supported through a combination of funds, such as some tax revenue, industrial support, individual contributions, membership dues, visitor sales, and/or special program grants from private and public agencies.

The facilities, exhibits, and programs of the science/technology museums differ widely. Some are quite large and elaborate, while others are small and almost intimate. In some instances, the exhibits cover virtually all fields. Other institutions tend to focus more on a few fields.

At the Lawrence Hall of Science in Berkeley, for example, considerable attention is given to computer education. It is possible for a visitor to use three time-share computers and 30 teletype terminals to solve mathematic problems, compose music, and play various computer games.

Across the San Francisco Bay at the Exploratorium, the emphasis is on individual experiences with light, optics, sound, and touch experiments. High school students—trained as "Explainers"—lead visitors through experiments similar to those seen at student science fairs.

In Dallas and Fort Worth, the science museums emphasize public health and preschool education. Both operate special classes for 3 to 6 year olds, with museum exhibits serving as classroom discussion topics.

The Oregon Museum of Science and Industry in Portland offers special science and math instruction in ghetto neighborhoods, and operates a wilderness camp for field trips. The Franklin Institute Science Museum actually has full-time classes assigned to it by the Philadelphia school system.

More than a third of the science/technology museums have a planetarium as part of their facilities. The planetarium is one of the major attractions in Boston, Philadelphia, Pittsburgh, Portland, and Rochester.

America's applied science museums have come a long way since Chicago's Museum of Science and Industry opened its doors some 40 years age. And they are continuing to change and improve their communication techniques as they reflect and interpret scientific and technological advances and respond to the ever-changing needs of society.

The Dilemma

Although not necessarily representative, the evolution of the science and technology museum movement provides insight into how museums have developed and the functions they perform for their constituencies and for society in general.

Unfortunately, because of differences in their nature, funding, management, and sense of purpose, wide discrepancies still exist in the quality of exhibit materials, presentation techniques, and overall operations among museums. The consequence is that most museums fall short of having the strongest possible impact on their audiences.

In some cases the museum simply does not reach members of their potential public. In other cases they may fail to meaningfully convey information about their specialty to the active museum goer. In both cases the effect is substantially the same. Museums must identify, understand and reach their audiences—whether schools, community, media, or other specialized publics. Until this critical interface begins to receive more attention, the museum, as an institution, walks the tightrope of failure as a meaningful cultural, educational, and entertainment resource within their communities.

COMMENTARY
Religion and Politics:
Shaping the Ideological Environment

The difference between *ideology* and *knowledge* is perhaps not as obvious as is often assumed. Most people would likely say that knowledge exists and is either pragmatic or factual in nature. Ideology, most would concede, is either "out there in the future," nonobtainable, or simply "not the way things work" in reality. From a communication perspective, this distinction is inconsequential, since the dynamics that are necessary to the creation, maintenance, and sharing of both knowledges and ideologies are essentially the same. The next two chapters focus on two mass communication institutions, the church and the political image-maker, as a means of exploring how our ideological environments come into being and react on our behavior.

In working with some of the concepts of this book in a basic course in mass communication, Professor Todd Hunt, of Rutgers, refers to the church and the political image-maker both as media for "marshalling abstractions." Both, he maintains, must attract and hold their audiences through the promise of a future state of affairs. Since neither can offer validation of that future condition prior to asking for a behavioral commitment, their messages necessarily focus upon abstractions. The church holds forth the promise of a more fruitful afterlife, while the political candidate promises the "Great Society," or the "New Frontier," or "Peace With Honor." Additionally, as with most causes and movements, both rely heavily upon symbolic modes—pictures and statues, processions and parades, vestments and short sleeves, communion and handshaking, and both adhere to and play out a set of elaborate and historically rooted rituals.

Religion and politics have throughout human history shared a stormy but obviously inseparable relationship. The nature of that association has ranged from complete unity of the two, such as with the Roman emperors or the papal rulers, to arrangements which painstakingly spell out a separation between church and state. The socially created realities regarding this issue are those revolving around the notions of "temporal versus divine" leadership. The communicational issue involved is the human imperative to organize one's environment and to evolve a sense of identity in terms of self, community, time and place. Politics and religion provide man with symbolic realities that lend him seeming control, present and future, over his environment.

Peter Berger has noted that there has always been a cosmic dimension in human organization, as a defense against man's mortality and vulnerability. The creation of a deity which has immortality and durability, allows mankind to identify himself with a much more long-term place in his world and in the universe, Berger suggests. In essence, Berger tells us, this cosmic orientation provides institutions, societies and, indeed, humankind with the ultimate legitimation. This simple observation alone explains the inextricable linkage between religion and politics. Whether we are dealing with the "divine kingship" or the "born again Christian" or the religiously devout president, the association clearly establishes a relationship between the temporal leader and the ultimate reality. Given such religious legitimation of power, Berger writes, such leaders are clearly aligned with a role which represents the fundamental order to the universe. And while perhaps many political candidates do not fully understand why they are required to adhere to a moral code more severe than those they represent—or why they seem compelled to include quotes from religious scripture in their political speeches—they do know that it works.

But as we noted in Chapter VI, all of our symbolic realities are created in social communication, and remain viable so long as they are maintained. Both of these processes, we noted, imply the existence of some mass communication institution. And while there has always existed a religious dimension in our communication environment, its maintenance necessarily has been rooted in the socially-based institution of worship. The effectiveness and life-cycle of such institutions depend wholly upon their ability to make relevant the relationship of their messages to the pragmatics of everyday existence. Failure to maintain social support for the symbolic reality—i.e., it becomes less "real" for the individual—means that, in this case, religion would no longer serve as a viable referent for determining behavior. Concomitantly, the mass communication institution supporting the reality is weakened, and begins its accelerated movement through the life-cycle toward institutional dissolution and displacement.

Chapter X on religion explores the historical development of "the church" from its rise to power as the dominant mass communication institution to its current position today in the emerging communication economy. The chapter pinpoints a number of challenges to one of the oldest mass communication institutions, and provides some important insights regarding its future.

Chapter XI provides yet another approach to creating an ideal through mass communication. Building an image of a viable and winning political candidate is a hard-nosed task. As the author points out in this behind-the-scenes view, candidate-making and image-selling is not a storybook process. It is a straightforward, incredibly pragmatic business pointed toward a single end: "make the sale and win the election."

In spite of the obvious difference in the perspective presented in the next two chapters, they are of a kind—they are only opposite sides of the coin. Together they provide us with valuable insights into some of our more ethereal and perhaps more venerated symbolic realities.

CHAPTER X

We Speak That We Do Know: Religion as Mass Communication

James Hitchcock

In one sense the history of the church as an agency of mass communication must be seen as the history of its diminishing influence in the West. That history ranges from medieval days when Catholicism was, for most people, the only comprehensive vision of life to which they were exposed, through relatively recent times when the pronouncements of religious leaders and Sunday sermons were still given regular coverage by the press, to the present situation in which there is a tendency to treat the churches as phenomena of diminishing and merely residual importance.

History of Communication Dominance

A comprehensive history of media would have to begin with the fact that until at least the eighteenth century the church was probably the major organ of mass communication, the only agency (not excluding the state itself) able to convey messages regularly to the majority of the population. As the social historian Peter Laslett has pointed out, for most people in pre-industrial societies, the church building was the largest structure they ever set foot in and the Sunday congregation the largest formal gathering of which they were ever a part. In many villages and urban parishes practically the whole population was present. The historian A. L. Rowse has suggested that, before the advent of mass education, sermons were perhaps the major experience of rational disquisition to which the illiterate masses were ever exposed.

The communication efforts of the church were not confined to verbal messages directed at audiences on Sunday mornings, however. Particularly in medieval Catholicism, but also in Judaism, the heart of religion was conveyed to the people even more powerfully and effectively through rite, symbol, law, and custom which, in the manner of the folk religion of virtually all times and cultures, practically saturated life and society, to the point where the communication functions of the church or synagogue could scarcely be distinguished from their mere existence. In European Judaism this pervasiveness was confined within the narrow dimensions of the ghetto. Within medieval Catholicism, however, it dominated the whole society in countless ways, such as by the churches which were the largest and most impressive structures in almost every community, by the public festivals and rites which recurred frequently throughout the year, by a calendar structured around religious feasts, by a moral code which sought to regulate every aspect of life and whose authority was acknowledged even by those who violated it, by the religious symbols to be found in innumerable public and private places, by the close link between the church and the great events of human life—birth, marriage, death.

The Schism of Technology

The emergence of Protestantism, and the concomitant splitting of the medieval church, coincided with one of the great technological revolutions of the West—the invention and spread of printing—and historians are inclined to see a more than casual connection between the two phenomena. The easily produced and relatively cheap book destroyed the communications monopoly which the Catholic Church had enjoyed and permitted the broad dissemination of heterodox opinions within a remarkably brief time. John Hus in 1415 had been able to win only a part of one country to his doctrines; Martin Luther after 1517 saw his challenges of the church carried to the farthest parts of Europe.

However, it was not merely the practical advantages of printing which supported the Reformation. As Marshall McLuhan has theorized, the "oral" culture of the Middle Ages was essentially communal. It was considered self-evidently right that the church should enjoy a virtual communications monopoly, since the church was the depository of all truth. Outside the church there was no salvation. Men achieved truth through participation in the communal life of the church, believing its doctrines, living according to its laws, participating in its rites and sacraments, obeying its leaders, honoring its saints. A heretic was someone who not only rejected the church's authority but, as Thomas More pointed out, cut himself off from the majority of believers of all times and places.

Within Christianity there had been, practically from the beginning, a source of religious belief potentially (although not by any means necessarily) in conflict with the official teaching of the church—the Bible. In response to Protestant attacks, the Catholic Church increasingly insisted that the Bible was not the sole source of religious truth; it was clearly, however, the major source. All through the Middle Ages the possibility existed that a lone individual might use the Scripture as a measure against which the teachings of the church could be judged. It was theoretically possible for a member of the church's audience, like the twelfth-century layman Peter Waldo, or one of its certified local representatives, like the priests Huss and Luther, to invalidate the official message on the grounds of its infidelity to the original source. The printing press put the Bible in reach of almost everyone. It also, according to McLuhan, helped destroy communal habits of thought and fostered individualism, so that the quiet perusal of the Bible in the solitude of one's room could lead the individual, as it did further, to question the entire elaborate structure of medieval belief.

Protestantism was also a part of the communications revolution of the sixteenth century in the impetus it gave to the growing tendency to make the printed word the major medium of communication. Reliance on the Bible as the sole rule of faith was both a cause and an effect of this. Beyond it, however, the Protestant critique of the medieval church tended to dismiss as superstitious and idolatrous most of the symbolic modes by which the church had communicated with the masses—pictures and statues, processions, vestments, elaborate rituals, frequent holy days, detailed rules of behavior, etc. Henceforth the sole truth was to be the Word, as communicated through words. The reading of scripture, and its exposition in the sermon, was to be the heart of religious life.

Divergence-Convergence

From the sixteenth century to the twentieth, therefore, the sharp dichotomy in Western Christianity between Catholicism and Protestantism was not only theological but corresponded also to two distinct views of the world and was reflected in two quite different approaches to the problem of communication—the religion of symbol, supported by the force of tradition and community, and the religion of the Word, scorning all worldly props and striving to remain faithful to an authority constantly requiring renewed purification of the message. Thus Catholicism remained, until the 1960s, relatively static and authoritarian in doctrines, worship, ecclesiastical structure, and symbols, while Protestantism underwent all manner of internal crisis, metamorphosis, variety, and multiplication.

At the same time the two principal streams could not avoid becoming more like each other in certain respects. Catholicism was forced to validate its message by greater attention to public rational argument, to become more concerned with its image and to be vigilant against scandals which were tolerable when it had no rivals. It saw the necessity of explaining its teachings to those who at one time had been expected to accept them implicitly. Protestantism for the most part did not succumb to the full logic of Puritanism and did not confine its message to the Word alone. It retained church buildings and music, and to a degree even rituals and vestments.

The conditions of modern life in the West have generally forced the churches to concentrate, first, on getting and keeping an audience and, second, articulating their messages in the most effective and explicit ways possible. The Protestant tendency towards verbalization, begun in the sixteenth century, was belatedly accepted around 1965 by the Catholic Church as well, in its momentous decision to render its ancient liturgy into the vernacular tongues. Previously the value of the Mass was thought of as participation in a timeless and mystical act, whose meaning was essentially ineffable and implicit. Now the stress was placed on hearing and pondering the words; the sermon has been conceded an importance it did not previously have in Catholicism; Bible-reading is encouraged as never before; and much of the symbolism and ritual have been pruned and streamlined.

Even in its most puritanical forms, Protestantism was never simply a system of verbal communication, in the same sense as an expository speech or book. The Word was proclaimed and was meaningful only as it took root in the heart of a believer. The greatest scholar, lacking faith, could not truly comprehend the meaning of the Bible's words or the words of the preacher. Ultimately, therefore, for Protestantism, too, the inner meaning of the message was largely ineffable and implicit. However, modern liberal Protestantism has tended to erase the distinction between believer and non-believer and to accept scholarly competence as a surer guide to religious understanding than personal piety. The message is in a sense more publicly accessible than before, just as the Catholic Mass is. The churches are less convinced that a special disposition on the part of their hearers is a prerequisite for the reception of their message.

In part, this is the logical outcome of the Protestant Principle, by which the church must constantly subject itself to criticism, must root out all evidences of "idolatry," must constantly "purify" its message by distilling it. More generally, however, it appears to be the result of social and cultural changes which are largely beyond the churches' control but which church leaders perceive as requiring fundamental changes in strategy.

Competing Media The most important is perhaps simply the surfeit of information from which modern Western man suffers, which renders religious messages less and less distinct and effective. This is true both of verbal messages, in an age of mass literacy and the electronic media, and symbolic messages, since the iconography of commercial advertising or of secular political life may be now more powerful than the ancient and venerable symbols of the church. An occasional preacher like Bishop Fulton Sheen or Billy Graham may compete favorably with the secular wordmongers, but on the whole sermons are not found to be moving experiences. The crucifix is no more familiar a

symbol than the *M.G.M.* lion, the rite of Holy Communion no more impressive than the stage show at Radio City Music Hall.

Paradoxically, ecclesiastical communication was evidently most effective when it relied on a special language and arcane symbols, and its decline roughly parallels its attempt to compete for attention in the general marketplace. Its declining influence primarily dictated the decision to compete, but the abandonment of dilution of theological symbolism reinforces the general impression that the churches no longer have anything unique or urgent to communicate. Vital religions depend, perhaps more than most kinds of societies, on the use of what the linguist Basil Bernstein calls "the restricted code"—a language of special meanings accessible only to members of a special group, a language which serves less to convey ideas or information than to reaffirm group identity and define the place of speaker and listeners within the community. Not only theological language, but, especially in Catholicism, religious symbolism has been of this kind.

Social Changes Social and cultural change have made it increasingly difficult, however, for religious groups to remain sufficiently self-enclosed to allow the restricted code to be effective. Increasingly, therefore, church leaders have adopted the "elaborated code," a language which is potentially accessible to everyone of minimal sophistication or education. Its advantage is seen to lie in the possibility of communicating the substance of the religious message to unbelievers who previously found it incomprehensible. The disadvantage, less evident, is the fact that it further reveals that religious belief is simply one facet of existence, to be scrutinized and judged in the same way as any worldly philosophy or movement. Catholicism in particular has depended heavily on a large number of shared assumptions and perceptions which had no need of verbalization and, often enough, could not be verbalized by most members of the community but which were made real through symbols as diverse as fish on Fridays, the strange dress of nuns, and medieval terminology casually introduced into ordinary modern conversation. Many of these assumptions appear no longer to be shared by the whole community, which necessitates a continuous search for explicit, verbally articulated meanings.

A Communication Paradox

Although the operation of the churches as organs of mass communication resembles that of other agencies in some respects, it partakes of one crucial difference—the conviction on the part of church leaders (now weakened in some denominations) that it is not simply one truth among many but possesses an absolutely unique and crucial truth which underlies all others. It is this conviction which, until modern times, made religious leaders loath to debate their beliefs in open forum, because of the conviction that they were thereby submitting to the relativization of their doctrine.

The central problem for the religious communicator is how a truth which is conceived as infinite and absolute, and also profoundly strange in the light of everyday experience, can be made meaningful to masses of persons in such a way as not to do violence to it or translate it in inappropriate terms. Like poetry, religious insight can only be translated at a discount; the very act of communication threatens to maim what is communicated. To a great extent, therefore, Catholicism has preferred not to emphasize verbal formulas too strongly and to rely on symbols. Some Protestant groups, those in the Pietistic tradition, have denigrated doctrine in favor of subjective emotional states of religiosity. A sophisticated conceptual understanding has been deemed necessary only for a relatively few people, although beginning in the sixteenth century the catechism was a means whereby complex verbal formulas could be transmitted to the masses in at least rudimentary form.

The earliest Protestants were shocked at the medieval church in part because it tolerated so wide a gulf between official teaching, which in the formulations of a Thomas Aquinas might be quite subtle and profound, and popular belief, which might be very crude and semi-pagan. The Reformation was in part a determination that this communications gap be closed and the true message of the Gospel be conveyed to the mass of believers with a minimum of loss. Even the partial achievement of this, however, had to wait the advent of mass education, by which time the influence of the churches had already waned greatly. The persistent danger of religious mass communication has always been that in transmission the message will be distorted and the persistent temptation for religious communicators has been to permit this to happen for the sake of a superficial "success." In Catholicism the most extreme form of this has been accommodation with primitive paganism. Whole tribes were baptized into the church with scarcely any instruction. Anthropologist Robert Redfield has distinguished between the "Great Tradition"—the full and varied riches of a major world religion—and the "Little Tradition"—one aspect of the former, usually rather peripheral, which is detached by the unlettered masses and made central to their own beliefs, mixed with alien elements. It is a phenomenon especially strong among Latin American peasants who have supposedly been Catholic for 400 years. Throughout its history the Catholic Church has been remarkably tolerant of this folk religion. The concept of "material heresy" refers to false belief arising merely out of ignorance or misconception; it is not thought to be morally culpable. An attitude of docility towards the teaching church has usually been considered more important than a careful and faithful assimilation of the substance of the church's message.

At the other extreme, modern liberal Protestantism has often settled for a humanized Christianity which avoids the problem of faithful transmission by limiting the message to what is easily comprehended by modern enlightened persons. Difficult notions like the Trinity, the divinity of Christ, miracles, and eternal damnation are either largely ignored or denied altogether. The substance of the Christian message is presented as having very little which is mysterious or disturbing in it but as being quite congruent with the best modern thought, especially in the area of ethics.

Assessing Message Effects The conviction of religious communicators that the message they convey is uniquely important requires them to look for evidence of their impact in a way in which reporters and commentators in the media, and even most teachers, do not feel constrained to do. Religious mass communication differs from other kinds in being decidedly not transient, at least in intention, since it is in the nature of religious communication to seek to have a profound influence on the recipient of the message, if possible to effect a deep inner conversion and change of life. There are many clergy who are content with routine signs of success, such as regular church attendance or adequate weekly collections, without inquiring into the spiritual state of their parishioners. The most conscientious may consider themselves failures if they do not perceive signs of mass spiritual awakening and personal reformation. The religious communicator never seeks merely to influence opinion but also action. However, depending on how religion is defined these actions need not produce any basic transformation of the conditions of daily existence but may be cultic acts largely separated from secular life. Most religions are also relatively tolerant of the behavioral lapses of their communicants (e.g., the Catholic practice of confession).

Altering the Transmission Through most of its history, Western Christianity rested on an authoritarian belief in an infallible expression of Divine Revelation communicated to man, which in the case of Catholicism was ultimately the Church and in the case of Protestantism the Bible. The duty of religious communicators was then to transmit this received deposit of truth to an audience, who were to respond to it humbly and with fidelity. The communicator operated from a stance which was, so to speak, above the world and which sought to pass judgment on the world. Communication was essentially a one-way transmission.

This remains the position of some churches. But with the development of liberal Protestantism in the nineteenth century the concept of an authoritative Divine Revelation weakened, and this spread to Catholicism in recent years. Some modern theologians have hypothesized that religion is essentially the working out of human longings for God or transcendence and that no sacred book, credal statement, ecclesiastical law, or religious rite is to be considered absolute; all are to be taken as human products in aid of the religious quest.

In this framework the task of the religious communicator changes from that of transmitting Divine Revelation to aiding his listeners in their own searches. The communicator no longer pronounces with authority before a humble audience but speaks tentatively, uncertainly, seeking to draw together many diverse strands of human history and experience in order to shed light on the commonly felt desire for higher truths. To some extent even authoritarian preachers do this, in that the attempt to apply infallible truths to concrete situations is not itself infallible and requires caution and humility. But liberal theology has drastically redefined the entire role of the churches, which are no longer seen as having any truth to communicate which their listeners do not already possess in some form.

The Heart of the Paradox This new definition relates directly to a central dilemma of the modern churches, which is their attitude towards "the world." Traditionally, Christianity has judged the world severely and has sought to convey to its followers the sense that their true home is elsewhere (conveyed not only in words but also, for example, by attempts to recreate the Heavenly Jerusalem in medieval church buildings). Liberal theology, however, seeks to place the core of religious life in the midst of the world. Hence the task of the churches is not to pass judgment on the world but to draw out from the world all its best potential (although severe negative judgments can still be passed on certain aspects of the world).

This new theology has created a problem which the churches have not yet solved, in the uncertainties which attend the religious leaders' attempt simultaneously to affirm and condemn the world. The dilemma of the religious communicator is between a stance of authority

and judgment, which may make him seem remote, doctrinaire, unfeeling, and irrelevant, and a stance of openness and humility, which may lead his hearers to conclude that he has nothing to say. It is a dilemma which is at the heart of the churches' present crisis of identity and authority.

The attempt of many religious leaders to shift to a stance of humble searching is fraught with difficulties because, in almost all times and cultures, religion has been conceived as incarnating authority and ultimate truth. There is a general cultural expectation that churchmen speak either with certainty or not at all. Religion has, in most societies, been intimately connected with tradition and with social sanctions; difficult beliefs have been given plausibility because of the weight of tradition behind them and because so many people appear to accept them. These factors, as much as the appeal of the church's own teaching, have induced acceptance. In the modern West, religion has been increasingly detached from broad social support except in very general terms (e.g., until very recently the common notion that church membership was good but with a refusal to specify the contents of a desirable religion). Correspondingly, the force of tradition also wanes. The popular mind, having associated religion with tradition and culture for so long, tends to conclude from this lessening that religion no longer deserves credibility. Bold religious leaders hail the churches' emancipation from the albatrosses of authority, tradition, and culture, but the emancipation makes even more anomalous their own positions as teachers. The liberal churches are increasingly put in the position of appearing to have nothing of substance to communicate to society, while the conservative churches seek to communicate a radically unique message which to large numbers of people seems implausible. The problem is illustrated in the dilemma of Catholic nuns, for example, whether to continue wearing a strange but powerfully symbolic dress or to blend as much as possible into the secular scene.

Modern pluralistic society has created a serious problem for the churches in that religion has always sought to convey a sense of the absolute to people, of ultimate truths and laws, and for it to accept modestly a position as one reality among many, one voice among many, is already to compromise its authority in a very serious way. The modes of communication directly open to the churches—the pulpit, the religious press, formal worship, religious symbolism—are less effective than they once were, especially in competition with the mass media and with the schools. Religious spokesmen sense that not only are they competing for attention but their messages possess no more authority than those of rock-music stars, television commentators, or politicians. More importantly, the secular media strive to create a common apprehension of what normal and satisfying human life is like, and religious spokesmen often find that the plausibility of what they have to say depends on the degree to which they can fit in with this common image. (For example, a call to a life of rigorous asceticism will go largely unheard so long as the media preach an easy hedonism.)

Interdependence or Independence: Determining Strategy

The importance of religion in society also tends to be judged in accordance with the degree of attention it receives in other mass media. If it is relegated largely to Sunday mornings, religious spokesmen may have difficulty convincing people that it has relevance to their entire lives. What great attention is bestowed on it, as was done to the Catholic Church during the Second Vatican Council of 1962–65, the media themselves tend to define what is important in it rather than the leaders of the churches. Popular concepts of religion can probably be affected more by its treatment in the secular media than by the messages sent out by church leaders. The total absence of religion from the public schools and from many of the colleges and universities says much about its perceived importance in society.

The need to compete for public attention presents a dilemma to religious leaders comparable to the dilemma of authority vs. humility. In Christianity, although not in Judaism, there has always been a strong impetus to convert the world, hence to address the largest possible audience. The ability to gain such an audience, however, requires the severe compromising of the message. The religious communicator cannot say anything which is too improbable, bizarre, or "fanatical" and stands the best chance of being listened to if he uses religious concepts to validate existing trends in secular society. He makes himself "relevant" by ceasing to be distinctive. Paradoxically, it is often those religious leaders who believe they have no unique message to convey who are most concerned about addressing a large audience outside the churches.

Most conservative religious leaders seem to have tacitly acknowledged that, at least for the time being, they will not convert the world and have chosen to concentrate their efforts on those within the fold, who are already more or less receptive to the message. Their task as teachers and pastors is thus to strengthen and deepen fidelity to the basic message (although conservative denominations usually also attract more converts than liberal groups). Aware that formal methods of communication tend to be ineffective in an indifferent social and cultural milieu, they concentrate on sustaining what the sociologist Peter Berger calls "counter-communities" of individuals whose values and beliefs differ significantly from those of the larger society but who reinforce one another in their deviations. The church is tacitly acknowledged to be a small world among many other worlds, although official theology may hold that its truth is actually the foundation of all reality.

Except in the most extreme cases (Amish and Mennonites, for example), these smaller religious societies are not immune from outside influence and are in constant tension between the distinctive beliefs of the group and the incompatible truths of the general culture. The solidarity of the group is to an extent dependent on its being relatively closed and fixed. But the secular media have the tendency constantly to enlarge the boundaries of the believers' world, making real hitherto remote phenomena like scepticism, frank hedonism, practical sec-

ularism, etc. Even conservative religious leaders are forced to take account of secular organs of communication and to modify their messages accordingly.

The churches are also in a paradoxical situation with regard to mass communication because, while religion finds its deepest and most creative expression in the lives of particular individuals (mystics, prophets, theologians), private religious experience is of little value unless it can be disseminated widely and rendered comprehensible to large numbers of people. Thus on the one hand religion generally urges an indifference to worldly opinion and the acceptance, if necessary, of a position of radical isolation from secular culture but must, for evangelical reasons, be concerned that its core insights, discovered by a few great individuals, be preserved, disseminated, and elaborated on a mass scale. The most radical critic of "the world," even Jesus himself, would be without sustained influence unless this dissemination were possible. Religious movements commonly flourish under the aegis of very powerful personalities with some access to organs of mass communication, although in their initial stages they spread largely through direct personal influence.

In one sense the secular communications media tend to weaken the influence of the churches by controlling the measure of importance conceded them in the public mind—the allotment of time and space clearly implies that religion is less significant than politics, and economics, even sports, entertainment, and cooking. It also tends to define what is significant in religion—contests for church offices between "liberal" and "conservative" factions, for example, which may not be what church leaders themselves conceive as most important. (The strictly spiritual aspects of religious life cannot be easily fitted into the "news" format.) However, the apparently declining influence of organized religion is traceable not only to "secularization," a phenomenon which some sociologists claim has been greatly exaggerated, but also to what is in a way its opposite—the sense that religion is all-pervasive in culture and hence is not by any means exclusive to the churches.

The Invisible Religion and the Identity Crisis

The "religious revival" of the early 1970s differs from the movement after World War II in not leading to a significant increase in church membership. Pentecostalism, Western adoption of Eastern mysticism, the "Jesus Movement" among young people, astrology, etc., have flourished outside the churches altogether or in only very indirect relationship to normal church structures. Part of this has been the logical outcome of liberal theology, with its insistence that man does not find God in an authoritative Revelation but rather searches for Him in the midst of the world; the churches can aid this search but cannot guide and direct it and may be cut off from it altogether by missing the signs of the times. Part is also the result of the fact that the secular media, in response to what is widely perceived as a general spiritual crisis, take more and more responsibility for the articulation of broadly religious themes, to some extent in competition with the churches.

The sociologist Thomas Luckman has defined "the invisible religion" as the general search for self-transcendence and ultimate values which engages practically all men, to greater or less degree, of which formal religion is only one part or manifestation. Everyone is in some sense "religious," therefore, although many reject the teachings of the churches. This religion, as a basic attitude towards life, is manifested in innumerable ways, including political creeds and symbols, moral values, family life, the forms of recreation, popular literature, etc.

Faced with the existence of this "invisible religion," church leaders confront the same dilemma which roughly divides liberal and conservative churches—whether to reaffirm the church's unique message and uncompromisable authority or to accept the role of merely facilitating the "religious" activities already going on everywhere in society. The liberal response, which is generally the latter, keeps the church from seeming to fall behind the march of secular history. But it paradoxically tends also to weaken the church's true "relevance," since the religious leader is often put in the position of seeming merely to echo or applaud ideas and movements originating elsewhere, rather feebly reinforcing the general drift of the culture. There is little to be heard from the church which cannot be heard in purer form somewhere else.

The more conservative churches attempt to maintain a stance of authority and uniqueness, which they are able to do with respect to a limited group of people. They may shun the general culture almost completely, or they may attempt to make compromises with it which are more or less workable (accommodating popular musical forms in worship, for example, or loosening strict moral principles without abrogating them entirely). Their most serious and difficult challenge comes not from militant secular opposition, which if anything promotes group solidarity and thus strengthens belief, but from the evident appropriation of the churches' own religious "property" by other agencies. Leonard Bernstein's *Mass,* which is quite different in spirit and intent from the traditional Catholic service, is a major example, along with the popular musicals *Jesus Christ Superstar* and *Godspell.* The religious leader now finds himself in the unfamiliar position not of preaching God to an indifferent or hostile world but of facing other communicators who in effect claim to preach about Him more effectively and authentically than the church. As Thomas Luckman has pointed out, increasingly people feel justified in appropriating various aspects of religious traditions for purposes alien to these traditions, using them in unstable syntheses which are put together to justify private existence. As yet the conservative churches have found no fully effective strategies for dealing with this tendency. The problem may exist even within a conservative denomination, as spokesmen appear who challenge the authority of officially designated leaders. The latter may find the difficulties of communication within the church almost as great as those posed by the larger society.

There is a communications revolution occurring within the churches whose final outcome is not yet clear and which contains within it certain contradictory elements. Part of it is once more the logical outcome of liberal theology—the sermon gives way to the dialogue, since the clergyman has no special knowledge not accessible to the congregation; traditional religious texts like the Bible no longer have a monopoly in worship, since God's truth can be found everywhere; rituals are no longer fixed and uniform, since each congregation must find what suits it best; traditional church buildings become an embarrassment and may be abandoned for living rooms and store fronts, since there should be no architectural separation between church and world; official creeds are tacitly discarded; traditional symbols are used in new and daring ways remote from the old meanings. In certain ways the logic of liberal theology is in fact the end of religion as a form of mass communication, since the churches are no longer assumed to have a core of unified truth which they can convey to their members in words, rites, and symbols. They are engaged merely in facilitating each individual's search for meaning, and hence are radically fragmented. Thus the nun who discards her baroque habit in order to be more "open" to laymen may soon feel she is no different from laymen and her role as a religious leader becomes highly problematical.

While the Catholic Church, at the time of the Second Vatican Council, appeared to accept belatedly the Protestant emphasis on the centrality of verbal communication—the virtual abolition of the Latin liturgy and a new emphasis on Bible-reading and preaching—the liberal churches have been moving in a somewhat opposite direction, based on an apparent conviction that word culture, as McLuhan insists, is losing its power and based also on the conviction (implicit always in Catholicism but rarely stated) that man's deepest nature is not communicable through words. Rock music, light shows, liturgical dancing, experiments in group dynamics, and psychedelics have all become part of the advanced religious scene.

Virtually all segments of organized religion now sense a profound crisis of identity and authority, which inevitably issues in a communications crisis—no one can hope to be persuasive who does not convey a sense of confidence in his own message, and this evident lack of confidence is perhaps the major problem now affecting religious leaders. They sense that, if it is now more difficult to believe in and communicate belief in religion than it once was, because of the weakening of tradition and social support among other things, it is perhaps also potentially easier, since an evident spiritual malaise has created a mood of searching and restlessness in many people, and there is a renewed openness to the power of myth, symbol, ritual, and mystical experience. The crisis continues, however, both in the religious leader's uncertainty as to how genuine or lasting this new atmosphere will prove to be and whether the leader should approach admittedly confused modern man as the bearer of glad tidings or merely as a perplexed fellow-seeker after truth.

CHAPTER XI

Political Campaigning and Image Building

Richard Redman

The overriding purpose of any political campaign is to win and as a consequence to provide the public with the political leadership it wants and needs.

We in the professional campaign business are not miracle workers. We are tough-minded professionals who use paid media and interpersonal means to present our candidate and tell our story. We help build a good organization—a warm, living, intensely human thing that makes people a part, gives them satisfaction. Only a good organization can seek out the voter person-to-person and say, "Come on, you want to, don't you?"

We see that the campaign is adequately financed. We are certain that our opposition is properly researched and that the opinion of our constituents is sampled and understood.

We put it all together into a well-planned, reasonably smooth running, carefully calculated effort to convince the voters that our candidate is the "best man." In short, we want to make the sale and win the election. The idea is to elect qualified people to run the government, but before even the best people can govern, they must first be elected to office. The old saying, "Losers don't legislate," makes the point clearly.

This chapter provides a view of political campaigning and image building and surveys the methods we use to communicate with and woo the voters. To put contemporary activities in perspective it may be helpful at this point to review briefly the history of professional campaigning and image building.

First, it should be noted that political campaigning and image building is by no means a new profession. The work we do in a political campaign is much the same as the work politicians and campaign man-

agers have done since the time of Caesar. Campaigning is central to the concept of the election and the decisions we have to make in our campaigns are basically the same kind as those made by political managers for centuries.

Modern political campaigning and image building, identical in function to earlier efforts, differ only in terms of size and complexity. One early example in U.S. politics is the election of 1840 in which William Harrison defeated incumbent President Martin Van Buren in a race which many historians termed the first modern presidential campaign.[1] In that election Harrison, a popular Indian fighter and the "Hero of Tippecanoe" ran as the candidate of the Whig Party. The Whigs concluded that their chances of winning depended upon the support of the Western states. They decided that Harrison should be styled as the "people's candidate" to run against the aristocratic Van Buren, a New Yorker.[2]

The Whigs carried their message to the voters with a frenzy. Their slogan, "Tippecanoe and Tyler too" has become an American legend. They held huge rallies and torchlight parades. They used log cabin symbolism to stress Harrison's frontiersman image, and the Whigs sang so many campaign songs that a contemporary claimed, "The campaign was set to music."[3]

The Whigs were more than good advertisers, though. They knew well what their voters wanted. Charles Sellers and Henry May wrote that the Whigs developed "an acute sensitivity to shifts in public opinion and became expert in building coalitions that would yield a majority or near majority."[4]

They maintained a strong campaign organization and a network of partisan newspapers that could get the campaign to the voters and get the voters to the polls. Their success at this is proven by the fact that the election of 1840 brought out 78 percent of the eligible voters—a proportion that Sellers and May hold "may never be equalled again."[5]

Since that time, many of the roles needed in a campaign have become more specialized. Politicians no longer feel entirely capable of handling every aspect of a campaign.

In *Professional Public Relations and Political Power,* Stanley Kelley, Jr. reports that commentaries on political campaigns before and after 1900 note the occasional presence of newspapermen serving as press agents for candidates.[6] After 1900, the practice of employing newspapermen as professional publicity managers increased and by 1928 the professional publicist was viewed a "necessary . . . element in the successful politician's entourage."[7]

Presumably, the first full-time, permanent publicity bureau for a political party was organized by the Democrats after their defeat in the 1928 elections. It was headed by a man named Charles Michelson, a newspaperman, who is thought of as the first to dramatize the usefulness of public relations in politics.[8]

Kelley claims that since the 1930s the trend has been for public relations specialists to involve themselves in politics. He states that public relations men were the moving force in Wendell Willkie's capture of the Republican nomination for President in 1940. In addition he writes that political campaigning has been influenced by the "merchandising experience of business enterprise."[9]

The first participation of an advertising agency in a presidential election race was apparently in General Dwight Eisenhower's 1952 campaign.[10] According to Marvin Weisbord, the author of *Campaigning for President,* the advertising agency Batten, Barton, Durstine, and Osborne played an active and important role in the campaign. ". . . A great public relations and advertising machine was assembling to put words, ideas, and beliefs into the General's mouth," says Weisbord.[11]

In the past twenty years there has been a clear upsurge in the use of communication and information professionals of all kinds in political campaigns, contributing to ever-increasing specialization and complexity.

Basic Elements of a Campaign

The five basic components that make up any campaign are: 1) The Candidate 2) Research 3) Funding 4) Advertising and 5) Organization. I want to examine each element and illustrate its importance and inter-connection in the overall effort.

The Candidate

You can't run a race without a horse and you can't beat a somebody with a nobody. Voters will generally vote for the candidate whom they consider to be the "best man." The fact is that if you run a "turkey" even the best of campaigns will end in disaster at the polls. It is therefore incumbent upon us, early in the game, to determine what makes a good candidate. What are the specific factors that create a good image in the minds of the voters? What are the factors that will cause voters to work for, speak for, and vote for one particular candidate over another? Is the person qualified to help sell his image?

Generally speaking it is these individual factors, synthesized in voters' minds, that constitute the candidate's "qualifications." Obviously, all voters do not weigh specific characteristics in the same way. But there are many common characteristics that are deemed to be important qualifications by most voters. What follows is a check list of possible assets or liabilities that may be helpful in evaluating a candidate's potential.

Personal Qualifications
1. *Physical appearance.* How does the candidate look? Is he tall, or short? Fat or thin? Is he someone who commands attention, or is he the kind of person who can slip out of a room without being noticed?
2. *Special training or talent.* Is the candidate skilled in public

address and debate? Does he know how to appear on television, on radio, or before an audience?

3. *Age.* Is he too young, or too old? Is he forty, but looks sixty, or is he fifty, but looks thirty?

4. *Education.* Where did he go to school? What degrees does he hold? Is a college degree particularly necessary for the office or the area from which he is running?

5. *Family background.* Does the candidate come from a family of bootleggers, or does he come from a family of distinguished, well respected people in the community?

6. *Occupation.* Is the candidate's occupation such that he will have time to campaign? Is his occupation logical for the particular position he is seeking?

7. *Ability to meet people.* Is he an introvert or an extrovert? Does he enjoy meeting other people, does he meet them easily, do they like to meet him?

8. *Sincerity.* Is he sincere? Does he appear to be sincere?

9. *Temperament.* Does he have an even disposition, or is he likely to fly off the handle at the slightest provocation?

10. *General health.* Is the candidate's health good? Does he have a permanent ailment which could cause him difficulty during the campaign or while in office?

11. *Leadership quality.* Has he demonstrated qualities of leadership in other capacities, in his church, in civic affairs, in business? Do people believe in him, do they want to help him?

12. *Administrative ability.* Has he shown in business, or as a volunteer that he can administer a program, serve as an executive, delegate responsibility, get a job done?

13. *Reputation among opinion makers.* Do community leaders like and respect the individual? Does he have a reputation for making the right decisions at the right time? Are his decisions based on fact and what is best for all concerned?

General Qualifications
1. A desire to serve, a willingness to devote adequate time to campaigning and service after the election.
2. Previous public service.
3. Knowledge of the district and its problems.
4. Knowledge of the issues.
5. Reputation with party regulars.
6. Degree of involvement in local issues.
7. Relative potential strength in the district.

Honest answers must be provided to the following questions: Is he of strong moral character, a law abiding citizen without a record of criminal or major traffic convictions? Does he fulfill all of the legal requirements to run for office, including citizenship and residency?

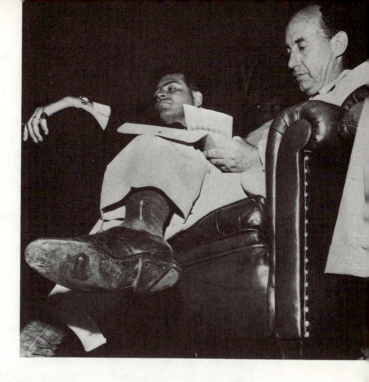

Does he have the training and experience to handle the office he seeks? Has he served honorably in the military service, and if not, does he have an acceptable rationale? Is he friendly and easily met? Can he speak and relate to large and small audiences? Is he well known in the community, having participated in community affairs? Is his running compatible with his financial capacity and obligations? Would he be subject to conflict of interest charges? Has he made public statements or had any prior associations which could be particularly damaging?

Considering the foregoing, we look at the candidate from two perspectives—first, his capacity to win the election, and second, his capacity to perform after he is elected. If the candidate ranks high on each item on the checklist, is a Republican, and is interested in our services, we are interested in working for him. We work only for Republicans because my personal philosophy is represented best by that party and feel that a definite conflict of interest would be created by working for one party and then the other.

It should be emphasized that right answers to the preceding questions are not a guarantee of success. Politics is highly competitive and unpredictable, and the picture is changed many times by factors outside the candidate's control. He doesn't always get to pick the issues of the campaign. For example, in 1964, many governors, congressmen, state legislators, and other candidates found themselves in the position of defending and explaining Senator Goldwater's position on a number of issues. Whether his position was right, wrong, or misunderstood, it still had to be taken into account. Similarly the controversies associated with the Nixon administration set an agenda which Republican candidates at all levels had to take into account.

Obviously, an incumbent Attorney General seeking re-election can be placed in a very difficult position by a sudden national crime wave, or other disturbing fact, which is totally beyond his control. A candidate for Congress in an agricultural district could well be in trouble over the price of hogs, a factor over which he has little or no control.

Next to the candidate himself, the primary source of personal appeal lies with the candidate's family. An articulate and attractive wife can be a highly effective campaigner. Another asset can be the candidate's children, although sometimes there is some reluctance to involve them in a campaign.

If we decide to use the candidate's family in a campaign we use them in a manner that is comfortable to them. Campaigns are bad enough on families. If they want to participate we let them do what comes naturally to them.

A good candidate must have an intense desire to win the election and a great desire to serve his constituency to the best of his ability. He must be willing to make both the personal and material sacrifices required for a vigorous campaign. He will be required to answer complaints he doesn't want to hear from the voters, to listen to advice he doesn't need from well-meaning but uninformed supporters, to speak to many groups that don't interest him, and to hold unwanted press conferences. All of this is necessary. When the candidate does appear, he must induce a genuine interest from his prospective constituents. If there is one thing you must prove to the voter it is that you are sincerely interested in him—concerned about him and his problems.

I am reminded of the United States Senate candidate who worked long and hard—probably the hardest working candidate I have ever known. Unfortunately during a long campaign he turned into a kind of "mechanical man," who went through the motions, met the people, shook the hands, made the speeches, had something to offer, but lacked the personal warmth and the sincerity necessary to make a voter want to vote for him.

Finally, in determining the image that our candidate will take to the public it must be remembered that there are three kinds of voters: (a) those who will vote for your candidate, no matter what; (b) those who will vote for your opposition, no matter what; (c) those who are undecided. And it is, therefore, upon the undecided voter that attention is focused. It is the undecided voter who must be won over to your candidate.

The undecided voter almost always asks two questions: Firstly, why should I vote for you? And, secondly, what's in it for me? I concur with experts who observe that there are seven basic ways to get the undecided voter.

1. He must like the candidate's theme—the platform—what the candidate is for.
2. He must be against the same things the candidate is against.

3. He must appreciate the candidate's image—family life, church affiliation, war record, etc.
4. There must be some difference between the candidate and his opponent that reflects favorably on the candidate and against his opponent.
5. The voter must recognize your candidate's name. He has seen it, heard it, knows it.
6. Your candidate has made personal contact with him. Your candidate knocked at his door. He heard the candidate speak. He feels an "I know him personally" relationship.
7. Your candidate should have third party endorsements. Mrs. Jones, the voter's neighbor is for your candidate. Therefore the voter will vote for your candidate because Mrs. Jones recommends him.

Research

Research is another vital function of campaigning; campaign managers who conduct too little research run the risk of losing out of ignorance. Campaign research can be divided into five basic categories.

Voter Turnout The first sort of research involves a very careful collection, correlation, and analysis of past voter turnout and voter registration figures. Allocating resources on a basis of where the most voters exist is particularly important in early planning. Although the contribution ratio method is a very simple kind of study, it produces some very dramatic results. For example, such a study shows us that fifty-six percent of the total Republican vote in New York State lies in seven counties.

A voter turnout study reveals election district turnouts in typical off-year and state-wide elections. It is quite common to find very substantial differences from one year to another—often varying as much as twenty percent.

In terms of planning for any given campaign, this kind of information is very important and must be taken into account. An attempt must be made to estimate what the voter turnout will be for a given year, it is not enough just to work with the total number of voters. It is necessary to have an estimate of how voters actually have appeared at the polls in each area for comparable past elections. Through such statistical studies we can determine for any given area the number of people who are likely to vote Republican or Democrat. Together they represent about seventy percent of the total vote. This means that the number of people to whom campaigns are important, the number of people who are going to be influenced one way or the other by what your candidate does, is not one hundred percent. Rather it is a small percentage of the total vote which we call the "swing vote" or the "influenceable vote." These people appear in irregular patterns throughout any district. A dollar spent in areas where the swing vote is over five percent will produce greater dividends than a dollar spent in one of the areas where little swing is probable.

Socio-Economic Conditions The second area of statistical research—analyzing the socio-economic characteristics of an area—involves data which is not easily obtained and is outdated quickly. However, census data can tell a great deal about the kind of people who live in the area where you are campaigning. By using district map overlays you can develop information about each of the major political subdivisions within the district, and get an idea where certain groups of people live.

Polling is another essential part of the research function. Although it is expensive, polling is one of the best forms of insurance known to a political candidate. A good poll cannot only indicate to us where our candidate stands in the race but why, and in the long run a poll can be a money saver because of the variety of information we can receive from it. Pollster Louis Harris in 1963 mentioned three sorts of information gathered from a poll that can be useful in political campaigns:[12] The first is in charting the anatomy of the voting public—a poll can indicate racial-religious patterns, nationality-group differences, occupational differences, etc. This information enables us to figure out how to put a majority together. The second major use of polls in campaign research is in determining what the electorate thinks of the candidate. This involves finding out how many people know who he is, and what the public thinks of him both as a man and a public figure. The third area of usefulness is in the definition of issues. A well-constructed poll can be an important tool in deciding what issues people feel are crucial and, equally or sometimes even more important, in what areas, and among which groups, particular issues are important. Having this information enables us to pinpoint the issues we want to talk about, and allows us to talk to audiences about particular issues with which they may be concerned.

Thus, for professional campaigners and image builders, polls can indicate how effectively we are doing our job of selling the candidate's message, and can tell us where we need to improve.

The Opposition The third major area of research is that which is done on the opposition, Particularly if you are running against an incumbent, the opponent's record provides a wealth of information, but you must have manpower to go after it. Newspaper morgues are very valuable for this type of research. However, for every real nugget you find, you will turn up a hundred items you can't use.

For example, a search of one opponent's voting record as a state legislator revealed that he had been a leading opponent of a thruway. In the entire upstate area the thruway was regarded as one of the great gifts of all time. From the opponent's view, as a "Big City" legislator fifteen years before, it was probably a wise decision to oppose the highway. But it was not a wise decision in light of his later interests. It took hours of digging to come up with that one kernel which could be translated into a useful political issue.

It is also crucial to know as much about your own candidate as the other side is going to. Know what he has said and done. There is nothing more embarrassing in a campaign than to come down to the last few weeks and have your opponent level a charge about a statement he alleges your candidate made ten or twelve years before, and have no one on your staff know whether your candidate actually said it.

Researching the Issues Major issue research is the fourth area. In every campaign a survey will indicate that there are certain overriding problems on the minds of the voters in your district. On these, of course, your candidate cannot avoid taking positions. These positions should be as full and comprehensive as possible.

Once a position paper of 40 to 50 pages has been prepared on a particular major issue, it must be "boiled down" to its essence. For example, a crime position paper can be worked into something the average housewife or man-in-the-street could read, understand, and be influenced by. Reams of crime statistics can be broken down to show how many crimes were committed every hour. It is frightening to read that in a particular city there is a murder every 14 hours, a reported rape every 6 hours, an assault every 6 minutes, and a theft every 3 minutes. This kind of thing makes the crime rate very real to a housewife whose husband just left to go bowling.

A critical function of major issue research effort is the dramatization of campaign issues. You are trying to cut through all the other messages directed at the public. Political campaigns never operate in a vacuum. People are being bombarded daily with thousands of advertising impressions. Your message has to have impact and must be directly related to people's concerns.

The fifth component of research deals with local issues, and is especially crucial in campaigns with funding limitations.

Issues which are of significance locally must be ferreted out. For example, one candidate wrote a letter to the traffic commissioner about the absence of a street light on a particular intersection at which a number of small children had been injured over a five year period. The local residents were so concerned for the safety of their children that they had organized a neighborhood association to petition the city to put in a street light. No action had been taken by the city, however. After the candidate sent his letter, his people talked with the head of the local civic association and it was agreed that association members would distribute the letter to every household in the neighborhood. Nine thousand flyers of the letter were printed because it was a highrise apartment area in a very congested part of the city.

This activity had great impact on the people living in the neighborhood because it dealt with an issue affecting their daily lives. The candidate probably cannot begin to shake hands with every person in his district, however, he can reach them in a personal way on subjects about which the people care deeply.

It is an unfortunate thing for a candidate to commit himself on issues on which he cannot deliver. Although there is always a temptation to make outlandish proposals, such proposals will come back to haunt. It is tough in a re-election campaign when an opponent starts talking about the things on which your candidate failed to deliver.

Fund Raising

Fifty years ago Will Rogers said, "Politics has got so expensive that it takes a whale of a lot of money just to get beat." Actually, however, the cost of campaigns is frequently overstated. For example, it has been estimated that in 1970 some $300,000,000 was spent on political campaigns—by both parties and on all individual campaigns for public office nationwide. By the same token, Procter and Gamble spent $275,000,000 on advertising in 1970.

Nevertheless, large sums of money are needed for campaigns and this money must be raised. There is no secret formula for raising political funds. The only way to get money is to ask for it, and the more people you ask the more money you're going to get. Who does the asking, when it is done, and how the approach is made are keys to the success of the operation.

Laying the Groundwork The first part of any fund-raising effort is preparation. A detailed budget must be prepared so you know how much money is needed. A budget also helps answer questions about how the money will be used. The income budget shows how much you plan to raise. Included should be projected incomes from larger giver solicitation, fund-raising dinners, door-to-door drives, and special projects.

It is critical to have a broad financial base for successful fund-raising. All of the money cannot be raised from the five richest people in town. Nor can it be raised with the buck-a-head approach alone, when integrated, these two approaches, with some intermediate levels, are effective. If a person can afford to give $5,000 or more, he should be asked. On the other hand, if a person is in the $1.00 category, he also should be asked. We cannot overlook the importance of large contributions, nor can we underestimate the importance of getting people involved by putting a few bucks on the line in support of something they believe in.

A list of solid reasons for contributing also must be prepared. Competition for the dollar is keen and prospective contributors usually must be shown why their participation is vital at this time. They must be assured that their dollars will be used wisely.

The over-financed Presidential campaign of 1972 and the subsequent Watergate scandal underscore most dramatically the need for broad-based fund-raising activity and support by large numbers of people. People like to back a winner and the 1972 Presidential campaign was a unique opportunity to support an almost sure thing, which is exactly what people did. There was a kind of frenzy to make a substantial contribution to the President's campaign and get on the "good" list of large contributors. Clearly the Watergate investigation raised serious questions and issues of widespread concern related to the whole spectrum of political fund raising.

Most people contribute because they believe in the cause or the candidate and they want to help. They do not expect favors in return. For each of the illegal gifts exposed by the Watergate investigation, there are tens of thousands of contributions which were given to support a conviction and with no strings attached. It is unfortunate that these things go unnoticed while a handful of alleged influence purchasers grab headlines.

Organization, Attitude, Accountability

The second element of fund raising is organization—people to communicate with other people to raise money. The better the people recruited, the better the organization, and the more successful the fund raising results.

Attitude is the third and most crucial component in the fund-raising effort. Little money will be raised if you and your finance organization don't think it can be. You should believe your candidate is the best. No one wants to put money on a loser. People want a winner and the approach has to be just that—one of a winner.

The fourth fund-raising ingredient is accountability. You must see to it that every one of your finance workers knows exactly what he is to do, whom he is supposed to call on, and how much he is supposed to raise. Check on him until he gets the job done. The people you recruited are likely to be busy individuals. Sometimes a friendly phone call every couple of days until the job is completed will suffice to keep your finance workers on their toes. You simply have to set up an organization and follow through until the job is done.

The fifth and final ingredient in political fund raising is hard work. It requires long hours. People who are going to contribute will not come looking for you. Nor will people you recruit be running up and down the street looking for work. You have to find people, encourage them, help them, and keep with them until the job is done. In short, fund-raising success wll not belong to the disorganized, the shy or the weak, but to those with a goal, a purpose, and a direct approach.

Political fund-raisers are always looking for new ways to stimulate contributions. A few years ago I was attending a breakfast meeting called for the purpose of organizing ticket sales for a $100-a-plate dinner called "An Evening With Art Linkletter." While I was there a fellow laughingly told me that he'd make a contribution if he could put it on his credit card. The remark kept rattling around in my mind. On the face of it, the idea seemed preposterous. But then it occurred to me that thousands of people charge dinners at Playboy Clubs, Sardi's, and other places. Why not a political fund-raising dinner? What's the difference? I tried it out on some business leaders and bankers and they were excited over the possibilities. So we figured out a system that would work.

Cards were sent out to prospective buyers of $100 tickets to the dinner. If a contributor wanted to dine on his "political credit" all he needed to do was return a card authorizing the party's central committee to charge it against his ",BankAmericard" or "Master Charge" account. The orders were then deposited in banks handling these two credit card systems and we had cash in the bank instead of no sale!

Advertising

The role of advertising in a campaign is not usually well understood. Advertising is a business which is much more artistic than scientific, more a matter of emotion than fact or logic. People in this business operate as much by the feeling in their stomachs as through facts from research or opinion polls. Their talent is producing images, words, and pictures while differentiating between importance and irrelevance. They are curious, inquisitive, skeptical, and mostly optimistic.

Advertising people believe that almost anything can be sold with imagination, and that in clumsy hands even the most acceptable propositions will crumble. Advertising is a business of selling. And selling, be it hard or soft, loud or quiet, in whispers or in blowing trumpets, must be in accord with individual insights as to what is required to make the sale.

This point is well illustrated by the imaginative approach that was developed for Robert D. Ray during his campaign for Governor of Iowa in 1968.

In November of 1967, an individual who was particularly interested in the Ray campaign was vacationing in Hawaii. He was poolside, soaking up the sun and listening to a portable radio. A song caught his attention. It was "Step To The Rear" from the Broadway show,

"How Now Dow Jones." The singer was Marilyn Maye, a native of Des Moines. That was it—the perfect campaign song!

Upon returning to Iowa he bought the record and played it for two or three key people, including the candidate. It was agreed! This was the song but the lyrics would have to be rewritten to personalize the effort. All the arrangements for the use of the song were made, and the song, sung by "Iowa's own Marilyn Maye" was introduced to the public.

The song proved to be a great hit. It was Bob Ray's theme song—wherever he went that song was played. In fact the song had such impact that during the last week of the campaign the opposition candidate was answering the commercials by pleading with Iowans not to "sell out for a song."

Most assuredly, there was a lot more to Robert D. Ray than a song. But the song was used to get people's attention, to set the mood of the campaign, to make them listen to what Bob Ray had to say. It was a proper accent for a candidate of substance and quality. It was an imaginative approach to winning an election in order that a highly competent and qualified man could serve as governor.

Advertising people are hired by candidates or their organizations to interpret to the public not what is, but what they suspect the people will want it to be; that is, not pure truth but a digestible version of it. This does not mean we hold the truth to be of no account. Knowing the truth is important because once we know it we can use it. The contemplation and assessment of evidence and facts is important because few new ideas come "out of the air." Advertising is selling a vision and inspiring a response.

If a candidate has an unpopular viewpoint on an issue of concern to the voters, he at least can express it in words that are tolerable. If a candidate does not like to shake hands, he can shake one hand well. A cameraman can record the handshake and it can be put on television. Candidates are never limited to what they are.

People vote on impression, on feelings they have about a man and about who they believe the man to be. Newspapers will not write "Joe Smith, candidate for the Senate, is a very sensitive human being." They will not dramatize what a candidate believes are his accomplishments.

Voters judge candidates on honesty, confidence, and charisma. When you get down to charisma, what do we do with a bald and pudgy man running against a Kennedy-like figure? Does he have a chance to win the election even if he is really the better man? What's wrong with trying to compensate for what are merely physical defects by skillful use of the camera? Why should a blemish keep good people out of office?

The public is not deceived. Shouldn't a candidate have one chance to tell his story in his way? Is it immoral for superficial defects to receive some amount of compensation? I don't think so.

Political image makers are frequently accused of giving irrelevancies, and of failure to give the substance of the issue. Of course we don't explain. We motivate. That's our job. We're not teachers, we're political managers. We're trying to win.

Elections aren't won or lost on the basis of hard news. They are won by how people feel coupled with the ability of the campaign organization to get its candidate's supporters to the polls.

As professional campaigners and image builders we deal with human nature. And people often use these frail criteria to determine for whom they will vote.

Take the late Senator Winston Prouty of Vermont. A wisened little man, he was running against a handsome opponent. Compensation had to be and was made. An emotional feeling was created about him through music. Some said it looked and sounded like a Whitman Sampler put into musical notes. But it was important. Is that wrong?

In addition to interpreting the candidate's message to the public and helping him to overcome his shortcomings both politically and as a campaigner, those of us involved in campaign advertising must know how to send our messages through those media that will reach those segments of the populace with whom we want to communicate.

Some media are more suited to one type of message than others, and some media attract different audiences than others. The planning of an advertising campaign must be done by professionals who have a knowledge of how to say what to whom at what time if the campaign is to be successful and efficient.

The financial position of a campaign, along with a host of other factors, can have a great effect upon how the candidate's message is taken to the people. A good example of this can be seen in Lawton Chiles' 1970 campaign for the U.S. Senate from Florida. Lacking the funding base for a heavy media campaign, Chiles was forced to work with media which were less expensive. In an imaginative effort, Chiles walked from one end of the state to another talking face-to-face with other Floridians.

His unusual style of campaigning achieved notoriety not only in the Florida press but all over the country. Thus he was able to gain free access to the mass media his campaign needed since the network saw his campaign as news, not advertising.

Organization

The primary function of any political organization is to win elections. Politics is a hard-nosed business. Merely calling some one on the phone to see if they have registered is not enough. You have to grind out the vote. There is no consolation prize. In politics you either win or lose! The organization is the vehicle through which the staff and volunteer workers are able to sell the candidate to prospective voters. The organization must identify the friendly voters, deliver them to the polls on election day, and insure that their ballots are properly counted.

The precinct is the smallest unit of the American political system. Out of these units are constructed the great pluralities that elect men and women to the highest offices of the land. To locate voters, to register them so they are eligible to vote, and to bring them to the polls, you have to reach them in the precinct. This has been true ever since the ballot box was invented. It's still true today. Even with television campaigning, mass meetings, newspaper advertising, and electioneering gimmicks, there is still no substitute for down-to-earth, house-to-house, person-to-person precinct work.

In order to accomplish these tasks each precinct elects precinct committeemen and committeewomen, the party leaders of these units. The job of the precinct committeewoman and committeeman is to work the precinct; to do all the things necessary to turn out the biggest vote possible on Election Day. The precinct committeeman and committeewoman are Mr. and Mrs. Grassroots.

Back in the 1840 Presidential campaign of William Henry Harrison, Abraham Lincoln, then a member of the Whig Party, wrote to some political friends in Illinois: "The whole state must be so well organized that every Whig can be brought to the polls. So divide your county into small districts," Lincoln continued, "And appoint in each a committee. Make a perfect list of the voters and ascertain with certainty for whom they will vote. Keep constant watch on the doubtful voters and have them talked to by those in whom they have the most confidence. On election day see that every Whig is brought to the polls."

His close attention to precinct organization, historians say, did as much for Abraham Lincoln as his famous stump speeches.

Political organizations depend upon volunteer workers for the "nuts and bolts" work of the campaign. Most volunteer workers are amateurs. They are not politically oriented but they have tremendous enthusiasm for the job and a great interest in your candidate. All that is necessary is for the campaign organization to tell the volunteers how to perform their tasks. They must be told how to operate an area headquarters, how to organize volunteers, how to register voters, and how to get publicity. They should be supplied with important statements by your candidate as well as his opponent's key statements. A volunteer must know what to say when his friends or neighbors praise the opponent or attack his candidate.

Most important of all, volunteers need a timetable. They are a very volatile group, wildly enthusiastic one day and terribly depressed the next. A stabilizing influence must be provided to prevent this. Just as many candidates have been defeated because their campaign organization became over confident on October 15 as have been defeated because their campaign organization gave up on October 15.

Even in this age of computers, automatic telephoning devices, satellite communications, high-speed presses, and Pitney Bowes letter machines, people who volunteer to work in campaigns remain the most important, yet least expensive, of all campaign commodities. While adding a great deal of enthusiasm to the campaign, volunteers can also indicate widespread grassroots support. They can act as pulse takers by feeding public opinion and reaction to "campaign central" throughout the race.

Conclusion

The preceding pages have touched upon the five basic components necessary to any political campaigning and image building effort. What should be remembered, however, is that an effective campaign is the product of good co-ordination between each of the five components.

Without a good candidate no campaign can hope to succeed. Without research the candidate is not as able to respond to the issues the public feels are important. Neither is he able to know what people think of him as a public figure, or where his support within the electorate lies. And without good advertising and a hard-working, competent organization that can get the voters out, the campaign will fail.

Any campaign that cannot raise funds is a lost cause. Without money there is no research, organization, or advertising. But, as we saw earlier, contributors would rather back a winner than a loser. Unless there is a good candidate, an effective organization, solid research, and advertising that gets the message to the voters strongly and accurately, potential contributors will not back the venture.

A campaign is a living, breathing thing. It depends upon the effective operation and co-ordination of all of its components. And the lifeblood of a political campaign is communication.

For those of us engaged in this exciting form of mass communication, we work constantly to be more skillful at our profession—to develop new techniques and to improve upon methods of getting a particular candidate across.

We consider politics the most important profession in the world. We feel you can't do anything more important. Preachers do a lot to save souls. Doctors do a lot to save bodies. But politics controls the lives of people. It determines whether people have freedom and practically everything else that is really meaningful.

And as we practice our profession these words turn over and over in our minds: "Winning may not be everything but losing is nothing."

Notes and References

1. Charles Sellers and Henry May, *A Synopsis of American History,* (Rand McNally: Chicago, 1969) p. 144.
2. *Ibid.*, p. 143.
3. Wilfred Binkley, *American Political Parties—Their Natural History,* (Alfred A. Knopf: New York, 1962) p. 175.
4. Sellers, *op. cit.,* p. 144.
5. *Ibid.*
6. Stanley Kelley, Jr., *Professional Public Relations and Political Power,* (Johns Hopkins Press: Baltimore, 1956) p. 28.
7. *Ibid.*, p. 29.
8. *Ibid.*, pps. 30–32.
9. *Ibid.*, p. 32.
10. Marvin Weisbord, *Campaigning for President,* (Public Affairs Press: Washington D.C., 1964) p. 151.
11. *Ibid.*, pp. 152–153.
12. Louis Harris' article, "Polls and Politics in the United States" from Donald Herzberg and Gerald M. Pomper, *American Party Politics—Essays and Readings,* (Holt, Rinehart, and Winston, Inc.: New York, 1966) pps. 175–179.

COMMENTARY
Architecture and Restaurants:
Creating the Physical and Contextual Environment

Our reformulations of the concepts of mass communication and mass communication institutions make it reasonably easy to deal with generalized notions such as knowledge or ideology. One can clearly see how such socially created constructs are born, elaborated, disseminated, reified, and ultimately altered or replaced. What is perhaps a more difficult transition is understanding such socially constructed realities when they are translated into physical form. Among the more pervasive elements of society's mass produced reality are its physical and spatial structures—buildings, parks, restaurants, landmarks—created to facilitate and shelter human activity. From the buildings in which we conduct basic personal functions, like sleeping and eating, to the structures which house society's most complex institutions, the role of the physical and contextual environment in our daily lives is substantial.

Architectural structures and their placement play a major role in shaping the symbolic reality within which the individual organizes, even in childhood as he/she learns where to sleep, what to sleep on, and develops a set of expectations about privacy. The choice and placement of furniture, the size, shape and decor of rooms, whether "homes" are contained in houses or multi-family dwellings, where such structures are located relative to other structures, and so on, all are important factors in shaping the symbolic realities of their inhabitants. And, what one learns in response to the physical and contextual environment varies from one home to the next, from one region to the next, and most dramatically, from one culture to the next.

This physical translation of our symbolic realities is, indeed, a most curious one. Our physical and contextual environment is clearly a consequence of symbolic realities brought about through social communication, and yet by its very nature it in turn fosters the perpetuation or alteration of those same symbolic realities. Beyond that, it serves as a spawning bed for a variety of new and related realities, many of which become so complex that they are beyond the grasp of most members of the society from which they evolved. Humankind's notion of territory and territorial prerogatives serves as one such example. The manner in which we have agreed to deal with property, to design "houses," to affix boundaries, and so on, has resulted in a highly complex web of real estate "laws" and legal procedures which the average citizen is incapable of either understanding or personally handling for himself or herself.

A very abbreviated list of related realities center on "codes of neighborliness," "upkeep," home and property "enhancement," "property values," selectiveness of inhabitants, racial and ethnic issues, "the local school problem," or the requisite (proper?) number of times one should fertilize the lawn each summer.

The next two chapters, at quite varying levels of analysis, address themselves to these and other issues involving the relationship of humans and their physical and contextual environment. The relationship between architectural structures and human behavior is the topic of Chapter XII, "Architecture: Medium and Message." Structures and spaces, the authors explain, are both mass communication messages and channels, more or less simultaneously. Structures and spaces provide a medium through which man conducts his life activities, as well as a set of messages regarding the behaviors which are appropriate in a particular culture, a particular place, and at a particular point in history.

The authors note, that, although the physical and contextual environment is pervasive in influence, that influence process is subtle, cyclical, often taken-for-granted, and may easily go unnoticed, much as the air we breathe.

One way to highlight the functioning of these particular mass communication institutions is to consider *a particular place,* its nature, form, and function. There are virtually an infinite number of such architectural artifacts one might select—highway systems, parks, restaurants, public housing, landmarks, office buildings, churches, etc. But for our purposes, we have chosen to focus on a single physical and contextual environment—Sardi's Restaurant in New York City—as an example of one very intriguing mass communication institution.

In our culture when one thinks about "places" to eat, words like restaurant, cafe, cafeteria, come to mind. The range of such structures and contexts is substantial. On one extreme are the "fast food restaurants," like McDonalds, which are painstakingly engineered to meet the audiences need for food, economy, and speed. On the other, are restaurants like Sardi's, which provide a carefully constructed context designed to send a variety of messages having to do with status, luxury, and fashionability, while at the same time meeting the desires of their audience "to eat." Further, while the success of restaurants such as Burger King depend upon the audience not conceiving of the structure as a channel for social interaction, the effectiveness of Sardi's messages demands that they do.

In Chapter XIII Vincent Sardi provides a case study which affords a number of insights into the subtleties of message design, channel selection, and audience segmentation, as they relate to the restaurant as a kind of mass communication institution. The analysis suggests many parallels between the activities of persons whose job it is to shape the contextual reality, and persons serving in more traditional mass communication institutions. The case study is useful in itself, and more importantly, we believe, suggestive of the sort of conceptual framework and mode of analysis which can be provocative for considering the range of mass communication institutions which shape, and are in turn shaped by, our physical and contextual environment.

CHAPTER XII

Architecture:

Medium and Message

Brent D. Ruben and Paolo Soleri[1]

Human history is fundamentally a saga of the manipulation of the physical world to produce myriad forms, small and large, private and public, lasting and ephemeral, humble and flamboyant, functional and symbolic. Those physical things make up man's environment where his children learn about normal behavior, peer-grooming, respectability and so on. Man molds himself by molding the physical environ, and his matrix fits closely with his physical matrix he inherits, and the one he himself is altering through his own existence.

In its broadest significance, architecture embraces just about the whole of this non-disposable, non-instant, and relatively non-obsolete world. *Architecture* stands for the alterations made upon nature by the organic, psychological, and spiritual components of man's consciousness and by social and cultural endeavor. Architecture, again in its broader scope, is not only a shelter for communication and information institutions—a medium—but also strongly and directly, at times over-bearingly, mass-information itself—a message—a multiplication of messages.

Architecture in this generic perspective, is not simply concerned with the structure of buildings but rather with the configuration and dynamics of human environments. One cannot even begin to enumerate the number and the specific identity of the most famous examples. A few at random: Babylon, Chichen Itza, Jerusalem, Karnak, Athens, Angkor Wat, Peking, Lhasa, Algiers, Carthage, Rome, Amsterdam, Istanbul, Venice, Florence, Paris, London, Leningrad, Calcutta, New York, New Orleans, San Francisco, and on. And there is the even more numerous group of smaller cities and then the small enclaves of towns and villages. For each of them there is a specific ethos that reflects uniquely the spirit of the inhabitants.

214

The physical world and the world of architecture is the objectification of the world of information in which we are all immersed as in an all-enveloping continuum; a continuum sensitive to our responses as much as we are sensitive to its challenges. We are, as any living thing is, under a constant assault of information, a limited part of which is verbalized, abstracted, and fed back to us to reinforce the importance of this enveloping environment. The most salient information for man does not come via verbal conceptualizations, but via odors, taste, sounds, light, and settings. Every one of us has felt the poignancy of a familiar and, even sometimes, not too pleasant smell. An olfactory datum triggers an avalanche of information, well forgotten but neatly stored away in the helix of our memories. In fact, what comes back is not the "objective" information but the subjective emotion shrouded around a past event.

Architecture as Medium

There is not, notwithstanding McLuhan, an unbreakable relationship between a medium and a message. Vietnam would have been with us even if the electronic conveyor of the messages were only the radio. But for the edifice or man-made environ it is a different story. There the media, the physical structures, are more than mediators between an event and the perceptional system, the person. The mediator becomes the actor, that is to say, it is actually information by itself and of itself instead of being a "remote" presence—a conveyor, as is the wire in the telephone, the transistor in the radio, or the picture tube in the TV set.

What makes a medium also a message is the non-mediatory character of the system itself. To "perceive" the taste of an apple is to taste an apple. The apple is then a medium which is also an information source. To attempt to "perceive" the taste of an apple by an hour long special on TV crashes head-on with the incapability of the medium of television to be specifically more than a message diffusion device. As such, it can deliver only that which can be abstracted from any event and conveyed through the mechanisms of its own nature. With television, this nature is visual, not tactile, nor tastable, nor smellable. It is oral, by the auxiliary of a sound system, and visual by definition. TV is therefore viable whenever an event can be dissected and abstracts of such dissections can be constrained into either the channel of sound or that of sight. It is versatile, but remote, because of the nature of the very process of dissection, abstraction, and re-construction. It is a manipulative, interpretative, confounding, and detached way of bringing the semblance of an event to a witness. Moreover, since the visual-oral dimensions themselves are only two elements of any event, even the visual-oral communication of visual-oral events suffers crippling limitations. Vietnam again has made the point. Ugly pictures and ugly sounds do not, cannot, compete with direct contact which involves personal suffering, participation, sacrifice and is durational in nature.

As any other technological medium, television is abstractional and a simplifier. It is abstractional because everything that comes on the tube and the loudspeaker has to be converted to signals which are transmittable by the technology. It is a simplifier because the channeling process itself can only be done by a reduction in the complexity of information.

Architecture as Message

In considering the edifice or a group of edifices and their interspaces, we see a much different situation. What they communicate is also what they are. That is to say, they are media that cannot stay away from intruding as a message. Architectural structures instigate, participate in, shape, and imprint the events that they contain. It helps little to say that in some measure this is also true for the TV. The influence of a technological system cannot obscure the distinction between medium and message. In distinction, the "ideal" man-made environ is a powerful presence which itself is acting upon the actors which it shelters. Thus, although it has purpose as a medium it has even a greater purpose as a message.

Modes of Architectural Transformation

The environment is a formidable teacher, indeed, of ourselves, the sensuous receivers-intensifiers-transformers-transmitters. Hence, the architectural milieu does not simply inform us, it acknowledges in

us our own identity by the coordination of our being with our becoming.

There are two different ways by which we transform "nature," producing a totally man-ordered environment: one way is agriculture. Immense sections of every continent, excluding perhaps Latin America, Australia and Siberia, are physically restructured so as to present a surface which only remotely resembles what used to be in eons past. To understand the scale of the transformation, one could try to imagine the Europe as it might have been before the appearance of large human settlements—a cross between the Amazonian forest and the Wyoming prairies—and the Europe of today.

A similar discourse could be made for the second way by which man transforms nature: Man the city builder, constructs his habitat and the places that contain and shelter the institutions of life, work, exchange, socialization, culture, worship, etc. It could be a similar discourse, if it were not for the fact that there is in this second way a special kind of intensity and the definite appearance of the "man-made." In a true sense, in this second way it is as if each stone and brick, each chunk of mortar, each splinter of wood, iron or bronze was imbued of the light and the heat of the struggle put up by man in the face of a stubborn nature.

If one looks for mass-information in its compelling and lasting results, one cannot but see the difference and the respective impact of the two modes; the early wilderness and the tamed landscape. In both cases, it is a kind of information whose pervasiveness itself makes it

difficult to be conscious of. As the liquid medium of water goes un-noticed by the fish, although it is responsible for its morphology and its existence, so it is for the information envelope which invests and makes man from his ancestral childhood.

Structure and Function

All but infrequently, architecture has been less concerned with its critical functions in the interplay between man and nature than with the technical and structural pragmatics associated with the planning of exterior and interior design, and the placement and landscaping of buildings. By design, more often by default, the environment has suffered from architectural thinking which has emphasized the structural and technological at the expense of the functional and spiritual.

This environmental reshaping has been undertaken with precious little knowledge of what we are doing to ourselves in the process.[2]

> The design professions ranging from interior decorators concerned with single offices to regional planners with entire river valleys are involved to varying degrees. . . . It is as if the structure itself—harmony with the site, the integrity of the materials, the cohesiveness of the separate units—has become the function. This is predictable in the case of the architect who, in his training and practice learns to look at buildings without people in them. Lavishly colored photographs in glossy magazines show empty rooms and corridors, tables fully set with plates, silverware, and wine glasses, an open book on the sofa, and a fire in the hearth but not a sign of people anywhere.[3]

The consequences of structure-centered approaches to architectural thinking surround us everywhere, whether we examine environmental manipulation at the level of global and national geography, agricultural and urban landscape, or neighborhood and home design. And it isn't necessary to venture far from one's personal experience to illustrate the point, as behavioral scientist Robert Sommer suggests in a discussion of classroom design in his book *Personal Space:*

> Interior classroom space is all too frequently taken for granted by those who plan educational facilities as well as those who use them. Designers lack adequate criteria of classroom efficiency; teachers and students tend to adopt a fatalistic attitude toward school buildings. There is agreement from all parties that a school's physical plant should mirror its educational philosophy, but the methods for achieving isomorphism are elusive. The present rectangular room with its straight rows of chairs and wide windows was intended to provide for ventilation, light, quick departure, ease of surveillance, and a host of other legitimate needs as they existed in the early 1900s . . . The typical

long narrow shape resulted from a desire to get light across the room. The front of each room was determined by window location, since pupils had to be seated so that window light came over the left shoulder. Despite new developments in lighting, acoustics, and structures, most schools are still boxes filled with cubes each containing a specified number of chairs in straight rows. There have been attempts to break away from this rigid pattern, but experimental schools are the exception rather than the rule.

The American classroom is dominated by what has been called the rule of two-thirds—two-thirds of the time someone is talking and two-thirds of this time it is the teacher, and two-thirds of the time that the teacher is talking, she is lecturing, giving directions or criticizing behavior. Movement in and out of classrooms and the school building itself is rigidly controlled. Everywhere one looks there are "lines"—generally straight lines that bend around corners before entering the auditorium, the cafeteria, or the shop . . . The straight rows tell the student to look ahead and ignore everyone except the teacher, the students are jammed so tightly together that psychological escape, much less physical separation, is impossible. The teacher has 50 times more free space than the students with the mobility to move about. He writes important messages on the blackboard with his back to his students. The august figure can rise and walk among the lowly who lack the authority even to stand without explicit permission. Teacher and children may share the same classroom but they see it differently. From a student's eye level, the world is cluttered, disorganized, full of people's shoulders, heads, and body movements. His world at ground level is colder than the teacher's world. She looms over the scene like a helicopter swooping down to ridicule or punish any wrongdoer.[4]

. . . As he grows older, he moves into cubicles with larger chairs and taller students. Even high schools provide few places for students to linger, so they congregate in the corridors, outside the locker rooms, or in the stairwells seeking refuge from crowd pressures and impersonal authority. Intimacy is discouraged. . . . A student learns his place in society and what others expect of him from the way that teachers and administrators conduct the social system of the school. He acquires attitudes that derogate self-respect and create the self-image of a pitiful figure at a standard desk whose physical presence is required by statute. These aspects of educational life are derived more from classroom form than from the new math or computer logic.[5]

Whether in the city or the classroom, the lack of attention to matters of function—the thoughtful matching of men to one another and to their physical environment—epitomizes a view of architecture as simply a *medium,* while ignoring the most fundamental respects in which it is one of mankind's most pervasive message systems, as well.

The classroom, the market, the town square, the shopping mall, the skyscraper, the city each in their own fashion both display and affect aspects of our psychological, social, cultural, and spiritual existence. In no small way, architecture functions to shape our values, our information sources, our interpersonal styles, channels, and habits, our customs, our rituals, our transportation systems, our religions, and our systems of economics. The complex patterns of information exchange and social networks characteristic among residents of the apartment complex are often virtually absent among neighbors who farm or own acreages. The fleeting patterns of non-ritualistic physical movement and information exchange which characterize the popular fast-food restaurant stand in dramatic opposition to the human dynamics of the fashionable supper club. The fast-paced movement of person and information demanded in response to the structure of the city bears only subtle resemblances to the behavioral demands of the architecture of the farm. Whatever examples one chooses to consider, it becomes clear that important differences in human behavior do parallel differences in the architecture in which they occur. With planning and by accident the alterations man makes upon his physical milieu do not simply *reflect* the ethos of his communities, his institutions and his place in time, but additionally serve as *powerful shaping forces* in the perpetuation (and sometimes change) of man's communities, his institutions—the very nature of human existence.

Philosophical and Economic Underpinnings

Undergirding the short-run, structure-centered perspective on environmental design are two premises indigenous to contemporary western thought—firstly, at least until very recently, we have assumed that we have and will continue to have unlimited resources and services at our disposal, and secondly, we have assumed that it is essential to divide, privatize, and individually own portions of the environment.

Consumption

Consumption characterizes a process of wearing out to the bone, or to the last thread, a specific thing, such as a tool or garment, container or content. *Kleenex,* the "instant" handkerchief, stands as a simple but clear symbol of the throw-away society. *Kleenex,* stored in the box, is thrown into the garbage and can find its way to the garbage dump by the instant intermediary of a nose.

A stroll through a shopping center will quickly show how unreal the world of affluent men is within the context of "a family of man" besieged by hunger, poverty, coercion, illness, ignorance, etc. But there is an even more fundamental reason for this unreality. A researcher has stated that the "housewife" has 140,000 optional items with which to "survive happily" in that no man's land called the "kitchen." Many people strive to do their best to go through the full catalog by direct experience. Of this mental dimness we are all responsible and all paying dearly, and at last, not incidentally but coincidentally, we put ourselves where we find ourselves now, in the energy bottleneck. The magic word is, needless to say, frugality. This frugality is not to be found in segregation; segregation of spaces, functions, institutions, activities, productivities, bloods, castes, relations, etc., but in the thoughtful integration of them in a truly interactive condition.

Ownership

The view that environmental ownership is sanctioned by God and therefore is to be held as a sacred right of man is absurd. It would appear that on this score man has stepped backwards below the animal level. Among animals hoarding is almost unknown and territoriality a flexible concept, since "territory" is an open field for all sorts of activities by other species, vegetable and animal.

In most general terms, one could contend that a direct consequence of a sanctified concept of private property at the human level is a pauperization of the environment. Under such narrow constrictions the environment becomes the locus where things are hoarded around increasingly withering selves, at the expense of the person and of the

society, to the point where the selves are not much more than petrified egos, and the physical landscape of society is reduced to the dread of suburbia. At such a stage the environment may well reach its lowest form; parasitically grafted to the dwindling resources of the earth.

Given our penchant for disposability, privatization, and individual or corporate ownership, architecture which suggests or requires

increased permanence, deprivatization, or alternative forms of ownership or management generally runs head on into our most basic assumptions about the nature of human dwelling, human institutions, indeed, human existence. The problem is simply that to the extent we are unable to consciously become aware of and come to grips with ourselves and assumptions, we are precluded from considering the functional needs of man in any logical way. We are constrained in our ability to imagine and give consideration to alternatives to traditions whose structures may have long since outlived their functions. From the least generic levels of architectural decision-making to those considerations which may lead to major changes on the face of the earth, the need to seriously reconsider our assumptions is great: Whether to utilize fenced or unbounded territorial borders; above ground, below ground, or mobile living modules, separate or communal living facilities in college dorms, secluded or exposed nurses stations, open or petitioned offices, cemeteries or parks are decisions that can and should be made in light of a framework which appropriately reflects the nature of human needs for the present and the future.

Concepts of Architecture

There are a great many frameworks in terms of which architecture has been viewed. For these purposes it may be most useful to utilize centrally the concepts of Christian Norberg-Schulz, who conceives of architecture in terms of space and its utilization. Introducing this perspective, Norberg-Schulz quotes Lucretius who appropriately sketched the dimensions of concern when he noted that: "All nature is based on two things; there are bodies, and there is emptiness in which those bodies have their place, and in which they move."[6]

The patterning of the relationship between man and space, to which Lucretius refers, begins for us early in childhood. From infancy, the newborn human begins a process of organizing him or herself with the physical environment. Consisting initially of orderings with small objects to be maneuvered with the fingers or mouth, the child's perview extends next to micro-environments—a place to eat and sleep, to bathe, and rooms containing the smaller structures necessary to these functions.[7]

Levels of Spatial Analysis

Norberg-Schulz[8] has suggested that the most elementary organizational scheme involves the learning of *places* or *centres* (indicative of proximity), *directions* or *paths* (suggesting continuity), and *domains* or *areas* (defining enclosure). From these beginnings, the organization of space to the child proceeds outward in a series of concentric circles, from the immediate to the remote, with the increasing universe of activity as that defined by the pebble, dropped into a placid pool of water. The centers of the activity—the first-encountered and familiar places, paths, and areas—increase in number and, broaden in scope from the simplistic environment which contained the first things of play and furniture for sleep, to the room, the home, and outward to other centres and areas, along new paths.

Proceeding from the lowest level of human interface with the physical world—that defined by the *hand*—we move to a level where the architecture of furniture has relevance.[9] At this level, the interface between man and the physical world is defined by the *body*. The house, at the third level, takes its spatial definition primarily from the extended movements and functions of the body. The urban level is defined through patterns of *multi-person social interaction,* while the landscape is defined by man's *interaction with the natural environment,* instrumented by his technology.

Whether one is concerned with the architecture of the landscape, the city, the shopping mall, or the house, or the room, certain regularities are observable.

The work of Kevin Lynch and Christian Norberg-Schulz provide a set of functionally-based concepts based upon space and patterns of human utilization. What follows is a summary of their category systems.[10]

Centre, Place, Node

Centre, place, and node are the points which serve as the foci to and from which man is traveling. It may be a house, a harbor, a town-square, a corner-hangout, the pretzel stand in the center of the shopping mall, or the shopping mall itself. A place, centre, or node has structural identity. You know when you're there and when you are not.

Path and Direction

According to Lynch,[11] "Paths are channels along which the observer customarily, occasionally, or potentially moves." They may be corridors, bridges, walkways, streets, elevators, transit lines, sidewalks, hallways, railroads, highways, doorways, traffic patterns in the home, bicycle paths, short-cuts through the woods, or international flight patterns.

Notions about direction and movement are crucial to space utilization and architectural design at a variety of levels: Up and down, front and rear, high and low, often connote meanings that are widely shared. Many aspects of the religious architecture for example, the steeple, reflect the concept of a relationship between the vertical and the sacred.[12] In a slightly different vein, the concepts of movement on the vertical plane are associated with notions of salvation and punishment, as with the Judeo-Christian concepts of heaven and hell. "To ascend," "to climb," "to be above," "to be one up," we generally understand to be preferable to "downward spirals," "descending," "falling," "being one down." Similarly, moving "forward," "progressing," "advancing" are desirable, while "moving backward," "going in reverse," "being behind the scenes," or "at the rear of the bus" are generally conceived to be undesirable spaces.

Edge and Boundary

"Edges are the linear elements not used or considered as paths by the observer. They are the boundaries between two phases, linear breaks in continuity."[13] Examples are walls, shores, edges of developments, hedges, and rivers. Boundaries are barriers which are more or less penetrable. They close one region off to another. Boundaries are important organizing features, particularly in defining areas, as in the outline of a city by water, or the house by walls.

Area, Domain, and District

Of area and domain, Norberg-Schulz says:
Paths divide man's environment into areas which are more or less well known. We call such qualitatively defined areas 'domains' . . . the distinction between place and domain is useful. . . . The domain can . . . be defined as a relatively unstructured 'ground', on which places and paths appear as more pronounced 'figures'. If we think of our own country, or of the earth as a whole, we primarily think of domains: oceans, deserts, mountains, and lakes.[14]

Generally districts are defined by a thematic continuity which may consist of a variety of factors including texture, space, form, detail, building type, use, activity, inhabitants and topography. Thus, within New York City, for example, there are numerous districts including Washington Square, Central Park, Harlem, Times Square, China Town, Greenwich Village, Queens College Campus and so on. "Natural" domains are combined with political and economical domains to create a still more complex pattern.

Landmarks

Landmarks function as points of reference, providing clues as to the appropriateness of one path or another given particular destinations. Lynch[15] indicates that they are usually rather simply defined physical objects such as a building, sign, store, mountain, roadside mileage marker, store front, doorbell, or mailbox . . . anything which functions for the individual as a sign post.

Interaction

While the components discussed in the foregoing provide a useful set of categories for considering the nature of architecture in a microscopic perspective, it must be remembered also that *place, node* and *centre* operate with *boundary, path,* and *landmark* to form an integrated whole in the world of our experience.

Dimensionality

Until very recently, the concept of two-dimensional, flat-surface living—characteristic of the city—has pervaded architectural thinking. We live in a period when populations migrate massively into two-dimensional, urban sprawls, while the quality and promise of urban life seem to be spiraling to very low common denominators. The phenomenon is probably nowhere more typical than in the United States, where the consequences of the premise that man must construct and inhabit dwellings in a small layer along the surface of the earth, is everywhere apparent. In part as a result, the major centers of population have grown "vertically" above successive layers of debris, waste, and decay.

Architectural designs utilizing a three-dimensional perspective are only recently beginning to emerge as a significant alternative. Multi-level, above-surface structures have become increasingly popular in response to conditions of crowding and rising land costs. For the most part, these developments are limited-function edifices designed to house a number of modules which are more or less duplicative in structure and more or less interchangeable in function, as with apartment buildings, condominiums, or office buildings. In a few cases, structures of an integrative-function variety have been developed, placing together in a single edifice components previously housed in single-function structures. These environments may contain not only rental or privately-owned dwellings, but offices, recreational facilities, parking facilities, and other services, as well. The goal in such instances is to broaden the traditional definition of the architecture of the *home,* as a single structure, to include nodes and paths typically associated with the architectural functions of *the city.*

A much less explored alternative, and one to be considered in some depth subsequently, is the three-dimensional structure which is constructed below ground-level, or combines aspects of surface and sub-surface construction.

Architecture and Ecology

The structural and functional center of man's existence has been the city. It epitomizes the complexity, diversity, and integration that characterize contemporary social existence. The emotional impact of the cityscape upon a person is a combination of the exhilaration of understanding and at the same time the anguish of realizing the massiveness of the unknown. But for a variety of reasons, the urbanization of man has been increasingly unkind to the city, and the city in turn is increasingly unkind to the man—the creator.

The dilemmas of our cities underscore the outcomes of our orientation toward disposability, one-dimensionality, privitization, ownership; our propensity for inadequate planning; and our tendency to emphasize structure to the detriment of function. We are faced today with the increasingly difficult choir of integrating the nature and demands of architecture with our emerging understanding of the requirements of ecology. Too often, we have been remiss in failing to coordinate our architectural endeavors with the larger scheme of climate, sun, wind, rain and frost action, water sheds, soil composition, vegetation, animal life and social environment.

One area where the consequences of our failures to consider these factors is particularly pervasive is earth moving. The earth's surface has undergone, and continues to undergo, a massive amount of arrang-

ing and rearranging, moving soil from here to there and later back again. All too often the reasons are more or less arbitrary, of short-run utility, serving almost always a very narrow set of interests. Most of the time the business of architecture should be the prevention of the moving of soil rather than the moving of it. Logically, the amount of earth moved should bear a relation to the thickness of the structure which is to be constructed, the short and long-run functional utility of that structure, and the number of persons who will be favorably affected by its construction. Large rearrangements of landscape, when for other than agricultural purposes, are simply not a justifiable manipulation of the environment.

Drastically needed is an approach to architecture in which the inseparability and interdependence of architectural and ecological phenomena becomes apparent. This sorely needed perspective may be termed *arcology*. The concept of arcology is an attempt to focus all the major problems of contemporary man: population, limited land, limited resources, limited energy, limited food-production, segregation, pollution, bureaucratization, technological mindlessness, waste, greed, cultural deprivation, and spiritual naught.

Questions about how, when, and to what end to alter the physical environment present a series of dilemmas which require our most careful consideration in light of the full range of alternatives. Conceiving of these decisions as arcological in nature—rather than either architectural or ecological—will hopefully provide the sort of generic framework necessary for reversing the trend of neglect and shortsightedness which has led to the pauperization of the environment in the name of progress.

Arcology

Arcology is both a philosophy and a methodology. As the former, its significance is the unification of the concepts of architecture and ecology. As the latter, *arcology* is a term which references what will be among the earth's first self-contained, urban environments. In a single structure, arcology will contain facilities for work, sleep, dining, social life, education, recreation, and spiritual worship, providing for thousands of people per square mile a structural alternative to the city.

Mesa City

The conceptual roots for the arcological methodology date the period of 1959–1964 and the design for Mesa City, conceived for development in the west of the North American continent or any other similar region. Mesa City was designed for a population of about 2,000,000.

> The city develops north-south in a band about 10 kilometers wide and about 35 kilometers long. At the south end of the main axis is the center for advanced study, encircled by secondary schools and dormitories. Directly north is a man-made park . . . widening then in a system of dikes and lakes, the edges irregularly settled by villages whose main activities are arts and crafts. Uphill . . . stands the theological complex; facing east is the theological university, a library-museum is in the center. . . . The center for advanced study, the man-made park, and the theological complex constitute the backbone of the city. Beginning again from the south and around the school complex is a band of villages and civic centers averaging 2.5 kilometers in width. Thirty-four villages of about 3,000 people each are grouped around civic and shopping centers in clusters of five. Each village is on a ground 1,000 meters in diameter; a garden 200-400 meters in diameter. There is an outside farming ground . . . for orchards and vegetable gardens. This whole band is crisscrossed by pedestrian and bicycle paths; there is no private car traffic of any kind. Each village is tied directly to the speedway through underground parking and repair-refueling facilities. High-density dwellings are developed on the east and west side of the man-made park. . . .
>
> Running in, out, and through the city are three continuous belts:
> 1. Closest to the center is the home industry system where workshops and living quarters are integrated along a circulation network.
> 2. The intermediate belt consists of the main network of speedways, roads, parking facilities, and a system of waterways for freight and passengers. . . .

3. The outside belt, sunk in the ground, holds second-hand stores, and markets, the blight of car dealers, the equipment dealers and renters, the junkyards. . . .

At the foot of the mesa . . . are processing plants where raw materials are reclaimed from scrap heaps. . . . An airport is on rooftop and taxi facilites are scattered all over the city. Another major airport is at the south end of the mesa connected to the city and the region by two main speedways.

The road system is mostly above and below ground level, and it is combined with a parking facility network including car storage, car silos, and normal parking. Within the structures carrying the roads are integrated road utilities such as motels and car services.[16]

Adjacent, are towns and villages, essentially rural in character, producing and processing foodstuffs and their derivatives. Industrial complexes would be located downstream of water reservoirs. Radiation, wind, water and tides were all to be utilized as energy resources. The plan for the city itself, called for placement along a man-made waterway, tied to the outer environment through a connective network of roads, railroads, and bridges.

Extensive drawings of the Mesa City design are presented in *The Sketchbooks of Paolo Soleri*.[17] Discussion of the conceptual underpinnings of the city is given in *Arcology: The City in the Image of Man*.[18]

Arcosanti

The next phase in the evolution of the arcological methodology is represented by Arcosanti. Mesa City was the plan for a city which would not do violence to the ecological context in which it would be constructed. Arcosanti is the design for the first uncompromising urban environment to provide a functional integration of architecture and ecology in a single, three-dimensional structure, and hence the first to truly fit the arcological paradigm. In a single multi-faceted structure, Arcosanti would integrate those functions of living, working, and community life, typically associated in scope with the diverse architecture of the city as we know it. Arcosanti was designed to be constructed on a ten-acre site. It would house roughly 3,000 persons, and would be 30 stories tall at its highest point. Like Mesa City, but now in a single structure, Arcosanti would contain facilities for education at all levels, recreation, transportation, theatre, shopping, arts and crafts, gardening, religious worship and manufacturing, as well as for eating, sleeping and work. Capabilities for recycling of resources would be integral to the structure. The dependence upon the automobile, characteristic of city life, would be virtually eliminated by internal systems of shuttles, electric sidewalks, and improved information-transportation systems.

At the end of 1970, following a series of arcological studies, Arcosanti, a town for 3,000 people was designed, and in 1971 construction began on a 10-acre portion of an 860 acre tract, 70 miles north of Scottsdale, Arizona, along the Agua Fria River. The construction of Arcosanti, which continues today, is being done with some professional guidance, by students who volunteer their services to work with the project. The volunteers each live in an eight-foot concrete cube fashioned from indigenous sand and gravel. Each living environment is furnished with built-in bed, desk, and bookshelves constructed of plywood. Round colored windows—roughly 7 feet in diameter—provide a visual continuity with the environment in which the cubes are situated. An octagonal building, 40 feet across, serves as a meeting place and a center for social interaction. The living cubes and community module will eventually become parts to be slotted together to form a portion of the overall structure of the Arcology.

Second Generation Arcologies

First generation arcologies—Arcosanti, in particular—are serving to loosen minds from the traditional moorings in which contemporary architectural thinking has been imbedded. Hopefully, the next generation of Arcologies, through research, will stimulate the conceptual development and resource allocation necessary for encouraging the construction and broadbased utilization of arcological designs.

One second generational project, now in an early planning phase, has been named *Two Suns Arcology*. In the next 2–5 years we will explore the design of arcologies especially suited to the ⅔ of the populated environment endowed with sunshine. Of this belt, optimum areas for arcological development will be those with small amounts of rainfall in the arid zones, because in those areas there are a high percentage of sunny days, the necessity of careful water management is a common concern, and high-density urban systems and local production of foodstuffs are desirable in these regions too. To the extent that arcologies can be designed which will accomodate these conditions, a major portion of the populated earth-space will have a viable alternative to the traditions of the urban sprawl.

Arcologies of the Future

Arcologies of the future may be as high as one mile and a mile wide, containing in a single structure a range of nodes, paths, and domains paralleled, at present, only at the level or the architecture of the city and the landscape. Perhaps more clearly, than is now readily conceivable, these environments will provide not only new and different media to house man's activities and his institutions, but more a massive and complex array of messages that will both dramatically reflect and shape the needs of man of the future.

To some, this concept of the architecture of the future is shocking, even distressing. It may evoke threatening images of man and his arcological existence that are similar to the relationship of the bee to his hive. For those who would have us believe we should strive to return to the innocence and simple life-styles and settings of days gone by, it is useful to remember that the natural man of today is a vastly different creature than nature man, or proto-man, of the Garden of Eden. Similarly, the impact and demands of the contemporary environment are different from those of pristine nature, surrounding, nurturing and harassing Adam and Eve. The illusions of Woodstock and the "Commune nostalgia" are short lived delusions at best.

Like the fish who goes about its life perhaps totally unaware of—and yet at the same time totally dependent upon and constrained by—the liquid medium in which it exists, so it is for man and the information envelop in which he takes his definition.

On this point, one cannot let go unnoticed the stark fact that a slightly different cosmic coordinate of earth, mass, distance from the sun, rotation and revolution, length, or difference in the nature of sun, would mean a *very* different kind of environment, a *very* different kind of life, and a *very* different kind of man. In evolutionary terms the environment—as channel and message—is truly the maker, and ultimately, the breaker.

Notes and References

1. Several sections in this chapter were authored solely by Paolo Soleri with only minor alterations by the co-author. These include the Introductory section—"Architecture as Medium," "Architecture as Message," "Modes of Architectural Transformation," "Consumption," "Ownership," (first portion), and "Conclusion." Other sections were authored by Brent D. Ruben. These are "Structure and Function," "Concepts of Architecture," "Levels of Spatial Analysis," "Cross-level Constructs," "Centre, Place, Node," "Path and Direction," "Edge and Boundary," "Area, Domain, and District," "Landmarks," and "Interaction." Other portions of the chapter are adaptations, abstractions, and interpretations of Soleri's work by the co-author. These include, "Architecture and Ecology," "Arcology," "Arcosanti," and "Second Generation Arcologies."
2. *Cf.* Robert Sommer, *Personal Space: The Behavioral Basis of Design,* esp. Chapter 1., Englewood Cliffs, N.J.: Prentice-Hall, 1969.
3. Sommer, pp. 3–4.
4. Sommer, p. 99.
5. Sommer, p. 100.
6. Norberg-Schulz, Christian, *Existence, Space and Architecture,* New York: Praeger, 1971, p. 10.
7. *Cf.* Norberg-Schulz, *op. cit.* pp. 18–19.
8. Norberg-Schulz, pp. 18–19.
9. Norberg-Schulz, p. 27.
10. The concepts presented in this section of the chapter are summaries of notions advanced by Kevin Lynch, in *The Image of the City,* Cambridge, Mass.: M.I.T. Press, 1960 (especially Chapter 3), and developed by Christian Norberg-Schulz, in *Existence, Space and Architecture,* (especially Chapters 2 and 3). The categories have been modified slightly for our purposes.
11. Lynch, p. 47.
12. Norberg-Schulz, pp. 21–22.
13. Lynch, p. 47.
14. Norberg-Schulz, p. 23.
15. Lynch, pp. 48–49.
16. Soleri, Paolo, *The Sketchbooks of Paolo Soleri,* Cambridge, Mass.: M.I.T. Press, 1971, pp. 1–2.
17. *Ibid.*
18. Soleri, Paolo, *Arcology: The City in the Image of Man,* Cambridge, Mass.: M.I.T. Press, 1970.

CHAPTER XIII

Sardi's:

Something Beyond Food

Vincent Sardi

Of course people eat at restaurants. Of course they expect good food for their money. And it goes without saying that no restaurant can survive, much less prosper, without serving its clients what they consider good food. But a substantial number of people expect restaurants they dine at to offer something beyond food. And Sardi's restaurant in New York City—by a kind of fate that has been understood, appreciated and nurtured by two generations of the Sardi family—certainly exemplifies the sort of restaurant that such people frequent.

Perhaps you can see it most distinctly on a winter evening during one of those New York blizzards that brings traffic grinding to a halt and keeps Broadway theaters closed because audiences can't get through the snow drifts. At Sardi's, the bar is the scene of lively conversation. Patrons are asking the bartender about an upcoming musical's chance for success. Many of the downstairs tables are occupied by theater people—actors, producers, costume designers, casting directors—some transacting business over dinner; others table hopping between courses. On such a miserable night you'd never expect an arriving patron to quibble over where he's to be seated. But even to a man seeking shelter from a blizzard, the position of his table at Sardi's can be more important to him at that moment than the mere fact that his shoes are filled with snow and his socks are soaking wet.

It is not that pneumonia is of no consequence to Sardi's patrons, but rather that they too understand something the restaurant's management understands. That "something beyond the food" that they expect is an institution and an "atmosphere" with long established expectations. The table hopping, the business transactions and the bartender's opinion are all part of that atmosphere, which has at its core the exchange of information. The location of the patron's table can

234

affect his participation—willingly or unwittingly—in this information flow. And, for that matter, the whole matter of table preference, and whether or not one succeeds in realizing that preference has in itself great information value—both to the patron and to other guests.

The problem in running a restaurant of this kind is that a meal can be made or ruined by such intangibles as whether or not a patron is seated under a certain one of the many hundred caricatures that cover our walls, or near the producer of an upcoming (or just folded) musical, or within earshot of an ex-wife, or at a table next to a favorite movie actor, or just simply in a section of the restaurant considered "chic" (and which other customers may not consider chic).

Beyond the seating arrangement, success of a given meal can depend on countless other items of information or contacts. For professionals in the performing arts, who represent a substantial portion of the restaurant's regular clientele, industry scuttlebutt passed along by bartenders and waiters can be valuable and useful, especially if it relates to the chances for success of a new show, or, better yet, the possibility of being employed by one.

Because of the sensitivity of these sometimes delicate communications, the headwaiter's position at Sardi's is one of enormous responsibility. That is why many restaurateurs (myself included) greet patrons personally at the entrance and seat them—hiring chefs and managers to run the "back of the operation" such as the kitchen, the business office and the maintenance staff. Certainly the owner must know his food, his purchasing, his kitchen machinery and his chefs (I sometimes think I can spot a bad chef even before he unpacks his knives). But the owner's main problem is "up front," where patrons are welcomed, introduced, seated and served.

Not only do I spend much of my time in the restaurant at the front door, but my most trusted employees perform as headwaiter in my absence. And a performance it is, especially in a restaurant like Sardi's that has 120 tables, only 15 of which are considered socially acceptable by a substantial fraction of its regular patrons.

But to fully understand the complexity of these networks in a restaurant such as ours, you need some understanding of the historical context of the basic notion of eating outside the home in commercial establishments. Fundamentally, these establishments derive from four basic types:

1. *the restaurant,* which is essentially a public eating house.
2. *the tavern,* a more informal establishment where liquors are sold to be consumed on the premises, perhaps along with some food.
3. *the inn,* which serves food and drink mainly as an adjunct to its main operation, which is to provide sleeping accommodations to transient guests.
4. *and the club,* which is an association of people as a rule for some common purpose, where members meet in a building or room reserved for their exclusive use.

Now, some of Sardi's patrons are so regular, they are sometimes thought of as living at the restaurant, even using it to receive telephone messages and mail. But I think of the establishment's main functions as that of *public eating place, tavern* and *club.*

Indeed, a number of real clubs have come to use the restaurant as their headquarters, including Actors' Equity in its formative years, and more recently various local civic organizations, as well as a group of sports car and racecar enthusiasts known as the Madison Avenue Driving and Chowder Society, which started as a gag back in the mid-Fifties and has continued meeting monthly at Sardi's for lunch ever since to exchange lively talk about automobiles and watch films of the latest races and meets.

Perhaps the most regular of the Sardi's regulars is the crowd at the bar, and to that group the well rubbed chunk of dark wood is their own tavern. In fact, one of their number went as far as stipulating in his will a specific sum of money to be used to buy drinks for his comrades at periodic intervals until the funds were used up. (His request was honored, of course, and it was subsequently imitated by deceased patrons of other fashionable watering holes in New York.) Transacting business at the Sardi bar is frowned upon, but good conversations and companionship are not. The lobby area near the bar has been the scene of many lasting friendships. It was there that actress Ann Jeffreys bumped into the man she subsequently married—actor Robert Sterling.

Above all, however, Sardi's is a public eating house. Theatergoers as well as performers know they can walk into the restaurant less than an hour before curtain time and be on their way, fully fed, without feeling rushed, in plenty of time to catch (or say) the opening lines. Performers generally prefer to eat after they work, as does a substantial fraction of the audience, particularly since curtain time on Broadway was moved up an hour to seven-thirty. But the fact that Sardi's is essentially a public eating place—an elegant one perhaps, but nevertheless an eating place—is a point of constant reminder when the kitchen is asked to prepare one of its specialties and rush it to a Broadway star's dressing room before a performance. Debbie Reynolds wouldn't go on stage, for instance, without her take-out dinner from Sardi's of sirloin steak and sliced tomatoes, consumed with gusto in front of her make-up lights and accompanied by the aroma of greasepaint. When Pearl Bailey had to eat onstage as part of her performance, she insisted on Sardi's chicken, and managed to wade through $2,496 of it in a successful run of two years.

Roots and Accidents of History

Thus far I have only talked about Sardi's from a more-or-less local point of view—how the restaurant is viewed and used by segments of the New York City community. There is yet at the same time, I think, quite a different Sardi's, one that provokes quite a different view from a much larger and certainly much broader audience. While the name Sardi's may not be a household word, our restaurant is one that enjoys a national reputation. A great number of people visiting New York for the first time would, for example, have a visit to Sardi's on their itinerary. Their reasons for coming to the restaurant would be quite different from those of our local and regular patrons, but at the same time, the kind of local clientele we serve obviously has a great deal to do with why an out-of-towner would come to Sardi's.

What determines a restaurant's identity in this regard is largely a matter of historical accident. We have often been typecast as an exclusively theatrical restaurant—the place where the stars go to eat and the public goes to watch them eat. This isn't precisely true. Our clientele—including the so-called "Sardi's set" (a phrase coined by Dorothy Kilgallen)—actually comes from all walks of life. But the largest single group is connected one way or another with the theater. One reason for this is that the restaurant is located in the theater district. Also, my mother and father, who began the business, worked together originally in a theatrical hotel and were well known there by a number of actresses and actors. When they opened their restaurant, they quite naturally made their friends at the hotel aware of it. That, in large measure, is why actresses and actors started frequenting the establishment from the first day it opened. And that is why Actors' Equity held some of its early meetings there. Realizing the fundamental importance of the restaurant's initial directions, my father fought desperately and successfully to keep Sardi's on West 44th Street after the building in which it was first housed gave way to the wreckers' cranes. It was, strangely enough, one of the great names of the theater industry, Lee Shubert, who helped secure the restaurant's current location by offering my father space in a new building he was putting up only a few doors from the first Sardi's.

So much for incidents of historical accident. As my father recalls in his biography, the new Sardi's wasn't exactly overrun by business. To the contrary, for the first several months things looked quite grim, and my father came close to closing down. It seemed that location and goodwill were not enough to bring success. It was at this point my father began casting for ways to make his restaurant more than a place to eat, for a plan that would make it "belong" to the theater people. It was during this period that our now famous collection of caricatures was conceived. My father contracted with a temperamental Russian immigrant artist by the name of Alex Gard to do the drawings. Gard was fiercely independent, and his renderings of his famous subjects considerably less than flattering, and all, many reluctantly, but a few celebrities signed their likenesses. In all, Gard produced some 700 of the drawings that now hang on nearly every nook and cranny of Sardi's.

Business began to build. More and more the theater people made Sardi's their home, and following them were the newspaper columnists, press agents and public relations men who, in reporting upon the stars, did much to create the image of Sardi's as a glamour spot. Undeniably, network exposure of the restaurant on the famous radio program, "Luncheon at Sardi's," an interview show which originated from the restaurant daily for a number of years, helped considerably to make our name well known throughout the country.

Sustaining the Message

Given these several historic roots of a modern restaurant, how does its owner set about maintaining and building upon them? Again, he must know food, for without good food his restaurant cannot possibly survive. But beyond the food, he must provide a place of comfort for his patrons. And they, in turn, will be comfortable if they find a combination of food, service, beverages and atmosphere at prices they can afford, yet not so commercially arranged they feel put upon. The net

effect of this is not merely to put food on a patron's plate; it is to do so while setting a tone for his meal that enables him to enjoy it all the more. At Sardi's, the main thrust of that tone is to communicate friendliness, conviviality and even a certain tinge of excitement, all without jarring the patron or impairing his comfort in any way. It's a delicate matter, maintaining this balance between comfort and excitement.

That's why we're extremely price conscious at Sardi's. We mean to convey this feeling of friendliness, and we're not going to do that if a patron opens the menu, takes one look at the prices, and has a heart attack. In a free enterprise system such as ours, we must make a profit to survive, obviously. But we try to carry out that task as painlessly as possible. This is most difficult to achieve these days because of escalating wages and food costs.

Still, Sardi's has become an institution. As such, it is as non-commercial as possible without being unsuccessful too. It employs headwaiters who are not money hungry for example. And they are paid substantially larger salaries than most headwaiters so they don't have to accept gratuities. To put it bluntly, a headwaiter who's in the business of selling tables and locations at Sardi's would quickly upset the delicate balance of the relationship between patrons and staff, as well as between regular patrons who drop by to see each other. Similarly, we try to eliminate the money hungry captain who sticks his hand in front of a patron's face and won't let him out without a tip. We try to have captains and waiters convey the feeling that Sardi's is a comfortable place to stay. In fact, the captain usually asks those at each table if they are planning to see a show. If they are, he attempts to provide appropriate service so the meal moves along comfortably and without delay in a seemingly effortless manner. If a patron has no such commitment, he sees to it that they're not rushed in any way. While it's true that some of the most beautiful restaurants in the world have been failures because their kitchens didn't achieve the standards of their dining rooms, it is equally true that some very successful restaurants with great food have been damaged by the attitudes of the owner, the headwaiters, or the personnel in the dining room.

Second only to the quality of its food and the collective disposition of the restaurant's staff, is its surroundings, which also communicate something. The decor is more than just a part of a good restaurant: it practically becomes part of the taste of the food.

Decor is mood. Decor is ethereal. It's not always clear why one decor works and another doesn't. But there it is, and it affects every meal served to every patron. Clearly, it is very important. The decor at Sardi's is probably the simplest in the world: four walls painted a strange terra cotta, unusually high dark-maroon leather bankheads, lots of caricatures, old-fashioned incandescent chandeliers and sconces, red table cloths covered by white table cloths, and waiters in bright red jackets. The goal of the decor at Sardi's is softness. This is in keeping with my constant urging of the staff to make patrons feel comfortable. We don't want to jar people in any way.

For example, take those high leather bankheads. For a person sitting against the wall, the dark maroon leather comes up behind his head, setting off his face with a certain softness. The lighting, most of it indirect, adds to this feeling. And I often meet patrons out on the street who look ten to twenty years older in the sunlight than they do in the restaurant. I'm convinced the lighting is a critical element in the decor of Sardi's, and I'm very sensitive to anything that affects it. My business manager once figured out that we could save quite a lot of money by eliminating our traditional red tablecloths, which are largely covered anyway by the white topcloths. We tried that for a short time and nobody complained or even noticed the change. But I sensed a bit of harshness to the lighting, and insisted we go back to using the red tablecloths. The decor is a restaurant's way of telling its patrons where they are. And we want ours to be completely devoid of harshness. For this reason we have no neon or florescent lights, which I think are simply horrible for the faces of women and especially elderly men. We have parchment shades around every light bulb, we bounce most of the light off the ceiling, and we raise and lower its intensity during the restaurant's hours so it doesn't look dingy at lunch hour, or overly bright in the evening. In short, the decor at Sardi's is adjusted to minimize jarring harshness and the main purpose is to communicate a sense of comfort.

The rows and rows of caricatures that have become a kind of symbol of Sardi's would be worth having on that basis alone. But like the lighting, they too serve a functional purpose as well. The faces in each caricature are approximately lifesize. And when the restaurant empties out at curtain time the place never feels empty to those who remain because of the hundreds of faces lining the walls. In fact, some regular patrons prefer to dine between peak periods and time their arrival just for this off-hour. The happy lifesize caricatures surround those who dine in these more sedate periods, in effect never allowing them to dine alone.

Even the paint on the walls is intended to communicate a sense of stability and reassurance. Originally that paint started out as completely different color than its present hue. But each time the restaurant was repainted, the fresh paint was mixed to match the *faded* color, not the original color. And more than half a century of matching faded coats, one after another, has left the restaurant with a peculiar terra cotta color that actually looks as faded as new paint can look. The idea here is that on the one hand, patrons virtually never notice a new paint job. On the other, the walls have acquired a lovely patina that comes with age. This leaves the place with the constant aura of permanence: of age without change. Certainly no decorator would mix terra cotta, maroon and red all in one room. But Father Time apparently has his own decorating rules.

Extending the Message: Influence and Persuasion

Beyond the important but admittedly circuitous vehicle of decor as a communications tool, there is also the more direct approach of restaurant policy. On many occasions, Sardi's has implemented special policies to bring across a point. An example that stretched on for years is the restaurant's early involvement in civil rights.

New York City has always had a number of fashionable restaurants. And for more than fifty years Sardi's has been fortunate to be counted in that group. It's no secret that people look to such institutions for indications of what is proper and what is not. And fashionable restaurants like Sardi's both *reflect* as well as *set* certain social trends. Dress, of course, is a prime example, and in a sense, women's pantsuits became thoroughly acceptable once they were welcomed as evening garb at leading restaurants in major cities.

But there are deeper social issues in society than evening garb, and a restaurant like Sardi's can be a power to reckon with on substantive matters. Such was the case when the United Nations headquarters were being planned for Manhattan. A group of concerned New Yorkers worried about the possibility of representatives and their staffs from distant countries encountering discrimination in New York because of their color. The group decided to form something called the Committee on Civil Rights in East Manhattan to ensure that members of the United Nations would obtain apartments near U.N. headquarters, even though virtually all of Manhattan's east side apartment houses were, in effect, segregated. I took an interest in the Committee's work and helped it branch into the restaurant industry. I started giving lectures to restaurant owners' associations, headwaiters' associations and similar organizations, in return for which I was often called unprintable names and my views were generally opposed. But I continued, insisting that Sardi's restaurant would show, by its example, that blacks and all others were welcome.

In retrospect it seems a mild enough crusade, because these days a black is every bit as welcome in virtually any New York restaurant as is his white counterpart. But not so in the early Fifties.

When black patrons were welcomed at the door and seated at Sardi's in those days, entire tables of patrons would get up and leave in protest. On occasion this amounted to a loss of ten or twelve parties getting up and walking out: I don't mean individuals; I mean parties of two, three and four, a dozen of which would get up and walk out the moment a single black was seated.

But we stuck through this period, honestly believing that if our policy put the restaurant out of business, at least it would be closing for good reason. We didn't have to close down though. The novelty wore off, public sentiment gradually changed and, as we had anticipated, other restaurants followed our lead.

But now a new area of possible civil rights concern was becoming clear. The lack of black personnel seemed all the more obvious when a black couple sat down to enjoy a meal. And clearly the restaurant was going to use its position and influence to insist on black employees.

"Insist" is the right word, because at that time waiters unions and other unions serving the restaurant industry were absolutely segregated. We insisted upon and obtained black employees, some of whom worked out and some of whom didn't. After several attempts we finally succeeded in keeping a nucleus of black employees. (We didn't wish to make the restaurant staff all-black, because we believed that would be a reverse form of segregation and would serve no purpose.) The restaurant presently has as part of its permanent annual staff four extremely competent and very personable black waiters. And it also employs Spanish, French, Puerto Rican, Mexican, Cuban and Irish waiters and busboys. We now see a pattern of integration spreading throughout the city, extending to unions in other industries.

Now in case you're tempted to think of Sardi's as an exceptionally bold example of a restaurant that disseminated information and takes what it considers a leadership role in these weighty issues of the day, an example of another restaurant in an entirely different part of the country should prove interesting. During the very period that Sardi's was attempting to promote integration of restaurants in New York, a restaurant owner named Lester Maddox was using his establishment in the South to convey his objections to the very thing we were fighting for. Apparently he too was quite successful in his own undertaking. The public exposure accorded the image of Mr. Maddox standing with an ax handle in defiance of integration was sufficient to subsequently elect him Governor of Georgia.

I'm sure there are thousands of examples of restaurants that have been a strong factor in community matters. And I know personally that the reputation of Sardi's has been put on the line in this way a number of times. Even just as a meeting place, Sardi's has been used by countless civic groups, such as the Mayor's Midtown Planning Group. And it has participated directly in matters specifically affecting both the Times Square area where the restaurant is located, and the restaurant industry. For instance, we formed a Greater Times Square Committee, eventually disbanding it when the Mayor followed with his own Midtown Planning Group.

To be sure, we haven't always been successful, and I would be the last to imply we have. For example, in trying to call attention to the need for greater city involvement for protection of the Times Square area, including the safety of people on the streets, we generated a great deal of publicity that backfired. Not only did it call the city fathers' attention to the shoddy and unsafe condition of the entertainment district, but it also brought the issue to the attention of the public at large. Obviously you don't make the streets safer at night by frightening the public away. So now we're trying to reverse the trend and improve the image of the area. Again, we have meetings planned with owners of hotels, restaurants, theaters and even taxi fleets to raise money for this project, and Sardi's is the scene of some of these meetings. The idea now is to show how New York's reputation as a city of crime has been grossly overstated. So while it too occupied an inordinate amount of time and effort to get the City's bureaucracy to reverse the decline, New York's downtown district never did sink to the deplorable state of decay found in many other urban disasters.

A Specialized Role

Perhaps the preponderant information function performed by Sardi's is that of "transmitter" within the theater industry, which has, as we noted earlier, traditionally used Sardi's as one of its meeting places. When a play goes into production, it is not at all uncommon for the producers to solicit opinions on its relative strengths and weaknesses from the restaurant's waiters, captains, bartenders, headwaiters, and even the checkroom lady. When I first started working in my father's restaurant, I interpreted such solicitation of staff opinion as frivolous. But over the years I gradually realized that these producers and directors were very astute. The observations of waiters and captains generally reflect a certain objectivity, unadulterated by close association with the show. And their taste in theater is likely to be considerably more representative of popular preferences than that of show business people. Finally, the staff at Sardi's inevitably picks up a great deal of information about a given show, much the way New York cab drivers would tend to come by information and opinions about a mayorality race, from the people.

In recent years I've come to view such exchanges of information almost as part of the service the restaurant offers its professional patrons. We make it a point to tell them exactly what we hear, without editorializing or twisting it around in any way. You should hear some of the questions we're deluged with as a play goes into previews—the last tryouts on Broadway prior to opening night. Actors ask us if people like their performance. Producers ask if word on the street seems to be favorable, and directors ask whether their key scenes are making the proper impact. Always, those associated with a production have their feelers out for comments. Indeed, writers tell me that many a Broadway show has been rewritten during its preview period right at a table in a corner of Sardi's.

Nor are we alone in this. Interestingly, our patrons recognize the informational value of several restaurants. If an actor passes through New York City, I am told he has only to drop in at Sardi's once or twice for lunch and once or twice after theater. Then he would go to a place like P. J. Clarke's bar late at night. He could also check out the Algonquin at lunch, hit the "21" Club bar, and spend a bit of time at Joe Allen's restaurant on West 46th Street. This done, he's virtually guaranteed to run into a large number of fellow actors and producers who also happen to be in the city. Sardi's has definitely become one of these hubs of communications for the performing arts, including theater, motion picture and television. And if you're in that industry and you've just arrived in town, that's where you go. That's one reason we are almost forced to hold mail for patrons in show business. And there must be thousands of restaurants serving other industries the way we serve ours.

But as the restaurant became more successful, other groups flooded in: businessmen, press agents, journalists, theater-goers and, in continuing large numbers, tourists. To this day, however, many of the regulars are still theater people and professional performers.

In 1946, I took over the restaurant from my father, and gradually the cross section of clientele started reflecting the influence of some of my own interests. I had been in the Marine Corps during World War II, and many of my ex-marine friends have made a kind of headquarters of the restaurant since then. Marine Corps formal lunches and dinners are often held here.

Another hobby of mine was sportscar racing, thus the Madison Avenue Driving and Chowder Society, the members of which share my enthusiasm for race cars and antique automobiles. What is enthusiasm, really, except a kind of animated form of interaction shared by lively people?

But still, Sardi's is mainly a meeting ground for theater people. Within two blocks of us exist six of the very best Broadway theaters. And these theaters—their performers and audiences—keep Sardi's alive. Nothing helps business at Sardi's like a hit show in one of these theaters. And had they been torn down and replaced by skyscrapers (as seems to be so much the trend in New York) Sardi's certainly would have died.

Fortunately, however, most of those theaters are owned by the Shubert family, and they're just as dedicated to keeping alive the institution of live theater in New York as I am Sardi's. As I said earlier, by historical accident the Shuberts happen also to be the restaurant's landlord, and they have cooperated with the Sardi family for half a century. One of the main causes of restaurant failure in New York is the lack of cooperation of landlords, who, in time of bountiful restaurant business, have signed owners of those establishments to leases that cannot possibly be met in harder times. Cooperation from the Shuberts, though, has been terrific. They look upon the theater not only as a business, but as a part of their lives; a form of art that they mean to maintain. In a sense, the Shubert family senses the greater good of the experience called "theater," that Sardi's on a decidedly less imposing scale tries to maintain for its patrons.

Effecting and Following

I should point out, however, that running a restaurant with an awareness of human interaction in no way insinuates that every possible form in which it may spontaneously effervesce is perfectly acceptable. Quite the contrary: we find there simply must be rules governing communications. I won't bore you with those pertaining to the New York City Board of Health Code for restaurants, and other such laws beyond the restaurant's immediate control. But even simple communications between staff and patrons and among patrons must be regulated to some degree.

For example, it would never do to allow a theater-goer, no matter how enthusiastic, to interrupt a star in the middle of his or her dinner for an autograph. Were that sort of thing permitted, no performer of any note would be able to make it through a single meal. So the staff is always alert to discourage those who would approach celebrities. Those who persist after being told are shown out of the restaurant. Another example—the staff is not permitted to wear political buttons during working hours. I have no idea what civil rights experts would think of that, but employees don't play politics on our time. There are certain things in which the restaurant simply must remain neutral. You might say, from the communications point of view, that a substantial portion of our clientele needs a wall to bounce ideas off, and the restaurant is that wall. As such, it can have no point of view of its own so to speak. In short, everyone should be welcome regardless of their point of view.

But some rules, alas, do change. A new thing in the restaurant business is the singles bar, where men go specifically to pick up women and vice versa. We have never intended to run Sardi's as a singles place, but nevertheless we've had to change with the times to some degree. Years ago we never permitted a man to pick up a lady at the bar, for instance. First of all, a woman was never allowed at the bar unless she was escorted, precisely to avoid such encounters. But now, of course, the bars have been liberated and we do have unescorted ladies at the bar. If a conversation starts, and we see that nobody is annoyed, we allow it to continue. But even so, we must be careful to avoid becoming a so-called pick-up joint. So in an approximate way the staff does monitor conversations between strangers at the bar just to make sure that business of a questionable nature isn't transacted.

Finally, the question arises as to how much of all this communication between a restaurant and its patrons is really accepted as coming from Sardi's as an institution, and how much gains acceptance on the strength of its owner—a distinction that blurs easily in a personal business like ours, one where the hand at the helm can easily be mistaken for the ship itself, so to speak.

In the case of Sardi's at least, most indications suggest the institution more than its owner is the source of persuasion and power. I might have been tempted to think otherwise when, some years ago, I grew sideburns and mustache to contrast nicely with my Yul Brynner-style bald head. Once the idea was accepted by my own family, I felt confident about it and watched to see how patrons at the restaurant would react. At first, businessmen coming in for lunch would joke about my fluffy sideburns and mustache. Then a junior executive at a big advertising agency told me his firm had sanctioned them for salesmen once the firm's president saw mine while attending a business lunch at Sardi's. Apparently, I thought, the owner of a fashionable restaurant can set trends in personal style on the sheer strength of his example.

That illusion was shattered, however, by what I call "the frozen vegetable episode." We were asked to endorse a new line of frozen vegetables created by the Bird's-Eye Division of General Foods. The first step was to film some television commercials in the restaurant and play them in test markets—specially selected sections of the country where consumer acceptance could be gauged.

One of the commercials centered on myself as the speaker, in what is known as a "stand-up"—me walking through the restaurant and talking about the product. The script allowed me to establish my identity as Vincent Sardi, owner of Sardi's, then I explained how I was proud to say we endorse Bird's-Eye frozen vegetables and use them in the restaurant. In the test market, this commercial did very poorly.

The same time that commercial was shot, the film crew also shot another. Same product. Same endorsement. Except this one opened with a man and his wife preparing a meal in their kitchen at home. She says: "these vegetables are just like the ones you'd be eating at Sardi's. You know, Sardi's, with all those actors and actresses. Think you're in Sardi's," at which point the scene quickly dissolves to the same table, but in Sardi's. The man says, "I'm thinking, I'm thinking," then launches into a testimonial about the frozen vegetables. Curiously, this commercial was successful beyond the sponsor's fondest expectations and sales were double what they anticipated. Apparently this approach communicated the glamor of Sardi's to the viewer, and this proved more potent and persuasive than the restaurant's owner giving a personal recommendation. It also associated the viewer in his own mind with the product, first by showing it to him in his kitchen, then transplanting him to the restaurant.

Taking a cue from this episode, we made a business decision recently to open a chain of dinner-theater operations instead of another restaurant like Sardi's on the West Coast. We had been offered the chance to open the restaurant in a new complex of theaters at Century City Plaza in Los Angeles. But success with such a venture, it seemed to me, would depend on my being in both New York and Los Angeles at the same time—something that is still impossible despite continual improvement in communications technology. Many of the same patrons who know me in New York would hope to see me out West.

Instead, we decided to start up a so-called dinner-theater out there. The idea is to charge each patron a flat price for his theater ticket and dinner. Dinner would come in the form of a buffet, so he goes to the buffet table and·brings back to his own table whatever food he selects. A waiter serves beverages, dessert and coffee, preferably during intermission of the show that goes on right in front on a stage.

Now it seems to me that the Sardi's dinner-theater conveys the glamor of the restaurant's association with the theater. Since I'm not an actor myself, though, I would hardly be expected to perform. And my presence would not be crucial. The resulting new operation depends for its success more on the weight of the Sardi name as an institution, rather than on my personal efforts and presence.

Well, that's how a restaurant communicates, and clearly this communication takes place on many levels. But if you want to get your own feel for some of this communication, you can test it out for yourself next time you're standing outside a strange eating place trying to figure out whether or not to go in.

What are you actually hoping to see as you peer through that window? The answer is a lot of things, most of them intuitive by the time you become an adult. But please allow me to remind you what

you're hoping the restaurant can communicate through that glass pane before you commit yourself by walking in the door.

First, you may notice that the window is dirty. Next, your instincts will probably be triggered by the lighting. Is it warm and friendly, or just dingy? Is it bright and cheery, or just a bunch of glaring fluorescent tubes? How do the patrons look? Neat and cleanly dressed, or rumpled, hung-over and beer stained? What about the walls? Have they been decorated with grease-stained odds and ends just to cover them up, or are they clean and nicely arranged? What about the tables?

Do they have table cloths that run up a restaurant's laundry bill, but make the meal a more comfortable experience by dampening the sound of flatware and plates and absorbing conversations at nearby tables?

What about service? In the few seconds you've spent observing the scene, have you seen waiters or waitresses moving about trying to satisfy patrons? Or are they off in a corner somewhere debating among themselves the great international issues of the day?

Now step back a moment. Is a menu posted anywhere in the window, and if so what does it say? A lot of flowery imagery about the virtues of the cole slaw cream? Or good information that will help you select a dish you might enjoy?

Do you want still more information? You might walk around to the side and check out the kitchen vent. Is it spewing out billows of grease fumes, indicating that virtually every dish is deep-fat fried, or is it issuing forth the somewhat more subtle aroma of a reasonably clean working kitchen which prepares each dish with some spices and a little care?

Of course, all this is what a restaurant can tell you before you even open the door. Once inside, you can discover whether the headwaiter or host greets you with consideration or indifference, or, for that matter, greets you at all. You can look the place over more closely, even to the point of examining dishes as they're placed before patrons at nearby tables. You can scrutinize the menu. You can chat with your

waiter, asking him about everything from the food to attractions of special interest in the area if you're in a strange town. You can smell the restaurant's odor and soak up its ambience, and before you ever pick up a fork, the place has communicated to you virtually everything it can except, of course, the quality and flavor of the food you have selected, and the service afforded your particular table.

But even while you're sitting there, hopefully enjoying your meal, you should remember that the food and decor aren't the only ways a restaurant communicates. It communicates with its own waiters and their union, if they have one. It communicates to and beyond its patrons in matters of taste, dress and even human relations. In the case of Sardi's, it has transmitted a message of its presence and its glamour to perhaps millions of persons who have never seen Sardi's, or perhaps are never likely to.

But if it should happen that on some blustery winter's evening you should find yourself in New York outside Sardi's, peering in the window, by all means do come in. If for none of the reasons we have outlined here, at least you can have a look at our faded terra cotta walls.

COMMENTARY
Performing and Visual Arts:
Creating Realities About Realities

In Chapter VI we discussed Korzybski's notion of self-reflexiveness, or the uniquely human ability to create information about information. This sort of "second-order" processing of previously mediated environment-data is perhaps most clearly understood in the next two chapters, which we call "Creating Realities About Realities." In many respects the arts provide us with perhaps the most vivid picture of how the process of human communication works. On the one hand, the products of the artist or playwright or producer provide us with a closeup look at how another individual processes environment-data into information. At the same time, however, viewing a painting or watching a play in itself represents the most fundamental act of human communication. To be sure, the artist's painting or the musician's score or the writer's play *are* his message—and to him that message is clear, precise, and meaningful. As well, he *intends* for it to have both meaning and effect upon those who view or hear his work. At the same time, as the chapter on visual arts will point out, the viewer or listener comes to that confrontation with his/her own understandings of, past experiences with, and symbolic realities about "art." We must assume it would be the rare rather than the expected event that the viewer/listener would find and understand the artist's message as intended. But we know from our own and others' experiences that the rare seems more predictable than the expected. We do find agreement and understanding both between artist and audience, and between one audience member and another as well.

That such coincidences of artistic experience do occur ought to tell us that much of what we call art are indeed legitimate mass communication institutions. Take, for example, the average citizen's visit to the Louvre for the purposes of viewing the *Mona Lisa*. What will he/she see? Will that individual somehow be able to communicate across the centuries with da Vinci through the messages he left on his canvas? Can such a viewer somehow sense in the portrait whether the artist sought to communicate pleasure or sorrow or sympathy or disdain? Yet most of us would see reasonably the same thing, and probably experience the same general feelings—or, at least, we would say roughly the same words about our experience. Why? The *Mona Lisa,* like hundreds of other works of art, is an institution. As such, it has and continues to foster and support a set of symbolic realities which are widely subscribed to. In most instances, such realities likely have little to do with those which evolve from the work of art itself. In other words, the average citizen comes away awed by the *Mona Lisa* not for its form, texture, colors, or because it represents a particular artist in a particular period, but because he/she has seen *it*. Seeing *it* provides a focal point (has provided such a focal point) around which interaction can take place, the scenario for which is already a deeply entrenched symbolic reality in our communicational environment.

If this were not the case, how could we explain people standing in long lines to pay money to watch a film? Or how do we explain a couple from Des Moines ordering tickets for a Broadway production that is sold out three months in advance? In either instance, the film or the play themselves are not, cannot be, the prime mover of the behaviors described, since neither the people standing in line nor the couple from Des Moines have as yet seen the performances in question. What has happened, of course, is mass communication. By mass communication we mean that process by which symbolic realities are socially constructed, nurtured, diffused, homogenized, and widely subscribed to, thereby evoking a behavioral commitment on the part of the individual based, not upon the event itself, but, upon the communicational realities created around that event. It is thus that many artistic artifacts assume full status as mass communication institutions.

What this process looks like and how it functions in an empirical setting is admirably accomplished in the following two and concluding chapters of this book. In the article on the legitimate theater, the producers of Broadway's longest running hit, *Grease,* recount the conception, creation and launching of a hit musical. More than that, the authors share the process of creating a reality about a reality, of making a single statement about a time and place that would at once evoke from individual audience members responses to many such times (all of the 1950s) and many places (each place at which each audience member individually experienced that time period). In so doing, the producers set for themselves the challenge of neither being so specific as to prevent the individual audience member from being able to generalize to his own experiences, nor so general as to prevent the same individual from being able to locate himself in the plot. The step-by-step procedures entailed for achieving this goal, which characterize the chapter on theater, provide an exceptional flow-chart for creating a potentially successful mass communicated message package.

The chapter on visual arts, in a similar manner, traces the evolution of the "private act of art" into an influential medium of mass communication. The author, himself a successful artist in more than one medium, provides an incredibly candid view of the relationship between an artist, his work, and the public. In preparing this chapter, the author shares with us some of his own work, published for the first time in this volume. He offers his drawings both as an artistic experience and as a focal point for his discussions regarding the artist-audience interactions which occur as the artist's messages become public.

CHAPTER XIV

Broadway: A Sound Heard Around the World

Ken Waissman and Maxine Fox

At sunset when most of New York City is closing up shop and calling it a day, the theater is just beginning to come alive. Dozens of marquee lights suddenly illuminate 44th, 45th and 46th streets as well as several other side streets along Broadway north to 54th street.

This is "Broadway," a small ten block area just west of Times Square; a culture industry set in a predominantly technological environment. Its average annual gross is about $60,000,000, quite insignificant when compared to many of the country's other industrial enterprises. In the course of a year, certainly no more than 6,000,000 people will actually attend a Broadway show, almost insignificant when compared to the country's population. And yet, standing in the shadow of New York's skyscrapers are the big thirty theatres from which rings forth a sound heard round the world!

A few days after a show opens on Broadway, and is acclaimed a hit, word spreads like wildfire throughout the land. Those involved with its production, including the performers, suddenly begin appearing on TV, and photographs of the show are published in magazines. Reviews are even printed in foreign newspapers and the new hit gets simultaneously launched across the seas.

If the show is a musical, and becomes popular, record albums will be sold in thousands. A song or two may become a hit on the radio. The lyrics for the musical will be available as sheet music in stores, and libraries will have hardbound copies containing the script of the play. In several months and for years thereafter, the show will be on tour and also be performed in summer stock, in repertory companies, and in local community presentations. And if it succeeds in getting international acclaim the show will be performed in many languages and in many countries. If it is a dramatic play, it may become a part of Ameri-

can literature. It may even win a Pulitzer Prize. All this emanating from 10 city blocks in mid-town Manhattan.

Beneath the greasepaint and glamor, the theatre is by comparison a small industry—a fabulous invalid—struggling for survival with the desperate need to create a communication through inexplicable vibrations between audience and actor. The majority of offerings in any given season fail to achieve that connection. They just die there, a bitter disappointment to both the performers and the audience. However, several times each season, what appears to be a miracle occurs. The communication is created and a hit show is born. The audience and the performers come together to form a mysterious energy shared by all. This is live theatre, a unique first-hand experience, unlike today's electronic media through which most of us live vicariously.

If you were to see a play on any given night, you would feel that it was all happening for the very first time. This is a carefully calculated effect. Actually, the process which culminated in the production you saw started many months before. To the audience, it all appears spontaneous, as if the actors were making up the lines as they went along.

For example, the show which my partner Maxine Fox and I produced, entitled *Grease,* about the Elvis Presley era of the 1950s became Broadway's longest-running musical.

In Search of a Beginning

Grease began with a phone call from a friend in Chicago. It was a hot night in August, 1971. Maxine and I had just finished reading the umpteenth script submitted to us that summer. Nothing we had read intrigued us enough to want to produce it. Fall was approaching, and although we had a national tour going out of Paul Zindel's *And Miss Reardon Drinks A Little* (we had co-produced the play), we were quite concerned by the fact that for the new theatre season in New York we might go unrepresented.

We had spent the summer looking at showcase productions, seeing various new plays being shown in stock companies, and reading dozens and dozens of scripts. We had seen a revival of *Anything Goes* in Ohio, a new rock musical at the John Drew Playhouse in East Hampton, and a reading of an old mystery play entitled *The Bat.* Nothing excited us.

It was about 11:30 in the evening when the phone rang. It was my college roommate, Phil Markin, now a dentist in Chicago. He and his wife had seen an amateur theatrical production in the Old Town section of Chicago. It was called *Grease,* and was being presented on weekends at a non-profit, non-professional showcase theatre called the Kingston Mines. "I don't know if this is anything you would want for New York," he said, "but it's all about the 50s and it sure brought back a lot of memories from our high school days." He went on to say that it dealt with the "greaser kids." I remembered them well. We always considered those kids the ones from the "other side of the tracks." He wanted us to come out to see it.

The next day Maxine and I checked with some other people in the business. Yes, many people had heard about this production and a few producers from New York had gone out to see it. However, the

general feeling was that it was a small, amateurish production not to be taken seriously at any professional level. But Phil, as we say in show business, was a "civilian," not connected in any way with the so-called "professionals"—and civilians make up the theatre-going public who buy tickets that make the hits. I could not dismiss his enthusiasm nor the fact that he and his wife had a good time seeing it.

We decided to review the production. After such a discouraging summer, we were more than aware this could be another wild-goose chase, so we didn't want to waste two airfares. The next morning I boarded a plane for Chicago, not knowing that that same evening I would have my first exposure to something that would soon become a very important part of our lives.

Everything we had heard in New York was absolutely true. The show had obviously not been directed at all. The cast, in spite of their enthusiasm, was totally inexperienced. Many of them could not even sing on key. The musical accompaniment was totally improvised, the songs were completely virginal, with only the barest suggestion of vocal arrangements. The book scenes were interminable. Yet, almost the minute the show started, some strange kind of magic began. The audience was forgiving of every fault. In fact, they seemed not to be seeing what was happening on stage. Suddenly the audience, myself included, sitting there on the bare floor of a converted trolley barn in humid weather with no air-conditioning, began seeing themselves as part of the activity unfolding on the stage. We heard the music we first danced to, the music we first "made-out" to at parties or in parked cars. The brown paper scenery painted with poster colors became our own high school cafeteria, our own gymnasium, our own hamburger drive-ins, and our own equivalents of the "Burger Palace Boys" and "The Pink Ladies." We recognized the girl who sang about the presents she got from her marine boyfriend in Korea. We knew the guy who sang about his primer-painted, souped-up '51 Ford. We knew the uptight girl who had just transferred to the public high school after having been dismissed from the Catholic school for wearing patent leather shoes (because the boys were able to see up her dress in the reflection from the shiny leather). And we all recalled the girl with the "bad reputation!" We remembered what she looked like, what her personality was like, and there she was. Here were all those kids, so long ago forgotten, with the "duck-tail" haircuts, the "pegged pants," the tight skirts, the cinch belts, and the pointed bras. Here they were, crawling out of the woodwork of the old trolley barn, and for just a couple of hours, they were alive once again.

However, in spite of this, I knew that the New York audience would be far more exacting in terms of professional theatre. In a tiny theatre that has an informal atmosphere, where the ticket price is no more than a couple of dollars, an audience doesn't mind doing the major share of the work themselves. They more easily ignore mistakes, faults and shortcomings. They fill in the things they think are supposed to be there. In New York at stiff "big time" ticket prices, the audience expects the performers to do all the work. They refuse to shortchange themselves by overlooking obvious faults. They refuse to supply what the production has not been able to realize. In short, they are totally unforgiving. In order to create the "magic" in New York that was communicated in the Chicago Kingston Mines theatre, the show would have to undergo a great deal of pruning, cutting, rewriting, and polishing. It would need professional performers plus the staging skills and talents of a professional director, choreographer, musical director, and set, costume and lighting designers. In addition, I had not yet spoken to the authors Jim Jacobs and Warren Casey, and Maxine had not seen the play. Certainly, as I sat there, no conscious decision had been made to produce it. Yet, somewhere inside, I experienced a very strong feeling that we would be presenting a new show that season after all. *Grease* would be our next project.

Maxine flew out the next day and soon shared my assessment of the play's potential. We spoke with the authors and told them we believed we could professionalize the show they intended *Grease* to be, and that we were definitely interested in obtaining the rights to produce it. We explained that ideally the show should be 60 percent music and it would be necessary for them to put an enormous amount of work into reshaping and rewriting the script, adding songs, eliminating songs, etc., first under our guidance, and then under the guidance of a director whom we would select shortly. They agreed. The fact that Casey and Jacobs were talented, knew their material and possessed a great deal of wit, was obvious for us from viewing the Chicago production. What we gambled on was their ability to pick up on ideas, rewrite quickly and improve upon their work. In putting together a show, the authors are always called upon to cut, rewrite and deliver material of improved quality. A producer gambles on his authors being able to do this. Many a play has gone down the drain because the writer was so married to each and every bit of his material that he was unable to see the forest for the trees. With the authors of *Grease* we were very fortunate.

In the beginning there were only four of us involved with the production—Jacobs, Casey, Maxine Fox and myself. To this group we began, one by one, adding the other members of the initial *Grease* clan. Today, there are over 250 people who make up the *Grease* family. These are all the people involved with *Grease* on Broadway, in the two national road tours, in London, and in Mexico City, where the show is called "Vaselina."

Building the Creative Team

After the producer has optioned the rights to a script, the first step is to sign a director and/or a star. For *Grease,* we did not want a star. It was very important to us that the audience feel the characters on stage were people from years past, people they could have known in their own communities. The familiar face of a "star" could, we felt, spoil that illusion.

In choosing a director, it was important to find one who would be able to envision the show exactly as the authors and we had conceived it. The four of us were of the opinion that *Grease* must have the over-all effect of a documentary. We wanted the show to avoid being "camp," or even a parody, but rather sought an affectionate re-creation of the people and the period in which they lived. We did not want the audience to feel the actors were portraying roles, but rather to create the illusion that the players were indeed from the "Fifties," that when the final curtain came down, they would leave the stage, hop into a '51 Ford convertible and head for the nearest hamburger hangout. A director is the key man on a production, and it was he who would have to take this rather abstract feeling we were shooting for, fill in the details, and translate it for the stage. In thinking of various potential directors for *Grease,* one name kept coming to the top, that of a young director named Tom Moore.

We had first become aware of Tom Moore three years earlier when we saw a production he directed at the American Place Theatre—a non-profit showcase theatre in New York. It was a two character drama, in which one character was confined to a bed for the entire performance. We were very impressed with the amount of action and energy he was able to exact as director from such a limited premise and by the very natural performances he got from his actors. We were also impressed by his sense of pacing and comedy, for mixed in this rather serious piece was a great deal of humor. Moore had worked in musical theatre directing resident theatre productions and in repertory, but he wasn't what one would call a musical-comedy director. This suited us perfectly.

Although *Grease* was a book musical (one that tells a story), we didn't want to approach its presentation with the attitude of a typical, plastic musical comedy. It was for this reason we were looking to create a documentary, pop-art look for the production. For example, we faced two prime concerns in writing the music for the show; firstly, because the show was taking place in the 1950s, we had to, through the music, recreate the whole feeling of that time period. The songs had to sound exactly like the songs we heard then on the radio or danced to at the school party. Secondly, since this was a book musical, each of the songs had to come out of a situation that was happening on stage, and the character doing them had to be doing so in the context of the story. Therefore, the trick was to compose a completely original score, rather than to borrow the music of the fifties, whereby the audience could conjure up the memories of songs from that era. For these reasons, we determined from the beginning to avoid choosing a musical-comedy director and to look instead for someone who was a little off-beat.

When we first met Tom Moore, shortly after seeing his production at the American Place Theatre, we learned that on many of his directing assignments he had worked very closely with the playwright on the construction and development of the script. This was also an important consideration in choosing him. There was a lot of work to be done with Jacobs and Casey on their book for *Grease.*

Moore agreed to fly to New York to meet with Maxine and myself and the two authors. After the meeting, Maxine and I were convinced that he should direct *Grease,* but both he and the authors had doubts. Moore wasn't sure that he was the right person for the job. Although he had grown up in the 1950s (he was 28), he had very few memories of the period. He didn't recall even being aware of the type of teenagers being dealt with in *Grease*. We explained we were seeking his directing knowledge and talent, not his knowledge of the 1950's, since the authors had enough knowledge of the period for everyone. On the other hand, Casey and Jacobs were worried that although Moore had numerous directing credits, he had never done anything in New York City commercial theatre. Few people had ever heard of him. We asked them to think about it, and we arranged a second meeting for two weeks later. This time, Moore had had more time to review the script and was able to go into much more detail and provide a number of good ideas about structuring the script. They all worked beautifully at that meeting and the decision was made.

The next step was choosing a choreographer. Maxine and I had decided, the moment we first saw *Grease* in Chicago, that Pat Birch would be our choice. Maxine had first met Pat in the Off-Broadway production *You're a Good Man Charlie Brown*. Her next show was *The Me Nobody Knows,* and Maxine had insisted that I go to see it. I, too, became very enthusiastic about Pat Birch as a talent. A wonderful, zany sense of humor and a sense of tremendous energy comes through in her staging. She also had a superb ability to take actors who are totally untrained in dance and make them look like experts. In addition, we felt that she, although a consummate professional, would be capable of leaving a certain "rough edge" to her work. In other words, she would skillfully avoid being too slick. All of these reasons combined to convince us that Pat Birch's talents would fit perfectly with our documentary, pop-art concept. She and director Tom Moore hit it off beautifully, right from their first meeting, and developed a collaboration that made for a uniquely creative team.

Simultaneous with these decisions, Maxine and I were considering choices for the other members of the creative staff. For costumes we chose Carrie Robbins and for the sets, Douglas Schmidt. Although both were active Broadway designers, they were contemporaries whom we felt could relate to the period. Also, they both had been schooled in repertory theatre, and this we felt would not only help them bring a fresh approach to the commercial musical theatre, but allow them to understand our concept and attitude toward the project as well.

Carrie Robbins, Maxine and I had all attended Forest Park High School together in Baltimore, so Carrie knew the types of kids we envisioned for *Grease* as well as we did. In fact, in describing some of the characters in the show, I would often say things like, "Carrie, remember Stanley so and so?" or "Remember Arlene so and so?" She would understand immediately, to the puzzlement of the rest of the staff.

To this group we now added the musical director, who would be responsible for vocal and dance arrangements, supervision of the orchestrations, and supervising music rehearsals, as well as conducting the band during the performance. In interviewing people for the job, it was important that we be convinced that the person possessed an affection for and excellent knowledge of the rock and roll music of the 50's, have the ability to collaborate with the rest of the creative staff and, equally important, be able to appreciate and share our sense of humor.

After several unsuccessful interviews with potential musical directors, a young man with good but limited credits was recommended to us. He was Louis St. Louis. The name alone was enough to make one interested, and when he entered the office with long hair, a full beard and an earring, topped off by a rather flamboyant manner, my immediate reaction was not exactly positive. However, thirty seconds after he opened his mouth we began to feel that here was our kind of person. His reaction and enthusiasm when we played him a rough tape of some of the music for *Grease* convinced us that our feelings were correct. After further discussion with him, and an opportunity for the rest of the creative staff to meet him, Louis St. Louis joined our expanding staff.

The next major decision we had to make was the choice of a theatre. For the audience, the show does not begin when the curtain goes up, but rather the moment they arrive in front of the theatre. The box office, the lobby, the auditorium all contribute to the atmosphere and will have an effect on how the show looks to the audience.

Because *Grease* was somewhat offbeat in comparison to the typical musical-comedy, Maxine and I decided not to open it on Broadway where the critics would expect something more conventional, and the audience would anticipate something more formal. We expected the initial audience to number about 35, predominantly consisting of those who like the informal and intimate flavor of "off-Broadway." However, the way we envisioned it, *Grease* called for a rather large production. All the off-Broadway theatres are quite tiny and, therefore, were unsuitable. We quickly thought of the Eden Theatre down on Second Avenue in Greenwich Village. This theatre had been the home of *Oh! Calcutta* and, more recently, *Man of La Mancha*. Although it was located in the heart of the off-Broadway theatre district, the Eden, with 1,100 seats and a large stage was equal in size to most Broadway houses. It was also recognized by Actor's Equity and other unions as a "Broadway" house and operated on full Broadway contracts.

Fortunately, it was available, and the perfect compromise was reached. We could have an on-Broadway-size production in an off-Broadway atmosphere. We set an opening date of February 14, 1972.

Creating the Reality

With the opening night set, we were now ready to begin casting. Over the next six weeks, Tom Moore, Pat Birch, Louis St. Louis, the authors and I auditioned over 2,000 actors and actresses to find the 16 that would make up the original Broadway cast. It was incredibly difficult. We were looking for people who could sing extremely well, act with considerable depth and credibility and, in addition, be able to dance. It is not easy to find young performers who are expert in all three categories. At times, we thought we would never find enough people. Equally frustrating were the occasions when a performer would turn up displaying wonderful talent and skill in acting, singing and dancing but had to be turned down because he or she lacked a certain unique quality, that had to be combined with the character in the script in order to create a new entity on stage.

However, by diligently auditioning every day from 10 in the morning until 6 in the evening for a six-week period, we finally put together what later proved to be an extraordinary cast.

During the audition period, Tom Moore was working each evening with Jacobs and Casey to prepare the script for rehearsals. In addition, there were constant production meetings at which we discussed costumes, set designs, and material being taken out or added to the score and the book. Now, with the preparation done and the cast complete, we were ready to enter the rehearsal stage.

Because the cost of rehearsing in a theatre is so expensive, Broadway shows conduct the bulk of their rehearsals in a rehearsal studio. Here, with masking tape outlining the set, and using fake props, the show is blocked-out, the musical numbers are staged and the characterizations are developed. Rehearsals continued in the studio for four and a half weeks. Meanwhile, the set was being built at a scenic shop and the costumes were being made and fitted at a costume shop. Also during this time, publicity on the new show was in full swing. One of the ways we decided to give the public a feeling for what *Grease* would be like and to create some anticipation for it was to invite the press to the hair-cutting session at which the male members of the cast had their long hair sheared into the famous duck-tail hair styles of the period. This "Back to Short Hair" event received enormous coverage, including a double-page spread in the New York *Daily News*.

For the first three weeks, rehearsals lasted eight hours a day, six days a week. Beginning with the fourth week, until the first public performance, rehearsals lasted 10 hours a day, with no days off.

During the fourth week, the cast moved to the Eden for technical and dress rehearsals, followed by two weeks of previews before the official opening. Tickets are sold to previews at a reduced rate. The preview serves as a work period—to cut, change and hopefully fix any problems so that the show will work by opening night. This is probably the most crucial period. No matter how good the show may look in rehearsal, there are always surprises when you get it in front of an audience. Things you thought would be funny simply fall flat. Numbers you thought would get a big hand get polite applause. The tension on the part of all the people involved reaches an all-time high during this period. Tremendous emotional control must be exercised by all.

The first preview of *Grease* was, in our opinion, a disaster! The show dragged, the rhythm was off, certain scenes seemed to go on forever, musical numbers we were sure would work got no response from the audience. This is the point very often where panic sets in. In

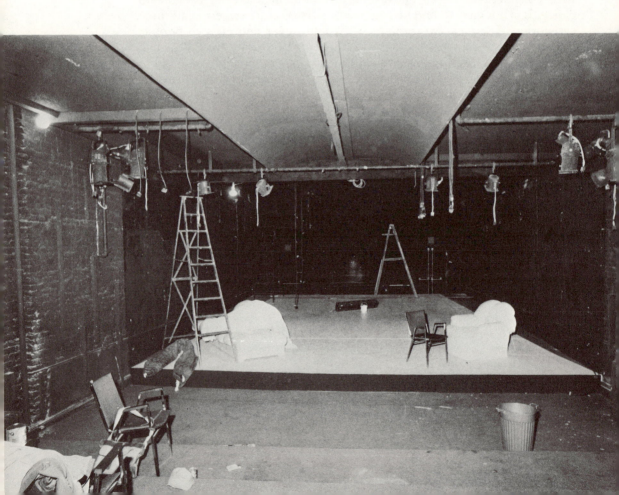

theatre jargon, we call it "flop sweat." Out of desperation, egos are trampled, the actors entertain delusions of being fired. The director, the writers and the producers seem to forget their unified objective for the show and mentally go off in separate directions. This sequence usually begins a downward spiral.

Fortunately, for *Grease,* this did not happen. All of us remained cool and meticulously set about the tedious job of "fixing."

When a musical number doesn't work, one of four things may be at fault: the song is just no good; the staging or choreography is incorrect; the scene that leads into it is wrong, or the actor simply isn't cutting it. It is important to not make a rash judgment and act prematurely.

In one instance in *Grease* where a number did not work, we decided that the song itself was not very good, and it was cut from the show. In another case, we felt that the song was really quite good but that it needed to come earlier. Also, we felt that the scene leading into it needed rewriting to set it up better. The authors were sent back to the typewriter and the song, "Those Magic Changes," about the basic chord structure of rock and roll music, was moved closer to the beginning of Act I. From then on, the number received a tremendous audience reaction. Another number that gave us trouble was "Beauty School Drop-Out," a song about a girl who flunks out of high school and then can't even make it through beauty school. We loved this song and we loved the set up for it in the book. Pat Birch spent many hours reworking the staging, and by the second week of previews she had delivered a show-stopper.

When a scene is not working, we consider several possibilities: it's too long, it has lost its purpose somewhere along the way and needs to be redefined, or sometimes its because the actors have not found the rhythm and pacing and have not yet gained confidence in their roles. It might even be that the lighting is wrong. If the lights are too low or give a sculptured effect, they can kill the humor in a scene. If they are too bright, they can kill the emotion in the scene. A balance must be found.

One particular scene seemed to significantly slow down the first act and break the flow of the show. We decided the original purpose of the scene (to show the boy-lead and girl-lead alone together in order to focus in on their relationship) had been lost. The authors wrote a whole new scene, and when it was incorporated in the show, it restored the necessary flow and continuity to Act I. Some scenes that seemed to be problems fell into place after a few performances when the actors developed a more natural pace and rhythm. A pajama party scene needed to be shortened, and the director pulled out his blue pencil. The scene that gave us the toughest problem was a basement party scene in the second act. The audience appeared to hate it. We discussed cutting the scene entirely, but it seemed necessary to the plot. There was also an important musical number at the end of it in which the tough, hard girl, Rizzo, reveals the vulnerable teenager underneath. We finally realized that this feeling must be presented as the underlying purpose of the entire scene. The audience must be able to see throughout the scene that although the gang puts up a tough facade, they actually are nice kids. When the scene was rewritten and redirected toward this end, it suddenly worked.

During the preview period the audience serves as your gauge. They tell you everything you need to know. When you overhear them talking during intermission or after the show, you have to listen with a trained ear to understand what they are telling you, because what they actually say usually has nothing to do with where the problem lies. You may hear them say, for example, that a particular part of the show dragged. You can't take that at face value. Maybe that particular part of the show didn't drag, but something that occurred before or after that particular scene caused them to think it did. A preview audience cannot tell you how to solve such problems, but we depend heavily upon them to tell us that something is wrong. Applause, laughter, silence, shuffling, intermission talk, end of the show talk are vital indications to understanding the nature of the product being developed on stage. And as we attempt to work out the problems, the audience by their reactions, will tell us whether or not we have succeeded.

Each day during the preview period we moved to correct problems with the set, the sound and with costumes. Rehearsals continued each day and with effective, restaging and further maturation of performances, the show improved bit by bit until, in the second preview week, it suddenly began to click as a whole. When this happens, you can feel a whole different level of response from the audience. A kind of electricity seems to go through the house from the moment the curtain goes up until it comes down at the end, and you know the "magic" has finally been created!

The Interface of Expectations

For many months February 14 had loomed ahead of us as the all important date, the official opening of the play. Finally it arrived. No matter how strongly an audience may respond to a show, the opinion of the critics will have a telling affect upon the final outcome. It is through the critics that word of the show first gets out to the public. One of the first impressions the theatre-going audience gets is from what they read in the newspapers the day after a show opens. This system has been highly criticized, since it results in a few people making their individual opinions the ultimate word on a new play. Regardless of its fairness, the potential audience does look to the reviews as a means of evaluating a new show, and so far no new system has been invented to supplant it.

So when opening night arrives, nerves and tension have reached their utmost peak. And when the curtain goes up, what happens on the stage will determine the fate of the show. In the case of *Grease,* fortunately, the morning-after reviews were good. Some were extremely enthusiastic, and some were quite favorable. There were, however, a few critics who didn't understand the show—because it was offbeat—

while others simply did not like it at all. Among the latter was Clive Barnes of *The New York Times,* who said the only thing he knew about the 1950's was that 1959 was a good year for Burgundy. A native of England, he later commented privately that he felt he had been watching a foreign language production. But he did mention in the review that he thought it was a very good production, and that if people understood it better than he, they might enjoy it. There were a couple of other reviews along this line. But because of the less than enthusiastic review by *The New York Times,* which from the theatrical point of view is the most influential paper, the show took several weeks to build up a capacity audience.

From the beginning, though, on account of the positive reaction we were getting from the audience, and the favorable reviews we had received from most of the newspapers, we had faith that within a few months the audience could build to full houses. Immediately after we opened we began playing to very good audiences, but certainly not full houses. As each week went by, the audience grew larger and larger until finally we were performing to capacity houses a month after our opening date.

During this time, which is the case with all new shows, we entered into a phase we call "housekeeping." Because each night is a live performance, each show must look as fresh as it did the night it opened. In addition, since we had a new show and many people were not quite sure what it was, the promotion of the show at that point became crucial. The reviews praising the show had to be made available to the public, and the image of the show had to be created in such a way as to entice theatre goers to first, come to the theatre and, second, to ensure the production lived up to those expectations once they got there.

Once a show opens, the stage manager takes over the director's job. He must watch the show every night, take notes, conduct rehearsals periodically so that if anything gets sloppy or any part of the production is starting to change, it can be corrected before the audience notices it. In this way, the initial vitality of a show can be kept. In addition to this, Maxine and I make a special effort to see the show at least once a week, and we can also take note of anything that might be getting a little bit off. Director Tom Moore and choreographer Pat Birch came back to the show at least once a month to conduct brush-up rehearsals, or to correct any sloppiness that might have crept in.

As word of the show got out and the excitement of the show began to spread, interest began developing in many different quarters. We not only started attracting teenagers, but older persons, as well as many of the larger groups who normally confine their theater-going just to Broadway. That started us thinking. Since we were classified as a Broadway show, and since we had made our entrance such a successful one, now might be the time to transfer the show to a Broadway house. By doing that, we would immediately make *Grease* accessible to segments of the theatre audience who wouldn't find their way to Second

Avenue—particularly out-of-town people, school groups, and others who want to see theatre on Broadway, not on Second Avenue.

So, on June 6, 1972, we moved the show to the Broadhurst Theater, a facility identical to the Eden in stage size, audience size, and the over-all shape of the house. Many people thought we were making a mistake moving the show to Broadway. We were told that *Grease* was not the typical Broadway musical, that the type of audiences we were attracting on Second Avenue would not follow the show to Broadway. But we felt that with the acclaim the show was receiving, the audiences going to the show at the Eden would most certainly follow us to Broadway. In addition, we believed there were considerably more people who wanted to see the show who would have greater access to it if it were right in the Broadway area. Fortunately for us, we were ultimately proved right.

The minute we opened on Broadway, business started booming. The advance for the following year started climbing so rapidly we knew we would be in for quite a long run. There was, however, no way to envision how long that run would turn out to be. You work very hard on a show to create an interface between actor and audience that will spark that so-called elusive "electricity" that makes a show a hit. Accomplishing that state will normally create a show that will have a successful run and make it popular with the general public. But that extra "magic" which allows a show to run 1,000 performances or more, that extra something that allows a show to become the longest running show on Broadway is something that goes beyond such a simple explanation.

As the show passed its 1,000th performance (in July, 1974, *Grease* became the 25th show in Broadway history to pass the 1,000 performance mark, and four years later still performs to capacity audiences), we began giving a lot of attention to why it might have developed such incredible longevity, both on Broadway and on the road as well.

Reflections on a Hit

There is, obviously, no single "formula" or reason to explain the enormous success of *Grease*. All we can do, really, is reflect upon what we have learned about the show through our audiences and the shape of our society during the period in which it became a hit.

Perhaps one of the first things we began to realize about the show was while its content deals with the 1950s, it communicates to the audience a kind of universal feeling that goes beyond those specifics. The show, on another level, takes a kaleidoscopic view of the problems of adolescence: the first date; being a member of a group; the constancy of maintaining your "image"; dealing for the first time with peer group pressures; the mercurial nature of adolescent emotions—the play in essence deals mainly with a series of "first-time-isms." The theme of *Grease* is one which everyone has been through or is going through. If you are 13 or 14, you are on the brink of going through it; if you are 15 or 16, the problems of the players are your problems; and if you are 30 or 60 years old, you can still recall the pain and the pleasure of having gone through it. That, we believe, accounts for why the play evoked the same kind of enthusiasm from such a wide range of age groups attending the same performance. The audience never seemed to laugh or show other emotions in unison, but there did seem to be enough for everyone at different points throughout the production.

Closely related to its broad appeal, *Grease* was primarily responsible for contributing a new audience to Broadway that had for the most part, previously been absent, young people. *Hair,* which preceded *Grease* to the Broadway stage, did bring large numbers of younger people to the theatre. *Hair* was not, however, a "book" musical—it was more of a concert. When *Hair* left Broadway, the young people left with it. *Grease* brought them back in droves. Not only did it bring in the audience, but the production demonstrated to the Broadway community that shows put on by younger people, for younger people could indeed deliver a previously untapped audience to the theatre district. Following *Grease* were *Pippin, Scapino, The Magic Show,* and several other shows which, while they appealed to more mature audiences, developed tremendous followings among younger people as well. The classical Broadway show—such as *No, No, Nanette,* or *Irene*—is really created by much older and more mature people for a much older and mature audience. Such productions are more readily identified with what one expects, or perhaps expected, to find on Broadway.

But if Broadway is to grow and continue to develop, it has to keep up with the times. Our concept for *Grease,* right from the beginning, was to give it a modern look. We intended it to be fast-paced and have a unique style that would make it fresh and for today's modern audience. Young people today think differently. They have grown up in a non-linear age. *A* doesn't necessarily have to be followed by *B,* immediately followed by *C* in order for them to understand what is going on. Both the range and nature of information younger people deal with today—television, jet travel, moon shots—require them to think both more rapidly and more abstractly than their counterparts of preceding generations. Today's youth can take what seems to be an illogical juxtaposition and make complete sense out of it. And they are used to seeing things happen rapidly—*Grease* was put together with that in mind. It's the kind of show that jumps from one thing to another, and today's modern audience can easily put it all together and flow with it.

Beyond that, *Grease* ignited a wide-spread revival of the '50s. Radio stations began playing records from the 1950s. We received considerable quantities of mail from colleges and universities holding "fifties" parties. The film *American Graffiti* about the 1950s era was released. Rock stars from the 1950s were revived across the country to give concerts, and soon afterward television got into the act by presenting a new series set in the 1950s. The rapid development and growth of this national nostalgic "mania" gave rise to even more speculation about the success of *Grease.* The most plausible explanation we could bring to bear upon how intrigued both young and older people were with the 1950s was that "looking back" had become kind of a contemporary theme for Americans. We all, it seems, have sort of an innate need to romanticize. Thirty or forty years ago that need was being fulfilled by romanticizing about great wealth and glamour. Most of the films of that era dealt with the glamourous life, the top hat and cane, and the Rolls Royce. The influence of that period can still be seen in our architecture, the remnants of sophisticated glamour hangs on in debutante balls, and in the folklore of the lives and behavior of the wealthy.

Fifteen or twenty years ago, when most of middle class America moved into the affluent society, our need for fantasy fulfillment shifted from glamour and wealth to something else still a bit out of our reach—space exploration and worldwide jet travel. The movies got into the act with the James Bond films, the glamourous life in and out Europe and the Orient, Alfred Hitchcock's "North by Northwest," and a variety of other travelogues. This new era manifested itself in the design of automobiles, the simplicity and streamlining of clothing styles, our hero worship of the astronauts, and our idealization of the "jet set."

Today, much of that, in one form or another, has become available to nearly everyone—we take moon shots for granted; almost anyone can budget a jet trip to Europe, and our fashion industry has mass produced the "mod look" so as to put it in reach of those with even the most modest incomes. Even so, our need to romanticize—seemingly a constant in our existence—has found new territory. What we seem to be doing currently is fulfilling that need by digging up our past and romanticizing and fantasizing about the good old days. Music today runs the gamut from Scott Joplin through Tommy Dorsey and Bill Haley. In clothing, everything from the "Gibson Girl" look to the Joan Crawford vogue to the James Dean image seems equally appropriate. The same is true of styles of architecture, movie-making, food preferences and merchandizing—we dismiss the large modern department store for the smaller boutiques and specialty shops which are much more personal in nature. In a few years, something new will present itself, some other dream slightly beyond our reach will capture our fancy; but right now that human need seems adequately fulfilled by nostalgia. Whether or not *Grease* was responsible for initiating the trend, or whether it simply rode an inevitable wave to its crest is something we most certainly cannot accurately determine. We are convinced, however, that the impact of *Grease* extended well beyond the doors of either the Eden on Second Avenue or the Broadhurst in the midst of Broadway. Those locations were only the source of a pleasant sound eventually heard around the world.

CHAPTER XV

The Private Turning Public: The Visual Arts as Mass Communication

Robert E. Mueller

Art begins as a private act. Unlike most mass media—television, books or newspapers—the interest of art is initially private and personal. It is one of the few intensely personal idioms left in an increasingly organization-oriented society. The artist works in his garret or studio, secretive to the point of neuroticism, involved in trying to articulate his feelings about his experiences. As Susanne Langer writes, "Art is the surest affidavit that feeling, despite its absolute privacy, repeats itself in each individual life."[1] It is this repetition that allows us in some way to share in the experience constructed by the artist, since each of us innately has the means to create a response.

Although the artist must preserve his isolation to chase the delicate hues of his art, lest like a rare butterfly or peacock the crowd might chase it away, he always displays his work. Eventually he goes beyond his work for his private ends, and takes it out and hangs it up for all the world to see. Paradoxically, if the artist's art is sufficiently private, it becomes something we all can share. The success an artist has in focussing our attention on his private insights measures the degree to which we all aspire to private expressions, and our opportunity to do so is heightened through his art. And when we grasp what an artist is up to, when we absorb his intensely personal vision, we share a new dimension of humanity through him. Art, therefore, ends as public property.

Cumulatively, all good art becomes known, and in this sense art is a mass medium. Everyone of us has a sense of Leonardo da Vinci's work, though he painted few oils and only some, like the *Mona Lisa,* have been widely publicized. We also know Picasso's double-faced women. One masterpiece often suffices for an artist to create a mass medium; time and notoriety take care of the rest.

272

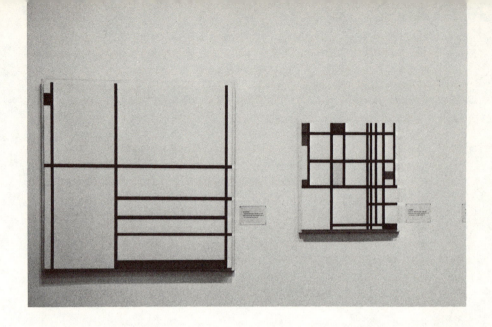

The manner in which movements influence the ebb and flow of general visual consciousness attests to the power of art as a mass medium. Piet Mondrian, for example, created extremely pure designs using only rectangles and primary colors. But Mondrian's example inspired the De Stijl group who worked in typography, furniture design and architecture, and we now feel the imprint of Mondrian's work on all aspects of modern design in the mass arena.[2]

The Art-Audience Interaction

There seems a direct parallel between the power that primitive art exerted over the primitive mind and how new modes of visual expression play upon our primitive subconscious. Much of our psychic heritage is invested in totems, images, symbols, works of art; we derive our storehouse of fundamental images from art, and therefore owe much of our imaginative world to that heritage of visual forms. More than we realize, our perceptual world is saturated with visual images, and it seems not far fetched to maintain that much of our "creative ability" flows through our absorption of visual art—the major repository and preserver of man's significant symbols. As Rudolf Arnheim suggests, it is our very ability to grasp visual form that has made possible the human capacity for creating theory and for generating intellectual structures of all sorts.[3] Since being able to grasp and comprehend art represents a broadening of our being at a very fundamental level of perceptual human awareness, we value art and seek it out, promulgate it, and fan its myth.

Perhaps, currently, we seek it a little too vigorously, and the art world, naturally, has responded with movement after movement. Cubism screams past Surrealism, Futurism flows into Abstract Expressionism, which dispels the image in Non-objective Art; Op Art gives way to Pop Art; Minimalism bows to New Realism, and so on.

The art world has been floundering around in these styles of storming images now for a decade or two, catering to public demands for images and modes that are in themselves now essentially grasped as mass expressions. While the public likely would not recognize the technical names, they would recognize mostly all of the images and forms noted above—they are now mass art and inexpensive prints widely available in book stores, "art shops," and even supermarkets.

Cumulative museum exhibitions, television, newspaper and magazine representations and criticisms, the subsidiary influence of design and decor, all permit art forms to reach out from the studio and gallery into everyday vision, forcing art to become as much a part of our sight and memory as Bill Cosby's face or the Laugh-In comics. The staying power of art images gives them a decided advantage over the images of other media, and for this reason they become important to all visual mass media. Art is designed to impress.

The Making of a Medium

Consider the series of sketches that follow. These are essentially private to me, although new to you, since they are the result of my personal involvement with linear form which has grown out of my

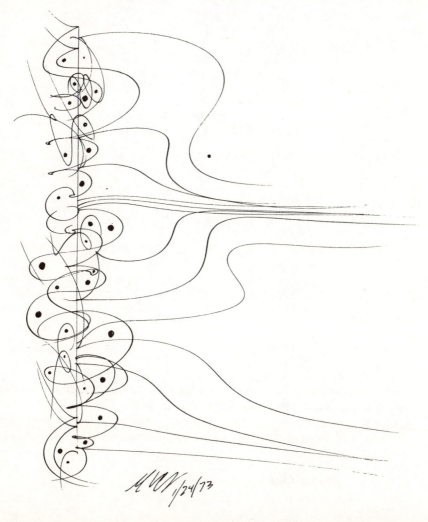

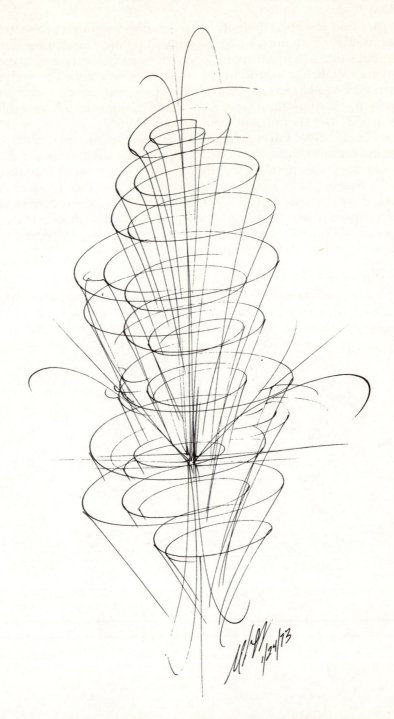

training in art as an Abstract Expressionist, but also from my immersion in mathematical form while a student at MIT. The abstractions represent visual structures cut to the bone of minimal means; simple sweeps of lines and occasional dots, defining neither space nor recognizable shapes, representing only themselves. How can such a sparse, abbreviated, highly abstract, primitive and private image ever hope to become public? The form of them is perhaps analogous in their simplicity to an unaccompanied flute or violin. The line, however, is no substitute in the eye for the vibrant tone of music in the ear; it, in fact, has even less quality than the most minimal music since all color is absent and all texture is removed. In short, the sketches are the minimal of the minimal in visual form, yet they are expressive. If such an art can find the means to become mass, even in your minds now, and if such a bare skeletal representation of creative structure can become comprehended, then other more highly endowed arts can too.

There is something potentially suggestive about even these minimal graphic schemata. I have discovered, after twenty years of creating them, that people respond to them with little visual experience. The

1/25/73

cumulative results of viewing these forms, in my estimation, amount to what might be called a mini-mass medium. Given time and the mode's integration into its rightful position as an art form, it could become highly communicative in its own right, which is about all we require of art and of emotions that we can only express in art forms.

Unlike mathematics I need not define for you the substance of the drawings; I need not say that a curl represents a sob of emotion, a dash of sprint of hope, and so on; you will not respond with such explicit feelings, but nonetheless you will respond with feelings. The most impressive characteristic of art derives from two qualities which I think are represented in my schemata: firstly, a heritage of previously existing structure which the spectator brings to the work and through which the forms can be grasped; and secondly, a sufficiently original and creative departure from that structural heritage to make the form interesting to behold.[4] The sketches I have generated lean on mathematical plots and families of curves which are prevalent in the mass domain today. Further, they advance the idea of simple expression of movement, flow, dissipation, and eruption, as in Fourth of July fireworks displays or as suggested in some kinds of music. Through contact with this form, the average spectator can begin to decide within himself some meaning, respond with some sense of emotion, both highly abstract, like music, get caught in the surface structure of a plane by the lines and dots. You then might sense, if I have been successful, the new departures and novelties of a new art expression, which dawns upon the consciousness until a new world of structure becomes illuminated. And finally, a new avenue for yet another world of mass ideas in structure emerges, which can serve as the basis for a new creative vision of form.[5]

For another example consider the Pop Art movement. The tenet of Pop Art is that art starts with common objects and refocuses our awareness of them by isolating them, either on canvas or in large, mock sculpturesque imitations. We are therefore led visually to see things we have forgotten existed. The common objects of our world are soup

cans, comic strips, the American flag, automobiles, hot dogs, and so on. Andy Warhol creates giant soup cans and other grocery store objects; Claus Oldenberg makes mammoth canvas kitchen sink faucets; Roy Lichtenstein enlarges the comic strip to gigantic single frames and perhaps fragments; Jasper Johns plays with variations on the American Flag; John Chamberlain turns crushed automobile bodies into sculpture.

The Pop Art movement opened up our awareness of the common modern object, just as Jean Chardin did for the precious china or delicate wooden objects of the 18th century in his genre paintings. Who are we to say that these objects are so banal that we cannot conceive of them as art? It has been said that the object of Pop Art was to create an image so boring that the spectator is forced to look for something else in the painting: the quality of the artist's technical performance, for example. Certainly Pop Art arose in response to the complaints of both critics and public alike that the art which preceded it was too esoteric, too concerned with the craft of the painter. It was painting for painting's sake. Its hallmarks were textures, splashes of paint, surface qualities and an almost random play of serendipitous elements, the cutting out of colored forms within large sections of spatial form.[6] William de Kooning's totally abstract giant brush strokes began to give way to figures of women, and Jackson Pollock began to drip out recognizable forms shortly before Pop Art's birth. Even so, Abstract Expressionism was then anything but mass—at least the public had no inkling of the communication involved; it was painting for painters, for people who painted and could take pleasures in the craft and the technology of oil paints.

If comprehension and perceptual understanding of form, and therefore communication, is indeed a "look-up" system, as R. L. Gregory has argued in his *The Intelligent Eye,*[7] then all mass communication depends upon a store of information and experiences within each spectator from which comparisons can be made and from which identifications are discovered and reformulated as they are perceived. Abstract Expressionism, being highly randomized swirls of colors and shapes, only vaguely suggested sky storms or nightmares in the eyeball, and it obviously could achieve little communication with the average spectator, much less ever become a mass medium. At least that is what we thought in those days when the form was first born, and so in the absence of an audience, we encouraged each other in our own private painting adventures. So when images were brought back, when recog-

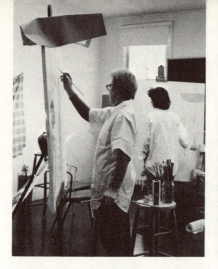

nizable things began to show up in museum shows and in galleries, everybody was happy—no matter that the image was so common as a Campbell's soup can, so common that it almost insulted the eye! Here was a mass form, a mass medium, already entrenched in the general mind by virtue of years of previous familiarity with the mass produced objects. Ironically, however, now even Abstract Expressionism, and even Non-objective art of the most highly refined kind—for example Carl Alber's squares of color balanced at some slight angle against other subtle colors—has become "respectable" today, which is tantamount to saying that it is a mass medium that everyone can grasp because they have learned the form's visual terms.

Pop Art quickly wore itself out—how mass can you get? One of the tenets of communication theory is that the redundant is as boring as the absent, as I have pointed out in my volume, *The Science of Art.*[8] Upon first meeting a radical new form, the mere act impresses—the use of common objects like Soap Boxes in art, especially in the museum environment, was quite a shock at first, and thus it was a unique communication. But once established, once the idea was seen, it all too quickly became like a poor pun, and failed any longer to arouse interest, except historically.

Op Art is another case in point. When optical phenomena are used by an artist—so-called "optical illusions" to which we all react out of a physiological necessity within the eye and brain—the art built is perforce mass influencing since we *must* react to it. By the same token, however, such art quickly becomes boring, which we might predict from another tenet of communication: that which can be predicted need not be communicated.[9]

From Context to Content

The art world, always eager to soak up new modes and new methods of using form, always seeking new outlets for the imagination, will inevitably—in spite of initial resistance—be profoundly influenced by movements. Pop Art cracked the stalemate of abstract art and let

flow many of the newer forms of art current today. It also allowed some of the older forms to reflower. When the rules of a current fad are broken, new rules always rush in to take their place, and in the process all rules, even those which once had been rejected come under re-examination. The re-emergence of Realism serves as an example. Pop Art was realistic, and through its popularity realism came back full force, allowing a fresh approach to the form; thus today Realism is again a respectable form of modern art.

The machine age, as well, set the stage for a new and long line of mass expression in today's art, which we all comprehend only too well. The sensitive artist of the time reacted to the machine as a sad joke on humanity. The tone was first reflected in the literature of alienation, and through it arose Dadaism, which took great delight in overturning mechanistic forms. But like so many alterations in man's existence and values over the centuries, the mechanical age, resistance notwithstanding, was not to be denied. Today the art world is manifesting the precision-like, automatic nature of the machine in many of its products, and indeed has turned to the machine as an artistic tool. One such offshoot of the era is computer art—although the results to date have been generally disappointing and, necessarily, lack the humanity which any machine production inevitably must.[10] But aside from bypassing the human imagination, the machine has opened up a common line of sympathy in all of us, which emerges more as a reaction to the messages of these nihilistic artists: We all sense the pall of alienation which the machine has cast upon mankind; we resent its unfailing accuracy and inhuman perfection. Both the intensity and immediacy of that response is deeply rooted in the work of artists bent upon suggesting the horrors awaiting the interaction between the relentless perfection of the machine and the imperfection of mankind.

But the Pop Art movement did more than break an artistic log-jam; it provided the public with a straightforward, uncomplicated art form with which it could identify. It released a new flood of simple, reproducible images. Although prints had been used before, under the influence of Pop Art, the concept of the poster exploded onto the modern scene and, for the first time, allowed art to become a competitive form of mass communication. Multiples have reached a new high in the current art scene, including a growing and lucrative industry of mass produced "original" oil paintings, sculpture, carvings, only to name a few. From its narrow beginning, the poster as a medium has placed a variety of art forms in places previously both unaccustomed and unacquainted with art.

The art print or the poster is a form of multiplication that has made art mass, and served the same function for mass viewing of visual forms as music multiplied by radio did for mass listening, or the printing press for mass exposure to the written form. When radio first abstracted sound for the person who created it, and multiplied it for mass distribution, the audience—used to seeing the source of sounds they heard—had to learn to deal with an abstract medium.[11] And while people had, to some extent, learned to derive meaningful, humanistic structures from yet another and earlier abstract medium, the printed word, radio most certainly must be acknowledged as the chief factor ushering in age of modern mass media. The addition of television, and the combined stimuli of both electronic media gave thrust to a form of communication that automatically multiplies the single object into many distinct and

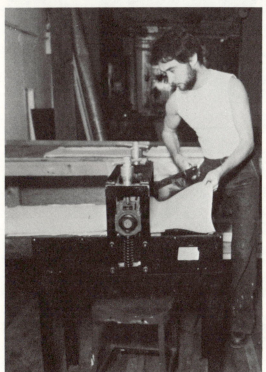

private minds. As McLuhan insists, the introduction of the new media has altered our sensoria. We perceive differently, the abstract has become the concrete. Our appetites have changed. The way was paved for yet another mass medium—popular art. Television carries sound, but the poster and print carries art, and the differences are due to the permanent effects of the latter over the fluid and temporary impact of the former.

The Evolution of Art Forms

The progression of art forms in the psychic-social evolution of structure, as I see it, is outlined as drawn in the flow chart on the next page. It begins when an artist creates his individual works, themselves necessarily the product of his own heritages of intellectual creative form, but brought to a new fever pitch of creative enlargement by his particular vision. Usually, the artist will show his work first to friends. The gallery next receives the work, and it enters the public domain through one-man shows and other gallery exhibitions. Museums then begin the slow, methodical exposure that begins to create the mass medium. Other media take up the publicity, and the works of art begin to exert influences upon other art, as well as upon related design-disciplines, and to influence form in general as the art is made plastic in all media. Next, the work enters the *History of Art,* and becomes a part of our cultural heritage. At this point in the evolution, the form begins to pass out of the conscious public domain and back into the highly personalized deep structural matrix that forms our private perceptual development. As noted earlier, the form becomes part of our storehouse of visual imagery, thus lending its powerful force to the

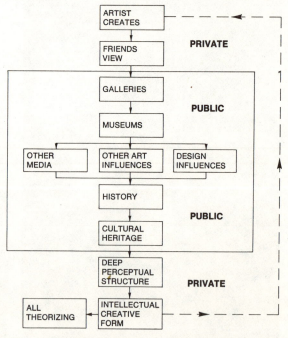

PROGRESSIVE EVOLUTION OF ARTISTIC FORM

creative development of yet further theory. The return to the heritage of the individual artist is inevitable, and it is a return at a level deeper than that of mere surface influence. At this point, the form becomes interwoven into the very intellectual, ontological fabric of the human mind.

This cyclic process, similar to that which I described in *The Science of Art*[12], proceeds in an ever-widening spiral, increasing human awareness of the creative and developing our imagination.

In the long run, this process affects all humans and can, therefore, be considered mass influencing in yet another dimension—through time, one generation to the next. But the impact of art on this plane does not, obviously, affect all people in the same way nor at the same pace. Art is both a creative and a creating medium. As such, as the flow chart indicates, it is both the *effect* and the *cause* of new modes of expression. Art is an agent of change and, therefore, often meets with considerable resistance. Humans exhibit a strong resistance to change and manifest an equal desire to preserve the status quo of conventional modes of ideation, because most of us lack the communicational equipment to cope with the uncertainties that come with change. Art shatters the conventional, but only by creating the unconventional to take its place, thus building a new mode for future conventionalities. John Hightower, director of New York's Museum of Modern Art, says, "Art should be kicking and screaming in the middle of contemporary society. . . ."[13] The mind, unless it is trained to observe art, or unless it is the kind of mind that thrives on unusually creative communication, tends to reject images that might replace older and more familiar ones, that summarize form and attempt to shape it into new content. The shape of content, of significant form with human worth, is not easy to apprehend. Inherently, then, art begins antithetical to most mass media, because it can reach only a few people. Some art remains so, private and eternally in oblivion. But increasingly greater quantities of art do not. In time, we do begin to become aware of its presence, to feel its force and, indeed, even to use it in subtly conceptual ways.[14]

The artist has become the graphic research engineer par excellence, and as everyone in advertising knows, it is the image that gets the most information across with the strongest impact. "A picture is worth . . . ," even so typography, layout, and design are powerful adjuncts to all visual images in the mass media. New styles in the graphics of advertising that have an impact of a novel nature can usually be traced back to the work of some artist, for instance, Picasso's contour drawings, Kline's bold abstract forms, Matisse's use of color, or Ben Shahn's lettering. What begins as esoteric arts, therefore, often become mass media over time. Whether they do so through interdependence upon other mass media or mass media technology is of little consequence. The museum is itself sufficiently frequented so that we can call it a mass medium. What is of importance is the process; that which shocks the eye of one generation becomes mass to the next—the private has turned public.

Notes and References

1. Susanne Langer, *Mind: An Essay on Human Feeling* (Baltimore: Johns Hopkins Press, 1967), p. 64.
2. C. H. Waddington, *Behind Appearance,* Cambridge: M.I.T. Press, 1970), p. 44.
3. Rudolf Arnheim, *Visual Thinking* (Berkley: University of California Press, 1969).
4. Daniel K. Stewart, *The Psychology of Communication* (New York: Funk and Wagnall, 1968), and also Claude S. Shannon, "The Mathematical Theory of Communication," *Bell System Technical Journal,* April, 1950, pp. 80–84.
5. Robert E. Mueller, *The Science of Art: The Cybernetics of Communication* (New York: John Day, 1967).
6. Andrew Ritchie, *Abstract Painting and Sculpture in America* (New York: Museum of Modern Art, 1951).
7. R. L. Gregory, *The Intelligent Eye,* (New York: McGraw-Hill, 1970).
8. Mueller, *op. cit.,* pp. 43–79.
9. *Ibid.*
10. Robert E. Mueller, "Idols of Computer Art," *Art in America,* 60:3, 1972 (May–June).
11. My *Radio Theory of Abstraction,* presented as an explanation of how the non-objective form can be given humanistic meaning, also indicates how art can become mass communication. See *op. cit., Science of Art,* p. 159 and p. 211. We carry over a great bulk of meaningful, humanistic structures from the most abstract media and build them to the point where all people can share them. The letters of the alphabet are examples of what I mean here.
12. *Ibid.,* pp. 64–79.
13. John Hightower, *Artforum,* December, 1971, p. 9.
14. Mueller, *op. cit., Science of Art,* pp. 303–325.

INDEX